# MANAGING EMPLOYEE
# INVOLVEMENT AND PARTICIPATION

# MANAGING EMPLOYEE INVOLVEMENT AND PARTICIPATION

Jeff Hyman and Bob Mason

SAGE Publications
London • Thousand Oaks • New Delhi

First published 1995

SAGE Publications Ltd
6 Bonhill Street
London EC2A 4PU

SAGE Publications Inc
2455 Teller Road
Thousand Oaks, California 91320

SAGE Publications India Pvt Ltd
32, M-Block Market
Greater Kailash – I
New Delhi 110 048

**British Library Cataloguing in Publication data**

A catalogue record for this book is available from the British
Library

ISBN 0 8039 8726-9
ISBN 0 8039 8727-7 (pbk)

**Library of Congress record available**

Typeset by M Rules
Printed in Great Britain by Redwood Books, Trowbridge, Wiltshire.

# Contents

*This book is dedicated to the memory of our friend and colleague Sarah McLeod. She is much missed.*

# Preface

Few would disagree that employees should have a say in workplace affairs. The problem is that there is far less agreement over the ways in which the voices of employees should be expressed. The three main directions identified in this book are initiatives which promote and reflect management concerns; those which aim to regulate relations between employees and employers; and those which propel united worker interests to the fore.

Management initiatives are often introduced on the understanding that relationships between themselves and employees are essentially tranquil and harmonious. Regulatory prescriptions aim to ensure stability and progress in industrial relationships through providing machinery which recognizes and resolves areas of conflict in pluralist management–employee relations. Radical perspectives contend that worker interests are inevitably subjugated to the needs of capital and can only be truly liberated within a restructured socio-economic system.

The practical effects of these different perspectives in enhancing or inhibiting organizational efficiency, at a time when competitive concerns are foremost in the priorities of both employers and state, are also subject to much dispute at present. In consequence, debates over the parameters of employee influence are circulating strongly within political as well as commercial circles.

This book has been written with the intention of examining, in detail, the different ways in which employee influence can be articulated at work, ranging from radical expressions of worker control to management insistence on limiting employee inputs to task-based and communicative issues under management direction. The effects of contrasting philosophies and practices are evaluated within a rapidly evolving industrial landscape from which manufacturing industry is gradually subsiding and in which enterprise networks are expanding on a global scale. Inevitably, issues of raising or containing employee influence are extending beyond national boundaries. We attempt to address this breadth of experience by examining involvement and participative policy and practice under both free market and regulatory regimes.

We endeavour throughout the book to explain what is happening in this vital arena of employee relationships, why certain features are prominent, and the possible consequences for the parties whose interests are at stake.

Though responsibility for the book is ours alone, we have been helped by numerous colleagues and friends who have offered support, criticism and advice. We cannot name everyone but we owe special thanks to Sue Jones for her continuing encouragement and counsel throughout the duration of this project. We would also like to express our appreciation to Debbie Cadenhead and Pat McTaggart for their word processing professionalism.

It is 'traditional' to conclude appreciations with expressions of gratitude to partners and families. We have no intention of breaking with this tradition, especially because we recognize that without continuing tolerance and understanding by Sabine and Margaret, this book would not have been written. Support was offered to us at a time when family commitments have been at their strongest, following the births of Matthew, Ewan and Connor and of Pierre, the newest arrival in January 1995. To our partners and families we offer our sincere and lasting thanks.

Jeff Hyman and Bob Mason

# 1

# The Context: Employee Influence in Organizational Decision-Making

> It is generally conceded in the liberal democratic world that working people should have a right to participate in the making of decisions which critically affect their working lives.
>
> R. Bean (1994) *Comparative Industrial Relations*

The deceptive simplicity and apparent consensus contained within the above statement masks one of the most complex, dynamic and controversial aspects of organizational structure and employment relationships in advanced industrialized countries. For when we examine the component parts of the statement a number of major issues are revealed. First, we could ask what is meant by the 'right to participate' and enquire as to which issues would be covered by this right. A related question would be whether in fact there is a universally accepted definition of a participative right. Second, we could consider what sort of decisions would be covered and who determines those which are critical to employees. Third, we could explore the expected outcomes from exercising participative rights and particularly how much influence accrues to employees or is lost to managers in consequence.

This book attempts to deal with these crucial issues by undertaking a close examination of current streams of thought and practice in offering employee access to decision-making within organizations. The timing is particularly appropriate as significant shifts have taken place in the environment of organizational decision-making in recent years. This has meant that whilst questions of making inroads into management decision-making at work have not retreated from the political left or labour activist eye, there has been a huge shift away from labour-driven initiatives to programmes advanced and operated by practical managers. In its wake, questions of defining and implementing 'industrial democracy', so hotly debated since the early days of industrialization, have virtually disappeared as a contentious issue for corporate governance. Instead, we are left with two principal, and in many respects contrasting approaches to defining and operationalizing employee influence, deriving on one hand from managers and their need to control effectively the performance of employees, and on the other from attempts by employees or by bodies acting on their behalf to gain and maintain a foothold in sharing aspects of high-level decision-making with managers. The book examines in detail the development of these two major streams of employee influence within a rapidly changing industrial and organizational context.

## Structure of the book

The early chapters provide a background and contextual examination of the principal concepts and issues surrounding workplace democracy and employee influence. The present chapter provides an account of contrasting arguments forwarded on behalf of workforce, employers and state in offering employee access to organizational decision-making. Radical views which link industrial democratic movements with widespread social restructuring are contrasted with reform-based pluralistic regulative traditions and with contemporary management orientations to employee influence at work.

Chapter 2 narrows its focus onto the two most visible manifestations of employee influence, namely employee involvement (EI) and employee participation (EP). First, definitions of each are offered; we then provide a systematic comparison of both processes in terms of their genesis, differing rationales and anticipated outcomes. The broad contours of each process in terms of techniques applied and patterns of growth are also outlined. Emerging from these comparisons, potential and overt tensions between involvement and participation are exposed, tensions which are particularly evident under the influence of strong market conditions.

Chapter 3 offers a detailed exposition of the shifting markets for products and services and the effects of these shifts upon demand for labour and for employee relationships. Pressures in the form of moves from manufacturing to service sectors and growing needs for product and service quality within increasingly competitive product markets are identified. Product and labour market deregulation which have been actively adopted by free market governments in pursuit of greater labour market flexibility provide added momentum to these changes.

Pressures are also evident on the labour supply side. Endemic skill shortages have been compounded by changing social trends in which enhanced educational opportunities throughout the industrialized world are attracting more people to participate in education for longer periods of time. Entry into the active labour market is thereby deferred and people enter with higher educational attainments and expectations for progress.

Organizational responses to such demand and supply pressures are reviewed in this chapter. These responses have been expressed in terms of organizational restructuring, rationalization of operations and, associated with these, the adoption of innovative or integrative approaches to employee management.

The following chapter argues that patterns of employee management typified by collective regulative systems such as collective bargaining are vulnerable to the volatile market conditions identified in previous chapters. In consequence, attempts by management to inject individualistic and unitarist patterns of employee relations can be observed. It is also argued that, as part of this reorientation, systems of employee management are shifting toward an emphasis on a human resource management (HRM) style of employee relations, which recognizes and rewards individual relationships within contemporary enterprises. Associations between HRM and employee involvement are established and contingent concerns for union-based participation are highlighted in this chapter.

The middle chapters of the book provide an analysis of current developments in involvement and participation. Chapters 5 and 6 examine contemporary patterns of employee involvement. Studies from different countries confirm a rise in the proportion of organizations which operate approaches to involvement; other studies indicate a proliferation of multiple involvement practices, particularly those of a communicative nature, such as team briefing, suggestion schemes and staff appraisal. Whilst coverage of involvement is undoubtedly growing, research reveals that at least some approaches are applied informally and can be somewhat superficial in effect, a finding which receives further support from the examination of equity-based financial involvement developments.

Chapter 6 treats financial involvement and participation as different concepts which arise from contrasting motives. Though both offer property rights through equity-sharing, financial involvement is expressed through the perspective of the employer who offers shares to individual employees with expectations that share ownership will incline employee behaviour towards an employer frame of reference. We assemble evidence that casts doubt upon the extent to which share schemes do influence employee behaviour. Financial participation involves collective employee ownership of equity, with the intention of offering employees substantial property interests to match those enjoyed by other institutional shareholders. The chapter demonstrates that collective financial participation has been subject to sustained ideological and legislative attack during the present competitive deregulative era and is unlikely to resurface as a dominant policy option under current configurations of employer and political influence.

Chapter 7 examines employee participation. It demonstrates that in those countries where a strong liberal economic climate prevails, such as in the UK and America, participation, even in its collective bargaining format, faces considerable obstacles. Nevertheless, in the USA, there are early signs that participation is becoming more acceptable to some sections of industry as a means to accomplish change within turbulent economic and trading conditions.

The chapter draws largely upon European experience in an examination of current participation trends. In European Union countries, with the exception of the UK, the political climate favours participation as a means to offer industrial stability through regulation of employee and employer interests. Principal participative measures include works councils and worker directors; the operation and effects of these bodies and constraints acting upon them are fully scrutinized in this chapter.

In the final chapters of the book, we analyse more systematically the rationales and responses of employees, unions and employers to involvement and
participative initiatives. In Chapter 8 we indicate that employees readily identify management involvement techniques as a means to enhance efficiency
rather than as an enlightened route to increase employee satisfaction. Perhaps
for these reasons unions have not readily collaborated in the design, implementation or operation of involvement initiatives. Fears of compromise with
involvement processes which have the potential to disrupt existing management–union channels of communication and influence are also cited as a
prime explanation for union reticence. At the same time, union weakness in
the UK has prevented the labour movement from persuading government or
employers to adopt participative approaches along the lines of those operated
within the European Union. Finally, whilst employees can be offered limited
decision-making experience either as individuals or as members of unions,
there is no doubt that a gender imbalance persists in industry, with women
facing considerable disadvantage in terms of access to both involvement and
participation.

Whilst involvement practice originates with management, we find little
evidence of a uniform or coherent rationale for the range of involvement
techniques introduced over the past few years. Moreover, lower-level managers, who are designated to implement and operate new EI practices, are also
most threatened by restructuring exercises and accompanying reallocation of
responsibilities, and these managers appear least enthusiastic to implement
involvement reforms.

In Chapter 9, we examine more closely the rationales and experiences of
inward investors in terms of their own practices and as potential influences
on host country management practice. Whilst we find that use of involvement techniques within a coherent involvement philosophy is widespread
among American and Japanese companies, there is less reason to be certain
about its infiltration into host country management practice. Adaptation to
host country norms by incomers occurs as well as implantation of overseas
practices. The directions of involvement practice are further complicated by
the rising number of joint ventures initiated between locally based and
incoming enterprises.

The final chapter distils the evidence and arguments presented in the book
to conclude that despite a general absence of strategic integration with other
managerial objectives, management-inspired employee involvement is on the
increase; and under pressure from employer action, representative participation at work is vulnerable. In turn, there is a danger that this vulnerability
could leave employees increasingly unable to articulate their collective interests if these become threatened by unsympathetic management policies or
practice. In these circumstances, the issue of emancipation of people at work
takes on a vital new significance, especially for national and supra-national
systems of political governance.

## Employee involvement and the new managerial revolution

The recent dominance of management in categorizing employee influence as a form of 'involvement' and in utilizing employee involvement in order to meet managerial objectives has overtaken many of the standard texts on 'industrial democracy' and 'employee participation' (see e.g. Clegg 1960; Blumberg 1968; Brannen 1983; Poole 1986) which were closely oriented, as the opening quote demonstrates, to examination of the potential for different configurations of employee participation to meaningfully influence high-level enterprise decision-making. One of the main themes of this book, therefore, is to trace the paths which this management initiative can take and to analyse the potential effects upon employee relations and organizational performance.

Since the earliest years of the Industrial Revolution social scientists, psychologists and management thinkers have endeavoured to discover and implement the most appropriate ways to treat people at work in order to motivate them in pursuit of high performance. After some 200 years of industrial organization, solutions to this problem of motivating employees to give of their best have proved to be surprisingly elusive and are still being relentlessly pursued by an army of organizational analysts and behavioural scientists. Motivational problems have come into even sharper prominence in recent years, as corporations of all sizes and in all fields face up to issues of heightened dynamic competition, ever-accelerating technological demands, and shortages of key technical and management skills, in a pervading climate of economic uncertainty and world recession. As a number of writers have indicated, the changed demands on organizations mean that they must become more manoeuvrable in the market-place (see e.g. Kanter 1983; 1989; Peters and Waterman 1982; Peters 1992). In order to survive, whole new activities have entered into the management lexicon as companies restructure, downsize, delayer, outplace and subcontract their satellite activities. In the absence of compensatory employee-focused practices, there is no doubt that these enforced changes would have significant potential to demotivate remaining employees.

One of the dominant themes to emerge from within this maelstrom of activity has been human resource management (HRM). We shall see in Chapter 4 that HRM can represent different activities and priorities according to different perspectives, but common to all formulations is, first, an understanding that people have the potential to provide competitive advantage and, second, that management styles should reflect the central importance of people as assets to be utilized in order to offer optimum benefit to the business. A main strand of HRM therefore proposes that in common with other capital inputs, employees should be treated as an investment, whose value can be enhanced through integrated systems of appraisal, training, development and involvement. Such an approach to people management locates at least some employees within the central core of organizational activity. In this respect it is not corporations but *employees* who must be flexible, adaptable and easily deployed throughout a range of activities; *employees* who must be drawn into the corporate culture and committed to its values and objectives; *employees* who must be capable of taking task-related decisions and be empowered to become self-managers rather than act as passive recipients to management plans.

But employers are faced with another facet to the same problem of competitiveness: they need to take decisions, often quickly and frequently and with harsh implications for the workforce, which derive from the market uncertainties of late twentieth-century capitalism. In responding to the urgency of market signals few employers can afford to be deflected by employee objections or encumbered by constitutional obstacles constructed by their unions. HRM seeks to find a solution to this conundrum by involving employees in task-based activities, but also alerting them to the precarious nature of paid work in a dynamic market environment through systems of communication and information provision. It might also be argued that HRM can serve to reduce or eliminate the potential of trade unions to materially interfere with management decision-making processes or outcomes (Lucio and Weston 1992; *Labour Research* 1994:5).

For these reasons, management attraction to personnel techniques which aim to reduce adversarial employment relations by involving staff in the financial fortunes of the organization and in task-linked areas of management decision-making has grown dramatically over the past few years throughout the industrialized world. Whilst the intention is to give employees a say in organizational affairs, the initiatives emerge from management and are linked, however tenuously, with the achievement of management objectives. We refer to this manifestation of employee influence enhancement as employee involvement.

## Rights to participation

Nearer to the democratic spirit of Bean's assertion is the strategy of many countries, notably in Europe, which have adopted, maintained and evolved approaches to labour relations which owe much to democratic or participative principles designed to invoke the rights of employees to question or influence the directions taken by their organizations, as distinct from approaches guided principally by their purported contributions to corporate performance. Of course, the presence of politically inspired participative schemes need not preclude (and arguably, could reinforce) the application of management initiated involvement schemes which are intended to raise levels of workforce performance. Techniques such as briefing groups and consultative exercises are applied throughout the industrial world, often extended to domestic enterprises from their use by multinational enterprises concerned to adopt a common labour relations culture across their plants (Peters and Waterman 1982:246). Moreover, under economic conditions which serve to reinforce management control over its labour resources, it would be questionable whether employee participation was also able to fully achieve its stated protectionist public policy objectives.

Despite these developments, there have been few recent systematic attempts to chart the scope or effects of these involvement and participative projects, whether in terms of meeting stated objectives of contributing to company performance or in terms of supporting employee rights at work. Furthermore, little is known about the strategic value attached to involvement programmes by managers or the incidence and effects of management mediation on participation programmes. This book aims therefore to explore contemporary patterns of employee involvement and participation operating under market conditions, but which are informed and structured by different political standpoints and priorities. It further seeks to examine managerial expectations which fuel different initiatives and to enquire whether, or in which ways, the techniques have helped to restructure or influence employment relations and organizational performance or to satisfy the wider political aims (such as to restructure the labour market or to raise levels of 'popular capitalism' through individual share ownership) which have been set out for them. Finally, involvement directions taken in different countries will be explored for signs of convergence or divergence.

Before considering contemporary developments in closer depth, we look at the history and background debates which have illuminated different routes for employee influence and by so doing have helped to make the subject so important today for managers, workers and trade unionists and for students of organizational behaviour.

## Pathways to employee influence

The principal participants in organizational activity are employers, employees and the state. Employers' over-riding concerns focus upon profitable production of goods and services, utilizing those resources (including people) at their disposal as efficiently as possible. Surveys have repeatedly identified that employee interests at work focus largely on pay, security (including health and safety) and satisfaction derived from their labour (Ramsay 1976; Allen et al. 1991:288; see also Fox 1971: Chapter 1). State concerns are spread more widely, embracing macro-economic performance, and using indicators such as competitiveness, productivity and price stability; but at the same time, and especially in social democratic countries, the state may wish to ensure that employees are treated fairly and in a non-exploitative fashion. Moreover, acceptable ideas of fair treatment may well shift over time, perhaps in line with rising levels of educational attainment, sophistication of industrial processes and organization, and alongside contemporary views on citizen involvement in institutional decision-making. A further factor is that, in most countries, the state is also a major employer in its own right and may wish (or need) to set an example to other employers as a 'model' employer in its treatment of employees (Clarke 1993:261). These contrasting broad objectives and aspirations ensure that employee relationships are subject to diverse pressures, and whilst all the above parties may agree perhaps in vague or general terms on the desirability of meeting certain ideal objectives of high profits, high living standards, low levels of unemployment, and exemplary standards of employee treatment, practical necessities dictate that these objectives are not necessarily compatible one with another; that people may interpret standards in different ways; and that conflicting ideas as to the most appropriate ways for their fulfilment may be in circulation.

A major concern for the parties within the employment relationship is the expression and effects of deploying employee influence at work. This is especially vital as the form and extent of employee influence may also impact upon the possible attainment of other highly sought objectives, and in this respect there are diverse and controversial views from which we can identify three main manifestations, associated respectively with labour, employers and the democratic state.

The radical supporter points out that employees enjoy no significant formal influence at work. This view derives from the purported material and control deprivations experienced by workers within a market economy, and through its call for democratic popular control over the means of production it throws a challenge to the existence, legitimacy or authority of capitalist management relations. This radical model has been historically associated with the concept of industrial democracy (ID), a term with little currency in contemporary market-driven economies where any worker or activist concern for industrial control has been fragmented and displaced by defensive struggles to retain individual employment and to protect employment rights. Unions, once seen by some as the architects for radical change, are in numerical membership decline and along with other pressure groups are facing new, highly complex agendas embracing global issues such as the environment, gender relations, technology control, activities of multinational corporations and, in some countries, renewed state hostility. The ignominious collapse of so many Eastern European 'worker democratic states' has exacerbated the lack of definitional and operational clarity to industrial democracy.

Further, counter-claims are made that worker emancipation has been achieved through capitalist market relations and the status of worker/consumer as sovereign in a competitive economy (see Eldridge et al. 1991: Chapter 6; CAITS 1994). A further strand of this argument contends that class-based distinctions between workers, managers and owners are no longer relevant on the grounds that: (i) unskilled work is in terminal decline, and contemporary work invariably possesses some managerial responsibilities under involvement and empowerment programmes; (ii) employee share schemes have dissolved barriers between owners, managers and employees, and under such schemes *all* employees are also owners; (iii) pension funds consist of the accumulated deferred pay of all employees and hence the bulk of commercial and industrial property is owned by workers. The eminent management commentator, Peter Drucker, considered that by the 1970s American capitalism had succumbed to 'pension fund socialism' as a quarter of the stock of American industry was owned by employees in their pension funds (Drucker 1976; for a critique, see Minns 1980). The concentration of pension fund property ownership is even higher in the UK. Moreover, to reflect this ownership dimension, UK pension fund trusts which legally operate for the benefit of their members (i.e. employees) usually have employee members, often in equal proportion to company representatives (Schuller and Hyman 1986). Arguably, under these circumstances, both ownership and control over the means of production are vested in employees and the 'revolution' associated with the democratization of industry has already taken place (Drucker 1976). Each of these arguments will be afforded further critical attention in the following chapters.

The conservative view is closely associated with employers and their sympathizers. It derives from managerial needs to direct and control the labour of subordinates, under conditions which can be alienating, insecure and poorly rewarded materially and motivationally (for an account of the drudgery and stress of much routine work, see Terkel 1977). On the other hand, enhancing the motivational content of work may produce positive benefits for employers. Indeed, many aspects of contemporary work rely upon high quality standards and dependence by management upon specialized and expensively trained staff whose commitment may be vital to economic success. Some writers propose that a positive relationship exists between job satisfaction and task performance and that task-based discretion and decision-making contribute significantly to both (see Rose 1988 for a discussion on these connections). In this book we refer to these management exercises in raising performance as employee involvement (EI).

From the state, procedures are advocated or introduced to regulate potential conflict between employers and labour, to address deprivations of employees or to lessen their vulnerabilities. Often, these procedures involve the formal participation of employees and their representatives in high-level enterprise decision-making or give them a say in distributive issues. Over the past 20 years or so, it has been the supra-state level of the European Union that has seen the most vibrant activity in this context. We use the term employee participation (EP) to encapsulate this model of decision-making in this book.

Each of these different traditions can be associated with, or derived from, the ideas and theories of different writers and movements.

## Thinkers in the radical tradition

The radical democratic school stems principally from the politico-philosophic traditions of British guild socialism, German social democracy, and European anarcho-syndicalism, which have all endeavoured, in thought and action, to make the concept of industrial democracy the central element of a new economic order in which production is dictated by social needs and managed under popular control (see e.g. Szell 1988).

For these movements, ID is primarily associated with a profound reordering of work relations which allows workers to secure access to control over the means of production. This social restructuring would also tackle the roots of alienation at work, for the development of capitalism and its subsequent maintenance have gone hand in hand with increased distancing of workers both from their ultimate product and from control over the processes of production. Advances in technology coupled with 'scientific' principles of rational management have also served to isolate employees from the processes of work in which they are engaged. The result is both technological and market 'alienation' of the worker, terminable only through the eradication of capitalist relations predicated by the domination of one class (owners or bourgeoisie) over the majority of workers or proletariat.

As early as the mid nineteenth century, Engels had described the desperate conditions of working people in industrializing England (Engels 1892). Together with Karl Marx, he concluded that the inherent instability and contradictions of competitive capitalism, which throws together ever-increasing numbers of industrially disenfranchised workers, provide the material conditions for its eventual overthrow by united workers (Marx and Engels 1848). The subsequent abolition of private property and its replacement by a truly democratic socialist society would bring with it the dissolution of the division of labour and the withering of alienation (Giddens 1971:63).

Major differences have emerged among radical thinkers over the ways by which the goal of superseding capitalism might be met. A crucial division has been over the revolutionary potential of mass trade unionism. Marx and Engels wavered from optimism to pessimism in defining a role for trade unions in the revolutionary process, but other writers took more determined lines. One school of thought cast unions as inherently conservative organizations whose opportunistic leaders would always acquiesce to the material gains offered to their members. Lenin, the Bolshevik leader of the 1917 Russian Revolution, was particularly pessimistic about the inevitable subjugation of trade unions, on the grounds that bourgeois ideology 'was older...more developed as a set of ideas, and it had vastly more resources available...than its socialist rivals' (Kelly 1988:30). Other radical critics such as Gramsci saw unions as both formed in the image and operating according to the needs of capital (see R. Hyman 1971:12). Michels' Iron Law of Oligarchy contended that the putatively democratic principles of unions would in practice be subverted by immutable sociological imperatives which ordain that union leaders become inexorably incorporated into a bourgeois life-style whilst their members, progressively estranged from their unions' decision-making processes, become increasingly acquiescent and apathetic in their dependence upon their leadership elite. Union leaders protect both their influence and life-styles by reaching accommodations with employers rather than risk confrontations with them (1971:14–17).

In contrast other radical strands were founded on the premise that trade unions were capable of wresting control by sustaining an offensive against the capitalist order. Syndicalist thought, which gained support in both Europe and America during their developing phases of industrialization, was founded on the notion that widespread and co-ordinated industrial action by trade unions could bring about fundamental change. An early, short-lived, example was the Grand National Consolidated Union, established in Britain in the early 1830s with the intention of forming a general strike in pursuit of gaining control over the means of production (Cole 1972:Chapter 2; Brannen 1983:34). In the twentieth century, manifestations of this tradition have tended to spring from the spontaneous actions of fragmented groups of workers, such as in the initial stages of the Russian revolutions of 1905 and 1917 (see e.g. Kochan 1966; Kollantai 1921), and in the years immediately prior to, and in the early phases of, the Spanish Civil War, between 1933 and 1937 (see e.g. Brenan 1950; Thomas 1977). In the period after the Second World War, the former Yugoslavia was pointed to by many as representing the most full-blooded example of ID through the practice of worker self-management (see e.g. Dunn and Obradovic 1978:1; Horvat 1969; Pateman 1983:114). More recently, though, the view has been expressed that trade unionism might be associated with a more 'tentative' form of 'workers revolt', as it challenges capitalist relations on two essential fronts, first by confronting economic exploitation and secondly by disputing issues of workplace control (R. Hyman 1971:38). Echoes of these diverse traditions lingered on in the UK into the 1970s, finding expression in such events as 'right to work' occupations, most notably at Upper Clyde Shipbuilders in 1971 (Foster and Woolfson 1986).

An alternative and equally fiercely debated route (or dead-end) for worker control has been the approach that unions should propose and support measures which enable them to gain experience of managerial functions and responsibilities through a process of 'encroaching control'. Armed with knowledge and experience of management, unions would be in a position to mount an increasingly expert and authoritative challenge to the profit-seeking intentions of capital. A number of the more recent formulations of industrial democracy, such as worker directors, collective wage-earner funds and worker co-operatives, can fall within this category. In addition to the formidable opposition of many employers and of the state itself, these schemes have also foundered on sharp ideological differences among union activists and socialist ideologues, many of whom would claim that, through incorporation into managerial functions, trade unionists who do achieve (or are granted) positions of eminence within capitalist enterprises will inevitably lose touch with both their members and, crucially, their principles. Anyone who does attempt to confront capital from within will soon become both isolated and exhausted (see Kelly 1988:Chapter 8). For the diminishing numbers of rejectionists, true industrial democracy can only be achieved through the overthrow of capital and capital can only be confronted through militant action.

Interestingly, most industrialized countries have been prepared to offer at least some of these 'democratic' approaches as part of their regulative and reform traditions, rather than as a vehicle for radical social and economic change. As we show later, the concept of collective wage-earner funds, promoted by Swedish Socialist parties as a means to restructure capitalist relations, was eventually diluted and then abandoned in the wake of considerable political and economic pressures. For these parties, it appears that the wage-earner fund agenda went beyond one of simple reform.

## Thinkers in the conservative tradition

The principal workforce challenges facing managers of enterprises can be summarized in terms of their need to:

1　define and confirm the legitimacy of managerial positions and decision-making powers, in a unitaristic framework
2　remove or contain manifestations of conflict
3　find the means to continually raise productivity, perhaps through gaining workforce compliance in terms of flexibility, effort and commitment and by reinforcing employee motivation
4　develop and refine enterprise consciousness among employees.

Each of these issues and their relationship to employee influence are now considered more fully.

### *Unitarism: confirming the legitimacy and authority of management*

The noted British industrial sociologist, Alan Fox, constructed a taxonomy of styles of employee relations management (1974:297–313). A popular style embraced (though perhaps constrained or modified in practice) by many employers is that of unitarism. The employee relations style of these employers has been categorized as 'unitarist' in that they endeavour to construct relationships within an assumption of unity of purpose and ideology between managers and their individual employees within a hierarchically led organization (see Ackers et al. 1992). In these organizations, the goals of leaders and led are assumed to converge, leaders using their expertise to expand profits for the benefit of all the enterprise stakeholders. Employment relationships are constructed on the basis of systematic assessing and rewarding of individual employee contributions to the shared goals through personalized remuneration and appraisal systems. Unitarism is a doctrine which unequivocally supports the evolution and maintenance of confidential relations between individual employees and their employer. The attentions of trade unions are viewed as an unwelcome and unnecessary intrusion which can only disrupt the internal harmony of the enterprise and their presence is therefore legitimately resisted or deflected by employers. Trade unions are said to capitalize upon the uncertainties and fears of employees, and conflict emerges from combinations of misunderstandings, lack of information and the activities of troublemakers. The conditions under which rabble rousing can occur are denied to potential troublemakers by preventing misunderstandings, offering reliable channels of information disclosure and ensuring adequate opportunities for individual self-fulfilment, expression of grievances and career progression. As subsequent chapters demonstrate, techniques which involve employees, either passively through information provision, or more actively through team affiliations, 'open door' policies and job enrichment, form a large part of the unitarist agenda.

Nevertheless, unitarist sympathizers may also acknowledge the existence of potential relational impediments to the realization of capital's profit-seeking objectives. For example, closing a plant may be perfectly rational behaviour from a company perspective, but persuading the employees affected to endorse the decision may be more problematic. Many unitarists believe that the provision of information through diverse channels, along with the other friction reducing initiatives described above, can defuse potentially conflictual situations by making employees aware of the harsh realities of economic life and sympathetic to negative consequences, even when they themselves are affected.

### The preservation of harmony and prevention of conflict

Many behavioural scientists and practising managers recognize that antagonisms *can* exist between capital and labour, whether at the level of the industry, organization or individual. They may have more difficulty in extending this to recognize that they *do exist*, as the articulation of conflict is more likely to be ascribed to frictional relational problems or systems failures (perhaps through failure to communicate management intentions effectively) as distinct from clashes between fundamentally opposed forces. For the management scientist, the problem has been to eradicate friction from the system, lubricate employer–employee relations and thereby, it is assumed, eliminate potential sources of conflict. Many of the approaches advanced to secure this objective merge into a single stream of individualistic techniques predicated upon a unitarist frame of reference for relations between employers and employees. Equally important, the assumptions underlying unitarism also provide crucial support for the authority and legitimacy of management actions towards employees.

However, as prescriptions for operationalizing the unitarist perspective on organizational behaviour developed, the dilemma of how employers should relate to trade unions, which had become established facts of industrial life, became more focused. In the early days of capitalist development, there were few problems as trade union activity was severely circumscribed by the state, on the grounds of fear of its revolutionary potential or its disruptive and hence restraining effects on trade. A combination of industrial development, involving progressively larger and more complex enterprises which made collectivization harder to subdue, social reform and a growing recognition of the reformist as opposed to revolutionary intent of trade unions (see above) helped to legitimize trade union activity in most industrialized countries. Nevertheless, against this background, individual employers were left with the problem of knowing how to confront union organization. The unitarist thesis, with its denial of sectional interests, pointed either to outright opposition to collective organization or to evasion or to both.

Opposition could take the form of simply refusing to recognize the presence of trade unions accompanied by sanctions against union activists. Avoiding unions is more subtle in that the employer creates an environment in which employees do not feel the need for outside protection. This may be accomplished by removing fears of insecurity by publicizing a no-redundancy commitment, by appealing to competitive instincts by rewarding individual endeavour, and by introducing a range of techniques designed to encourage 'enterprise consciousness' as opposed to the 'class consciousness' underlying employee collectivization. Employers might engage in both 'pull' and 'push' activities towards their workers, pulling employees towards them through offering appropriate inducements, whilst at the same time pushing, if necessarily forcibly, against organizers and activists within trade unions. A common example of this approach has been the periodic popularity of profit-sharing which employers might deploy as a means both to reinforce their relations with employees and to deter union organization by excluding union members from the scheme (Ramsay 1977; Bristow 1974).

Based upon these observations Ramsay has developed a 'cycles of control' thesis, in which he contends that over time a pattern can be witnessed in which employer use of these involvement techniques is heightened at times of strong economic performance and intensified union agitation and challenge to management control. Once the critical phase has passed, management interest in involvement passes. The 'cycles' thesis has been criticized for its lack of relevance to contemporary employee relations in which management-inspired employee involvement has adopted a historically high profile at a time of considerable union weakness and disarray within the labour movement (Ackers et al. 1992). Ackers and his co-workers contend that managers can introduce their involvement techniques for a multiplicity of reasons, not necessarily connected with labour control. Nevertheless, there is little doubt that managerial interest in involvement is closely related to organizational need to respond effectively to the demands of the product market, and that this largely impacts upon gaining workforce commitment despite restricting numbers of employees, intensifying their work or altering job content. More fundamentally, Ackers et al. question the validity of the oppositional interest and zero-sum assumptions underlying Ramsay's argument, claiming that both workers and managers can and do benefit from the imposition of involvement techniques. An important question, though, and one which is not really confronted in the Ackers critique, is the *cui bono?* of the involvement paradigm: for whilst not denying that employees can benefit from share schemes, for example, it does appear that employees also stand to lose out, perhaps through weakening attachments to their unions, and employers also expect to derive an unquantified motivational benefit from schemes which they have unilaterally introduced.

*Productivity and motivational objectives*

One common issue to be confronted by all employers, especially in an unsophisticated, developing and highly competitive industrial context, is that of raising productivity through increasing employee output. In more developed economies or industries, the emphasis may shift toward consideration of performance criteria, such as quality enhancement, rather than simply raising output alone.

An early and influential attempt at resolving the output problem was made by F.W. Taylor, who believed that workers were motivated primarily by monetary reward and in consequence argued that work should be structured through deploying scientific principles of management to encourage workers to maximize their income, by relating their earnings directly to individual output produced and by offering appropriate physical conditions to encourage peak production levels. The subsequent 'Fordist' techniques of assembly line production also leant heavily upon Taylor's prescriptions.

In the early years of the present century the attentions of occupational psychologists focused almost exclusively upon improving the physical conditions of work in order to encourage optimum output levels (Rose 1988:Chapters 2 and 3). The emphasis began to alter by the 1930s following the revelations of Elton Mayo and his co-workers, whose Hawthorne experiments indicated that work performance was more sensitive to social factors, such as group affiliations and supportive leadership, than to the optimization of physical conditions. Their findings also cast doubt upon the validity of the Taylor thesis of a straightforward 'rational economic' motive for worker effort (Fox 1985:81–93). 'Human relations', as it became known, developed into a major stream of management thought and in its later formulations gave prominence to the ideas of Herzberg, Argyris, McGregor, Likert and other neo-human-relations advocates in their espousal of concepts such as job enrichment, where employees are offered greater areas of task discretion and rewarded with praise through person-centred leadership approaches.

### Enterprise consciousness amongst employees

Abiding echoes of unitarist human relations principles can be found within contemporary constructions of 'human resource management'. These principles have gained further prominence through contemporary organizational concerns for quality and reliability, which cannot easily be imposed but must be associated with values internalized by employees themselves. Many companies now offer share ownership schemes, convene quality circles and conduct regular employee attitude audits in order to maintain congruity between their objectives and those of the workforce.

### The regulative tradition

The regulative tradition emerges from reformist actions of the democratic state in which macro-economic interests in maintaining efficient production and distribution are balanced against social concern for citizens as producers and employees as 'industrial citizens' who, under hierarchical management authority, enjoy only restricted democratic rights at the workplace.

The operation of a market economy assumes interest differences between purchasers and sellers. Hence, a principal effect of the operation of market forces is the generation of interest conflict between the exchanging participants. Between producers and purchasers these conflicts of interest are maintained and resolved through the combined actions of the price mechanism, laws of supply and demand and availability of legal redress for either party in the event of contractual disputes between them.

In relations between employers and employees as buyers and sellers of labour, however, the potential problems are more complex, for employers not only 'purchase' labour power but control its deployment within a continuing relationship, itself mediated by unpredictable or unforeseen external events such as technical developments and market recession. These, together with the economic resources at the disposal of the employer, tend to place the employees in a vulnerable and dependent position *vis-à-vis* their employer. Hence, the potential for conflict between capital and labour, and arguably for exploitation by employers of individual employees, is continually present. Under strong economic conditions, it is also possible that employees, represented and co-ordinated through trade unions, may be capable of exploiting conflict in pursuit of economic advancement or in confronting specific aspects of management control.

Within these potentially unstable circumstances, most industrialized (and indeed industrializing) countries have taken some responsibility for providing protection for both employees and employers. Often these protections take the form of defining and then ensuring a balance between rights and obligations shared between the parties and enshrining these in law. Hence, in some European countries, there is a legally protected right to strike, but this is matched by a platform of conditions under which industrial action may be taken. Nevertheless, for the reasons indicated above, employees are generally more vulnerable than their employers and more reliant upon them, and a range of protective rights, such as information provision, consultation and union membership promotion, have been introduced by the state in many countries in recognition of this imbalance. In Britain and America, the emphasis has been more on legitimizing the representational and negotiating role of trade unions within a generally abstentionist framework of state action. The state may become more actively involved if it believes that the balance has become too strongly inclined to one party or another or if the actions of either or both parties are regarded as obstructive to broader economic policies or damaging to political stability.

In contrast to the unitarist emphasis which inspires much of management thinking and action, the role of the state in ensuring and promoting balance between the interests of employers and employed generally stems from more pluralistic concerns that recognize the presence of competing interests, which may best be protected or promoted through representation and negotiation between collective entities such as trade unions and employers. Conflict under these assumptions is neither abnormal, nor pathological, as assumed by unitarists: through appropriately channelled forums, joint regulation can contribute to the well-being not just of participants whose interests are being protected and advanced but of the economy itself.

Pluralist regulation has a long history. In Britain it found expression in state attempts to institutionalize processes of collective regulation, as witnessed in the findings of the Whitley Commission in 1917 which recommended the establishment of joint union–employer negotiating committees at national level, supplemented by regional negotiating bodies and workplace consultative councils. This machinery has remained as a standard feature of public sector industrial relations for many years. Confirmations of the value of collective bargaining between free participants resurfaced with the findings of the Donovan (1968) and Bullock (1977) Reports. The Donovan Report was also strongly influenced by academic considerations on pluralism, a line of thought which was articulated in Clegg's view that independent trade unions and voluntary processes of negotiation represent the most appropriate form of 'industrial democracy' within a plural society (Clegg 1960).

Similar considerations helped to motivate the evolution of collective bargaining in America. Speaking of the passage of the National Labor Relations Act in the United States in 1935, Kochan et al. comment that:

> The labor policies adopted in the 1930s as part of the New Deal were designed to introduce greater stability and order and to lend a degree of permanency to union–management relations. Unions had presumably achieved a position of legitimacy in American society since collective bargaining had been chosen as the preferred mechanism for worker participation and representation in industry. (1986:5)

A number of recent American writers have continued to postulate positive synergy between the presence of trade unions, their representative responsibilities and productive efficiency (Eaton and Voos 1992; Kelley and Harrison 1992) and we return to this issue in greater depth in Chapter 7.

As we shall also see in subsequent chapters, European countries have tended to promote the construction of protective representative employee bodies such as works councils and worker directors as the means by which pluralist influence is expressed at work, with collective bargaining also available to address and resolve economic differences arising between the parties. The Social Chapter, which embodies a code of protective rights for employees extending across the European Union (with the exception of the UK), is the most recent pan-European attempt to regulate participative relations between employers and employees.

## The search for definitions

To each of the three patterns of employee influence described above, we can attach appropriate, and associated, models of employer–employee interaction which reflect both the degree of employee influence available, and the desired extent of that influence within industrial organizations.

The radical tradition postulates that atomized employees are alienated from the processes of organizational decision-making and as such are vulnerable to treatment as pliable and dispensable units of production. From this polar position, the call has been made for democratic procedures to be injected at the highest organizational levels in order to restructure authority relations within industry and thereby to make all aspects of industrial decision-making available and accountable to the majority of participants who are disenfranchised by existing structures. For this reason, as noted above, we have labelled this far-reaching approach to altering the foundations of relationships between employer and employees as industrial democracy.

At the other extreme, adherents of the conservative tradition might acknowledge that, *en masse*, employees do have little opportunity to exercise strategic influence within their employing organizations. They might counter, however, that individual employees are employed on a contract which does impute specific rights to employers and their managers to control employee labour, and obligations upon employees to acknowledge these rights. They might also add that the same contract provides any dissatisfied employee with the right and freedom to terminate the contract. Traditionalists also argue that employees have shown very little interest in engaging in organizational affairs, preferring to leave these specialized activities to those qualified, whether through expertise or by status, to undertake them (see Brannen 1983:74). Extending this argument, they might also add, in a unitarist tone, that employees willingly submit to the authority of management on the grounds that managers seek to fulfil organizational objectives to the benefit of all participants within the enterprise. Finally, managers and their sympathizers contend that employee influence interests are task rather than organization based, and in this narrower area management has done much to promote heightened discretion as well as information provision through processes of what we term employee involvement.

In contrast, institutional reformists recognize the democratic shortcomings of unregulated market relations at work and advocate means by which the imbalance of influence over strategic or organizational matters might be addressed. They might also adopt the pluralistic line that employee–employer relations are potentially conflictual and hence endorse or introduce similar measures which serve to regulate conflictual tensions. Again, as noted above, these approaches, which include collective bargaining and other representational forums, we term employee participation.

The paradigm of employee involvement (EI), employee participation (EP) and industrial democracy (ID) is essentially one of ascending levels of control by employees over their work and organizations. There are clearly problems inherent in adopting a classification of this nature, as the application of employee influence is highly political in that its exercise either restricts the exercise of managerial prerogative or, in its more radical formulations, removes it altogether. Even the management-oriented conservative tradition is unlikely to find favour with all sections of management, some of whom may well feel threatened by 'empowering' techniques which have implications for delegating management responsibilities and hence for overall numbers of management.

The use of terminology becomes an important resource in helping to define and give shape to the scope of employee influence. Employers have traditionally rejected not only demands for industrial democracy, but even usage of the term. In more recent years their demarcation has become even more marked, as demonstrated in the UK where political backing for state intervention in support of participative employee representative initiatives has lessened as part of the governmental shift towards reinforcing free labour market conditions. Managers now tend to talk exclusively in terms of employee involvement.

## The demise of industrial democracy

Industrial democracy as represented by a 'thorough-going change in the structure, aims and hierarchy of the enterprise' (Eldridge et al. 1991:144) which provides workers with a strategic or commanding role in enterprise management has only spasmodically surfaced in Western countries. Often it has been linked to broader political movements, such as with the Móndragón workers co-operative network established in the Basque region of Spain (see Poole 1986:102). Nevertheless, though supreme control of the enterprise is vested in the workforce, in practice the co-operatives are run on hierarchical lines, with little potential disturbance to management control (Brannen 1983: 138–9; Whyte 1991:91). In other Western countries, where regional and political associations are less pronounced, co-operative ventures have often been promoted or have emerged as an alternative to failed traditional enterprises or as marginal operations to fill small-scale niche markets, such as wholefoods (Hobbs and Jeffries 1990).

On a similar note, the experience of Yugoslavian self-management, as noted above, once hailed as a potential model for state–industry relations prior to the cataclysm which struck the region, also offers little optimism for industrial democracy based upon collective management, as a combination of state interference and bureaucratic controls combined to weaken the effectiveness of these joint enterprises (Thompson and Smith 1992:14). Further, there is little doubt that, like co-operatives, self-managed enterprises offered little tangible influence to employees, whose works councils tended to be subordinated to the requirements of management objectives.

Other 'socialized' economies, which witnessed and promoted innovative if limited programmes of organizational restructuring, have themselves undergone radical transformation. In these countries, where employee decision-making powers were very much tied to state ideological concerns and performance requirements (Bean 1994:166; Pravda and Ruble 1986: especially Chapters 1 and 11), the transformation seems to have left little enthusiasm for maintaining existing democratic or participative structures in industry, let alone embarking on new ones, especially in those countries like the Czech Republic where a new breed of capitalist is threatening to assert control. Indeed, Pollert and Hradecka note that, following liberalization, 'many of the new Czech employers . . . quickly shifted to the neo-classical right' (1994:561).

Moreover, Central and Eastern European countries are now heavily reliant upon incoming investors, whose terms of entry could include restrictions on employees rather than the granting of greater freedoms. For instance, in Hungary it has been suggested that 'some foreign investors have been quite open in their anti-unionism and sought political support for this position before committing further capital investment' (Hughes 1992: 294–5).

More generally in Central and Eastern Europe, trade union structures and membership have been greatly fragmented since 1989, matched by a growing atomization of employer interests, as privatization has created a plethora of diverse interest groups amongst both employers and employees. Prospects for employee influence on decision-making in the new Central and Eastern European industrial relations appear to be following two trends, neither of which conforms with the concept of industrial democracy. At national level, tripartite forums have emerged in a number of countries, most notably Poland, the Czech Republic and Hungary, involving new trade union con-federations and employer representatives from both the public and the private sectors. This neo-corporatism, however, masks a different trend within enter-prises: collective employee representation (not least through works councils) has experienced a growing marginalization as employers introduce Western-style EI into their organizations in order to stimulate employee performance and organizational efficiency to meet the new demands of integration into an increasingly competitive world economy. In other words, whilst some groups of employers in Central and Eastern Europe recognize the political merit of working with government and unions at state level (partly to ensure a rea-sonable degree of societal stability), decisions and policies emanating from these forums may well become increasingly divorced from the reality of work-place industrial relations in this region, where the extent of employee influence on organizational decision-making is restricted to shopfloor pro-duction matters (see Mason 1994).

## Conclusions

From the point of view of this book, it is recognized that the focus of interest in employee decision-making, whilst retaining its intensity, has shifted from concerns of industrial democracy to those of employee involvement and par-ticipation. Arguably, the extent to which these processes become anchored within organizational and political systems will help determine whether industrial democracy will be condemned to become part of the heritage of the labour movement or will provide an inspiration for fundamental change in employment relations. It is to these major developments that we now turn our attention.

# 2

# Employee Involvement and Participation in a Competitive Climate

The entry point for our enquiry resides in the nature of employer responses to heightened levels of competition encountered by organizations during recent years. These responses will be both guided and mediated by the political and economic environment in which commercial activity is undertaken. Hence, taking the UK where pursuit of 'free enterprise' has dominated political thought in recent years, government action has concentrated on sharpening competitive forces and on encouraging employers to respond in cost-effective ways to the competitive climate. In pursuit of these objectives, the state has tended to promote forms of employee relations designed to offer flexibility and freedom of choice to employers and to steer industrial relations practice away from costly and time consuming workplace decision-making agreed collectively with trade unions towards unilaterally employer determined working arrangements. As the concept of participation has traditionally been associated either with worker and union attempts to dilute management authority or with government policies to democratize the processes of industrial decision-making (Lane 1989:225), it is not too surprising that both right-leaning politicians and employers encourage practice of the (apparently) less politically charged 'involvement' concept in preference to 'participation'.

In this book, therefore, in order to distinguish between processes which in terminology and practice can too easily become blurred (see Marchington et al. 1992:6–9), *participation* will refer to state initiatives which promote the collective rights of employees to be represented in organizational decision-making, or to the consequence of the efforts of employees themselves to establish collective representation in corporate decisions, possibly in the face of employer resistance. This definition would include collective bargaining over terms and conditions of employment (see Bean 1994:161). *Involvement* will refer to practices and policies which emanate from management and sympathizers of free market commercial activity and which purport to provide employees 'with the opportunity to influence and where appropriate take part in the decision-making on matters which affect them' (CBI, reported in *Labour Research* 1991b:12).

**The scope of employee involvement**

There are a number of features which can help to distinguish the two processes. In involvement terms, 'opportunities' for employees tend to be those which encourage them to conform with and adjust to patterns of product market activity. It is for this reason that information provision to employees, which in practice tends to be an essentially passive form of EI which aims to alert employees to the dynamics and effects of market forces, has become a major element of involvement practice. Similarly, with markets in a state of flux, involvement practice inclines to be low level, assuming 'matters which affect' employees to be those which are located within reach of individual employees or their immediate workgroups, but which extend little or no input into corporate or high-level decision-making: they do not 'involve any de jure sharing of authority or power' (Marchington et al. 1992:ix). In similar fashion, involvement tends to be based on individual issues or managerially defined problems (such as quality) rather than on offering employees a systematic route into corporate decision-making (Eldridge et al. 1991:165). For this reason, many forms of direct employee involvement might also be interpreted as 'job involvement' which tends to be unilaterally management initiated with little or minimal collective employee contributions (see Poole 1986:Chapter 3).

It is within this restricted framework that the British Employment Department unambiguously describes its motives for promoting employee involvement as 'part of the Government's drive to improve the flexibility and efficiency of the labour market' (HMSO 1989:3). As a potential contributor to the government's flexibility project, involvement can be seen as an ingredient of its wider market-driven policy, other aspects of which include repressive legislation against union activity, removing 'barriers to employment' by providing employers with wide discretion to recruit and dismiss workers, and dismantling regulatory and protective controls such as wages councils and training boards (*Employment for the 1990s* 1988; Trades Union Reform and Employment Act 1993). Within a voluntarist or free market framework, there is little in the way of public policy which might bind employers to formalized involvement arrangements and thereby detract from management's capability to respond to market signals.

**The scope of employee participation**

An alternative state response to the uncertainties associated with market fluctuations is to offer employees a measure of protection against the harshness of unfettered market forces by providing them with some say in events which could disrupt or otherwise affect their working lives. It could also be argued that repercussions of market developments strengthen the case for employee protection. The rise in part-time and unconventional employment patterns serves to increase the dependence of employees upon organizations whose prime motivation is to respond effectively to market signals. These employment patterns have emerged in order to facilitate such responses quickly and without regard to the needs of affected employees. Also, the rise in computerized information systems can serve to distance commercial operations and their effects from the influence of employees, especially in global concerns. In his study of banking, isolation of information technology from operational processes has been identified by Cressey as one of the key factors which help to explain 'negative involvement of staff' in that sector:

> the computer services section or electronic data processing divisions were physically separate and distinct units, apart from the retail body of the banks. Their staff had different qualifications, training and career structures. This meant that the opportunity for extensive involvement about the form and functions of the technology was, in the main, denied. Technical development of both hardware and software was highly centralized, and 'gifted' to the branches ready-made: it came in the form of a black box, as techniques to be learned, or as new disciplines to be mastered. (1992:185)

In order for a protectionist process to serve a useful function for its intended beneficiaries, appropriate mechanisms are needed to inform employees or their representatives of high-level company intentions and to offer an established route which empowers them to influence those intentions. Participation under these conditions is likely to involve representative employee membership of higher-level decision-making bodies which formally equips them with opportunities for more profound inputs than are found with the narrowly defined market adaptation processes associated with employee involvement. For this reason, statutory backing may well be necessary to ensure consistent and uniform employer compliance with these objectives. Works councils, which have been established in many countries, especially within the European Community, for a number of years (discussed at length in Chapter 7), provide one recognized mechanism for participation delivery (see EIRR 1991b). Collective bargaining, and state support for it, is another participative approach which can provide employees with opportunities for decision-making which extend beyond joint determination of pay and conditions of employment.

Though participative approaches aim to provide employees with protection, in their non-collective bargaining format they might also derive from a less adversarial industrial relations perspective than that which gives rise to employer dominated involvement. Where the need for adequate systems of representation of collective interests is recognized and accepted as a valuable contributor to long-term industrial harmony, participation might also form part of a system which positively *encourages* employers to plan for the future through investment in plant, technology and people, and to include human resource development as part of long-term planning and investment strategy. In these instances, whilst providing employees with a measure of security, participative arrangements would also conform with a pattern of industrial decision-making typified by reference to long-term performance objectives. The shorter the time horizons by which companies operate, the less likely it is that they will wish to engage in binding collective determination of long-term employment issues. In the United States of America, a group of economists associated largely with Harvard University has extended this participation supportive argument to embrace union activity, which in pursuit of its employee objectives provides an effective workplace collective voice; this is seen as doubly beneficial in that employee morale is expected to be higher as a consequence of representative participation, and also there is an incentive for management to invest and train for efficient and cost-effective production (see Nolan and Marginson 1990; Kochan et al. 1986:144; Deutsch and Schurman 1993).

## A systematic comparison of EI and EP

We are now in a position to compare and contrast the two processes of involvement and participation more systematically. It can be seen that EI is associated directly with employer requirements for an adaptable workforce, receptive to production needs in terms of flexibility and commitment. To establish and reinforce these qualities it is assumed that employees will respond positively to information disclosure by and through management and by opportunities for enhanced discretion over narrow areas of work. EI is essentially a *process* of management which derives from unitarist ideas which construct a hierarchical ordering of workplace authority in which involvement seeks an instrumental outcome in terms of individual employee responsiveness.[1] By contrast, EP emerges from government or workforce attempts to address market inequalities by inserting provisions whereby employee interests over company decisions may be addressed.

The main distinguishing features are shown in Table 2.1. From the table it is clear that EI and EP share contrasting and to some extent, conflicting, characteristics as reflected in the main objectives associated with both processes. It is perhaps for these contentious reasons that interest in EI and EP has sharpened as employers attempt to utilize their resources to best advantage and employees strive to offset the effects of an increasingly difficult labour market through existing participative procedures.

## Employers' rationale for employee involvement

In an increasingly internationalized and intensified competitive climate for goods and services, pressure upon management to operate effectively becomes manifest. One expression of increased attention to comparative performance is that an increase in productivity, or more specifically in labour productivity, assumes mythic proportions for both managers and government policy-makers. Numerous contemporary studies have documented the attempts made by managers in both the UK and elsewhere to raise productivity levels through industrial relations reform (Metcalf 1989; 1990; Nolan and Marginson 1990).

Whilst companies can adopt a number of measures designed to enhance

Table 2.1   *Employee involvement and participation compared*

| Employee involvement | Employee Participation |
| --- | --- |
| Management inspired and controlled | Government or workforce inspired; some control delegated to workforce |
| Geared to stimulating individual employee contributions under strong market conditions | Aims to harness collective employee inputs through market regulation |
| Directed to responsibilities of individual employees | Collective representation |
| Management structures flatter, but hierarchies undisturbed | Management hierarchy chain broken |
| Employees often passive recipients | Employee representatives actively involved |
| Tends to be task based | Decision-making at higher organizational levels |
| Assumes common interests between employer and employees | Plurality of interests recognized and machinery for their resolution provided |
| Aims to concentrate strategic influence among management | Aims to distribute strategic influence beyond management |

labour productivity, two main approaches can be identified, the first coercive in nature and the second more integrative. Both approaches are likely to be preceded or accompanied by overall staffing reductions (see ACAS Annual Report 1990) and in practice, of course, both approaches can be operated in parallel in the same organization, as company contraction requires that the smaller numbers of remaining staff perform at optimum levels. Also, an initially coercive approach might serve to weaken the influence and standing of union representatives, opening the way for more individualist exercises in employee involvement.

The first approach then is of a forceful nature in that it encourages harder work through the application of an implied or explicit threat to the continued employment of employees. Examples of a directly coercive approach can be witnessed in the attempts at 'macho management' exemplified in the early 1980s in Britain by the activities of employers such as Michael Edwardes at BL, Rupert Murdoch at News International and Ian McGregor in the coal industry. Reports of similarly confrontational managerial approaches have become widespread in the United States (see e.g. Meyer and Cooke 1993). Less directly coercive approaches might endeavour to lower employment security through the use of temporary, part-time and subcontracted labour in employment practices associated with the 'flexible firm'. Notwithstanding the publicity attracted by the cases cited above, the extent to which 'coerced flexibility' has been adopted has been questioned. Studies have indicated that the highly publicized abrasive management style adopted by Edwardes and others has not become a dominant feature of employment relations. Also it has been pointed out that such approaches are more likely to be adopted for initial 'shock' treatment but are unsuited to form the basis for a longer-term motivational programme when workforces have been depleted, high-cost technology has been introduced and quality-based competition is rising (see MacInnes 1987:Chapter 6). Even the extent and directions in usage of flexible non-typical employment patterns involving temporary, part-time and subcontracted staff have been subject to question (Pollert 1988; Blyton 1992).

Work flexibility may also be sought by restructuring the range of tasks and responsibilities of employees through a process of 'job involvement' or 'quality of working life' (QWL) policies which require workers to take on added responsibilities or tasks in order to accomplish management defined objectives (Kochan et al. 1986:153). The added discretion which accompanies job involvement may encourage management to introduce or extend appraisal systems into manual job categories as a means to maintain managerial control over revised work practices less amenable to traditional monitoring and supervisory techniques (see Randell 1989). Performance-related pay allocated according to management discretion might also accompany these changes (Anderson 1992).

A second approach toward enhancing performance is more 'integrative', in that techniques are injected into employment practice with an intention to encourage improved employee performance through establishing or reinforcing a sense of common purpose between employer and employees. These approaches, described more fully below, also conform with features associated with the 'human resource management' school of employee management, which argues that the investment potential of valuable human resources may best be realized through individually centred commitment inducing techniques (see Chapters 4 and 5). The use of integrative approaches would also be consistent with the flexible 'job involvement' exercises noted in the preceding paragraph.

## Approaches to employee involvement

As employee involvement derives from the voluntary actions of individual managements, there is likely to be a wide diversity of approach adopted in practice. Nevertheless, three main directions to EI may be identified (see Marchington et al. 1992; Tillsley 1994):

*Downward communication flow EI*   This form of EI can be subdivided into communication from management to groups of employees, and communication with a focus on individual employees in the organization. Techniques of individual downward communication include house publications, newsletters, video presentations and chairman's forums. Group downward communication is demonstrated by the use of team briefing or briefing groups.

*Upward communication flow EI*   Individually focused techniques which could be included within this category are employee suggestion schemes and attitude surveys. Group forms would include quality circles and other related quality-centred techniques.

*Job restructuring* This category would include 'traditional' job enrichment and quality of working life initiatives as well as the more recent 'employee empowerment' moves publicized by some employers.

Employee involvement will be considered in greater depth in Chapter 5. In addition to these main streams there are a number of EI techniques which are slightly more difficult to categorize either because of their hybrid nature or because of their borderline status between involvement and participation. An example of the former would be performance appraisal which is often intended to act as a two-way, vertical communication bridge between individual managers and individual employees. While individual share schemes serve to inform employees about their company and its market position, their appeal to management can be based on the rather more substantial ideological ground of property ownership. For this reason the impact of financial involvement is assessed in depth in a separate chapter (Chapter 6).

There are some approaches which are more difficult to categorize owing to their (potentially) contestable nature. These activities can be included under the broad definition of 'joint consultation', which for the purpose of exposition will be discussed in Chapter 7 in our examination of employee participation, and can be seen from management's point of view as a form of 'representative' or 'collective' involvement.

**The growth of employee involvement**

There is a growing body of evidence that, in aggregate, usage of the involvement techniques outlined above has increased throughout mainland Europe (Bean 1994:183), the United States (see e.g. Deutsch and Schurman 1993) and, as we shall now show, especially in the UK. Since the 1960s in Japan there has developed a range of quality-based involvement techniques and informal communicative practices, which have also helped to influence practice in America and the UK (see Oliver and Wilkinson 1992:Chapter 2).

The Workplace Industrial Relations Surveys (WIRS), conducted in 1980, 1984 and most recently in 1990, provide a comprehensive view of developments in workplace industrial relations in Britain. The findings show that in the early 1980s managers reported a higher increase in the introduction of all forms of employee involvement between 1980 and 1984 than in the three years prior to 1980. Overall, the proportion of managers reporting 'any initiative to increase involvement' rose from 24 per cent to 35 per cent with particular emphasis given to 'two-way communication systems', a trend confirmed by worker representatives in the survey. It was also believed that the *variety* of involvement initiatives had grown (Millward and Stevens 1986:165–7). Between 1984 and 1990 the growth in involvement continued, with newly introduced arrangements reported by 45 per cent of all establishments, in contrast to 35 per cent in the previous survey (Millward et al. 1992:176). This most recent survey hinted at some qualitative changes in involvement practice in that the incidence of collective-oriented consultation had declined from 34 per cent in 1984 to 29 per cent of establishments in 1990, whilst task-centred or employee-passive initiatives such as briefing groups and communication techniques continued to grow (1992:180).

Further recent evidence for the prevalence of consultative and communicative forms of involvement in Britain is provided by the 1990 ACAS survey, conducted in 576 private sector establishments (ACAS 1991); the 1990 CBI survey (*CBI News* 1990); and the Employment Department (ED) 1991 survey of 377 British companies employing more than 250 people (*Employment Gazette* 1991). Qualitative case study research in 25 organizations conducted by Marchington and his colleagues (1992) reveals that four-fifths of EI schemes operating in their case study organizations had been introduced during the 1980s. In common with the 1990 WIRS study, the latest ED study showed a decline in the numbers of formal consultative forums from 60.0 per cent in 1988 to 43.5 per cent in 1991. Whilst WIRS pointed to structural explanations for this decline, the ED suggested that the increase in *individual* communication and involvement techniques might help to explain the apparent drift away from the more collective nature of joint consultation (1991:663–4). Findings which indicate the trends for individual involvement practices as revealed by these recent studies are presented in summary form in Table 2.2.

Table 2.2  *Employee involvement in Britain: findings from recent studies*[1] (*per cent*)

|  | WIRS 1980 | WIRS 1984 | WIRS 1990 | CBI 1990 | ACAS 1990 | ED 1991 |
|---|---|---|---|---|---|---|
| Joint consultative committees | 34 | 34 | 29 | 47 | 40 | 44 |
| Quality circles etc. | NA | NA | 35 | 24 | 27 | 16[3] |
| Suggestion schemes | NA | 25 | 28 | 35 | 36 | – |
| Attitude surveys | NA | 12 | 17 | 20 | 31 | – |
| Company literature | NA | 34 | 41 | 46 | 53 | 41 |
| Team briefing[2] | NA | 36 | 48 | 36–62[4] | 55 | 24 |
| Establishments (no.) | 2,040 | 2,019 | 2,061 | 943 | 576 | 377 |

[1]  The minimum establishment size in the WIRS was 25 employees and in the ACAS survey was 50 employees. No size data were provided for the CBI survey. The minimum company size was 250 employees in the 1991 ED study. The use of involvement techniques grows with establishment size, meaning that the generally higher proportion of the above techniques recorded by the ACAS and ED surveys may not be representative of practice in industry as a whole.

[2]  The apparent variation in the use of briefing groups may be explained by definitional differences between the studies. For example, the WIRS study in 1984 referred to 'regular meetings between junior managers/supervisors and all the workers for whom they are responsible' but only elaborated this definition into 'briefing groups' or 'team briefing' in the 1990 survey (Millward et al. 1992:165–6).

[3]  The ED study included quality circles and suggestion schemes as a single category.

[4]  Formal team briefing reported by 36 per cent of respondents and team briefing exercises by 62 per cent.

*Sources*: Millward and Stevens 1986; Millward et al. 1992; *CBI News* 1990; ACAS 1991; *Employment Gazette* 1991

In summary, it appears that pressure from competitive forces, combined with favourable environmental conditions which serve to undermine collective labour resistance to change, has offered opportunities for management to evaluate their approaches to employee control. Whilst there is disputed evidence of shifts toward more forcible deployment of labour in order to establish greater functional, numerical and financial flexibility in employment, management moves toward techniques aimed at employee integration through involvement have become increasingly visible in recent years.

## The rationale for employee participation

The previous section demonstrates that employee involvement evolves unambiguously from management objectives to utilize organizational resources in ways which are compatible with evolving market and technological needs. Employee participation, conversely, emerges from a collective employee interest to optimize the physical, security and aspirational conditions under which employees are contracted to serve. These ambitions are likely to be supported and promoted by political ideas, systems and parties sensitive to the potential deprivations which accompany unregulated market operations, but resisted by employers whose freedom of action may be curtailed by protective participation procedures.

An example of employer prejudice to employee participation proposals is well demonstrated by the UK experience. Tensions between the contrasting interests of employers and labour became evident in the UK during the late 1970s: during this period, political expediency to mobilize union support was articulated by a strong (if patchy) union impetus toward participative arrangements which were capable of propelling employee interests beyond the areas bounded by collective bargaining alone. Together, these movements manifested in proposals for worker directors, planning agreements and joint representative councils. The most ambitious of these initiatives was undoubtedly the attempt to introduce a participative framework based on worker directors using the formula of a unitary board composed of equal numbers of shareholder and union appointees supplemented by a minority of 'neutral' directors. These proposals, made by a majority of the members sitting on the Bullock Committee established by the Labour government,[2] were subsequently frustrated by internal divisions in the union movement, a lack of political will by the then ruling but tottering government, and the concerted opposition of employers and Conservative politicians toward the threatened erosion of managerial decision-making and hierarchical prerogatives (Cressey et al. 1981; Brannen 1983:102–3; Eldridge et al. 1991:162). In brief, the confrontational stances implicit in traditional voluntarist industrial relations as expressed in a preference for collective bargaining were unable, ideologically or practically, to accommodate the joint concessions required by the parties for the adoption of alternative participative arrangements. The subsequent emergence and realization of the 'Thatcherite' enterprise economy effectively removed any formal government policy attachment toward collective participation in the UK during the 1980s and early 1990s.

Though underdeveloped and strongly contested in the UK, support for formal collective participation in individual European countries and within the European Union remains strong. It appears that the following are necessary (if not sufficient) contextual features for participation. First, the political environment is supportive toward a balance of worker and employer influence through collective participation. In addition, political preference for collective participation may arise from allegiances between labour and governmental institutions, for as Lane reminds us: 'labour has usually achieved significant gains during the assumption of government power by social democratic or socialist parties' (1989:225). An example is provided by the Swedish Democratic Party which introduced its Co-Determination at Work Act in 1976 following pressure from both manual and white-collar union confederations (Martin 1984:268–78; Long 1986). It is consistent with this relationship between political and industrial influence that many of the Swedish participative reforms have since been subject to critical review and subsequent dilution following hostility of employers and the ascendancy of more conservative administrations since 1976.

A second and related point is that continuity of participative process is contingent upon a measure of broad political consensus for the concept and practice of participation. An important factor may be state acceptance of (or preference for) regulation of an otherwise undisciplined labour market. Third, many participative initiatives are buttressed by supportive legislation; institutionalization of participative procedure ensures consistency of application and helps protect the interests of the more vulnerable partners to the participative arrangements (see Poole 1986:174). Fourth, stability is encouraged by an assumption that 'participation in decision-making entails a sharing of responsibility for company performance between the parties involved' (Lane 1989:225), an assumption which was fatally lacking from the UK proposals for worker directors noted above. Underpinning this assumption is a belief that open confrontation between representatives of capital and labour is not necessarily the most beneficial approach to meet the longer-term interests of either party. Long-term issues can be identified and resolved constructively through collective problem solving forums which recognize both ultimate interdependence of the parties and their sectional interests.

The enthusiasm with which employers are likely to endorse such measures will be examined in subsequent chapters. At this stage, however, we could note that as these initiatives are mediated through the organization, there is likely to be scope for some manipulation by employers and senior management. To offer examples, following the growth in interest in boardroom participation in the 1970s in the UK, worker director experiments were established in the nationalized steel industry and in the Post Office; in both cases, however, worker directors were unable to confront strategic issues through a lack of union support and an inability to move beyond the workplace issues with which they felt most comfortable, a role that was 'validated by other members of the board' (Eldridge et al. 1991:160). Similarly, managers were neither encouraged nor trained to embrace a more participative decision-making approach when dealing with their worker directors (Taylor and Snell 1986). The comments of the General Secretary of the National Communications Union involved in the Post Office experiment readily confirm the difficulties faced by worker directors in gaining acceptance from their management counterparts:

> management was able – without much difficulty – to keep real decision-making out of the supervisory board, withdrawing into formal or informal management-only fora. Many important decisions were therefore merely rubber-stamped by the board, and as the worker directors had not been party to managerial discussions they found it difficult to influence the direction of the company. This tendency was helped by the general acceptance of 'management's right to manage' on the part of the independent directors. (Young 1991:78)

Similar weaknesses can be found in the many pensions trusts established by company pension funds following the Social Security Act of 1975 which encouraged pluralistic administration and supervision of pension payments and investments. Research shows that it is rare for employee trustees to take on anything other than a minor role which focuses chiefly upon personal and discretionary payments to pensioners, leaving strategic investment and financial decisions to the 'experts' (Schuller and Hyman 1986). In the early 1990s Mirror Group scandal we have seen that a lack of accountability in occupational pensions trusts can lead to disastrous consequences for potential beneficiaries.

It is also clear that the existence of a framework of participative legislation need not preclude the employer from embarking upon involvement schemes aimed at reinforcing management control over employees or of subverting participative intentions. Indeed, employers might be *encouraged* by these policies to introduce schemes which serve this function. It has been suggested, for example, that the impact of wage-earner funds introduced in Sweden in 1984 has been softened by the parallel implementation by Swedish employers of company-based share schemes (see Chapter 6). Also, a surge in employer endorsed involvement initiatives occurred in the UK as an accompaniment to the heated debates over the Bullock proposals (Cressey et al. 1981) and again in the 1980s partly as a counter to common participative measures proposed for the European Union (see below).

### Approaches to employee participation

Whilst collective participative practice varies in structure, scope and responsibilities from country to country, three main categories can be identified in the form of works councils, board-level worker representation and collective financial participation. The contours and influence of financial participation are reviewed in Chapter 6 and the impact of works councils and worker directors is considered in Chapter 7.

### Works councils

Works councils are found in the majority of European countries. Eleven out of 15 countries examined in a recent study have provisions for works councils or similar structures (EIRR 1990a). Though considerable diversity in structure and range of responsibilities is apparent, conceptually, a works council is a representative body composed of employees (and possibly containing employer representatives as well) which enjoys certain rights from the employer. In general, the principal rights laid down for works councils are (a) a right to receive information on key aspects of company activity and (b) a right to be consulted on issues prior to their implementation by management.

### Board representation

Unlike the Bullock proposals which advocated a unitary board of directors representing shareholder and employee interests, most countries which legislate or provide for employee board membership do so through a two-tier structure, where employee representation is applied at the higher 'supervisory' board which meets infrequently to formulate and monitor overall policy, strategy and progress. Supervisory board decisions are passed for implementation to an active management board of senior executives where employee representation is either lacking or offered on a minority basis.

### Collective employee share schemes

One of the economic and social inequalities faced by employees in their relations with employers is the imbalance of wealth and property ownership. For this reason, labour movements in a number of countries (and notably in Scandinavia) have advocated wealth accumulation schemes based on collective ownership and administration of company shares, which would offer institutional influence to union shareholders similar to that enjoyed by pension funds and other collective bodies. The British TUC and Labour Party both tentatively addressed the issue of collective funds in the early 1970s at a time when union influence in the political domain was strong, but have since withdrawn to positions more supportive of company-based employee share ownership combined with extended rights of union-based participation (Baddon et al. 1989:54).

### Recent initiatives for participation

Two main interrelated influences may be discerned in guiding the main directions of participative thinking, policy and practice in any country. The influence of the state is important in the extent to which it aims to regulate (or liberalize) the activities of industrial participants coupled with its commitments to maintain a perceived balance between the rights and obligations of capital and those of labour. The state of power relations between these participant parties provides the second factor; as we have seen this relationship is not necessarily a stable one, but will be shaped and mediated through the changing political, economic, legal and competitive environment in which it operates.

The tensions inherent in the emergence of participative or involvement practices are clearly demonstrated by the struggles over the ultimately abandoned attempt to introduce worker directors in the UK and over the scope and operation of wage-earner funds in Sweden. When the debate switches to a broader international canvas, the complexities multiply. This has become apparent with regard to the tortuous and, at the time of writing, unsuccessful attempts to introduce a common platform of participative procedures throughout the European Union. These struggles have centred around policies for board representation, procedures for information disclosure and more latterly the adoption of the European Social Chapter for employees.

In 1970, prior to the UK's entry into the Community in 1973, proposals for a 'European company' with employee representation on the upper of a two-tier board and a works council were under discussion by the central Council of Ministers (Brannen 1983:59). These discussions were suspended inconclusively in 1982, but a new framework for a European Company Statute was launched in 1989 including plans for employee participation compatible with the Fifth Directive on company law which was first introduced in draft form in 1972.

The Directive called for management (upper) board-level representation from companies employing more than 500 people. Under combined pressure from employers and their Conservative allies in the UK, the draft Directive was never ratified and in 1983 the requirements were altered to invite member states to provide employee participation either through supervisory board representation (one-third to one-half of seats), or through works councils offering similar rights to information and consultation as board membership, or through 'any other collectively agreed provision which included employee participation at supervisory board level' (EIRR 1990a:6). Despite protracted discussions, the continuing opposition of commercial interests and Conservative ministers has led as yet to no conclusive action.

Moreover, there has been no resolution to the information and consultative proposals first drawn up in the so-called 'Vredeling' draft Directive for large and complex enterprises. These proposals would require company management to disclose statistical information to employee representatives on an annual basis as well as to reveal to representatives details of corporate decisions with serious implications for the workforce. Initial obstacles were faced as a result of problems encountered 'because of British obstruction' over confidentiality and because of the fears of multinational corporations, whose parent companies would be obliged to disclose and consult over operations based in Community countries, that competitiveness would be undermined as a consequence (Wedderburn 1990:37). These doubts were confirmed by a failure among the Council of Ministers to achieve the unaminity required to adopt the proposals.

The Social Chapter 'seeks to reconcile the free market with a socially responsible state' (Hepple 1991:10) and has been adopted by all member states with the exception of the UK. The Social Chapter provides for 12 fundamental rights to workers and these have been operationalized in the so-called Action Plan which accompanies the Social Chapter. Eighteen draft Directives are included in the Action Plan and numbers 17 and 18 deal generally with rights to information, consultation and participation in decision-making. The Action Plan proposals for information disclosure and consultation closely follow the Vredeling initiative outlined above, and have received the expected hostile reaction from UK Conservative ministers and company representatives.

## Conclusions

Organizations are operating under increasingly competitive conditions, leading many to take responsive action. In the UK, companies have also been sheltered by political and legal changes which favour the development of an ethos of enterprise and a culture of individualism, encouraging the adoption of unitarist principles and flexibility through individually oriented involvement practice. Under these political and commercial conditions, collective employee participation has fared poorly; in countries like the UK and the USA, it has received no domestic political endorsement and little sustained support from a weakened union movement.

Continental Europe has witnessed a greater political commitment to regulation of market forces through the imposition of legal provisions for social controls over working conditions. Opposition between ideologies of liberalization and regulation has been expressed politically in the impasse within the European Union over the directions to be taken by employee participation.

Two initial questions are raised by these developments. First, what are the practical effects of different involvement techniques on employee relations; are they, as their proponents contend, exerting 'dramatic effects' on the performance of companies through restructuring employment conditions and relations? Second, we need to examine the approaches which have been adopted to employee participation with the question in mind as to the effects they too exert on employment relations and company performance. Specifically, we need to question whether the fear on the part of many employers of a unified platform of participative rights is justified. These questions will be addressed in the following chapters.

## Notes

1 The fact that some EI techniques aim to broaden the discretionary powers of employees over their work tasks might appear to imply that supervisory duties may pass to subordinates, thereby disrupting the managerial hierarchy of responsibilities. In practice, where such practices have been introduced, supervisors and/or line managers have been expected to move from routine

supervisory and disciplinary tasks to assume broader, more 'facilitatory' responsibilities. The threat to these managers comes not from an invasion of their supervisory territory, but from the fact that fewer supervisors may be needed to carry out these redefined duties or that they (or *their* managers) may feel that existing supervisors are ill-equipped through training or aptitude to carry them out satisfactorily. The challenges faced by supervisors are well considered by Storey (1992:Chapter 8). A company case study examined by Clarke (1993) further illuminates the problems.

2 The 1974 Labour government established the committee chaired by Lord Bullock to examine the most appropriate ways by which worker directors could be established. The committee reported in 1977 with recommendations to set up a unitary board of directors in large concerns with more than 2,000 employees. The board would be composed of equal numbers of employer and employee directors with a smaller number of mutually acceptable 'neutral' directors. This main report was accompanied by a minority report, largely drafted by employer representatives, which distanced itself from the recommendations contained in the majority report.

# 3

# Industrial Structure, Work Organization and Employee Involvement

The present chapter aims to illustrate the effects that changing patterns of industrial structure are having upon employer demands for labour. The significance of these changes for systems and practices of managing employee relations is then considered.

Taking the UK as a model for the multiplicity of industrial changes occurring in the 1990s, we first investigate the broad sectoral shifts which have taken place within the economy and the changes in occupational structure which have followed or been associated with these shifts. We then examine forecasted changes for industrial structure and the concomitant adjustments in labour utilization which are expected to be needed in order to meet industrial reorganization. As alignment between these shifts is neither simultaneous nor frictionless, current pressures upon labour supply are apparent and may well intensify. In turn demands for new areas of expertise and employee adaptability pose questions for approaches to employee control and work organization which many employers are currently seeking to address.

## The scale of industrial restructuring

The first point that we would stress is that industrial restructuring, represented primarily by the decline of large-scale heavy industrial enterprises and the rise of service sector and small-scale light industry, is a common phenomenon among the established industrial countries of Western Europe and the United States. Table 3.1 demonstrates the similarity of patterns of change between industrial and service employment for selected countries between 1963 and 1990. Agricultural employment in all these countries has also been in long-term decline (Hill 1988; Bamber and Whitehouse 1993).

More detailed studies show that manufacturing industry has been particularly affected. In Germany, for example, manufacturing employment declined from 44.1 to 33.7 per cent between 1960 and 1990, whilst employment in the service sector rose from 40.2 to 56.8 per cent over the same period (Jacobi et al. 1992:225). In America over recent years, 'manufacturing has contracted enormously while growth in the services has exploded' (Deutsch 1993:329).

Sectoral shifts and their associated effects upon occupational structure have also been instrumental in hastening decline in union membership in most of the developed market economy countries (see Bamber and

Table 3.1   *Changes between industrial and services employment for selected countries, 1963–1990*

| Country | Proportion of civilian employment (%) | | | |
| | Industry | | Services | |
| | 1963 | 1990 | 1963 | 1990 |
| --- | --- | --- | --- | --- |
| France | 40 | 30 | 40 | 64 |
| Germany | 48 | 40 | 40 | 57 |
| Japan | 32 | 34 | 42 | 58 |
| Sweden | 41 | 29 | 46 | 68 |
| UK | 46 | 29 | 49 | 69 |
| USA | 35 | 26 | 58 | 71 |

*Source:* Bamber and Whitehouse 1993:283

Whitehouse 1993:310; Bean 1994:78). In the United States decline has been considerable, with overall density falling from about 30 per cent of the employed workforce in 1970 (Visser 1992:19) to between 13 and 18 per cent in the early 1990s (Bean 1994:78). As much of American participative practice focuses upon collective bargaining between employers and unions, the potential weakening effects upon collective bargaining as a consequence of these developments are readily apparent (see Kochan et al. 1986:54).

In the UK, industrial restructuring has been particularly evident and the drift away from manufacturing is predicted to continue. Further, this pattern is being replicated, to varying degrees, throughout the industrialized world. Therefore, rather than attempt a superficial and repetitive exploration of industrial restructuring and its effects among different market economies, in this chapter we concentrate upon the experiences of one country, the UK, which has undergone substantial industrial and employment shifts.

**Reasons for industrial restructuring**

The reasons behind sectoral changes are well known. First, there has been the well-documented rise in the global economy, with the result that competitive forces have stiffened at both international and national levels, as well as internally within enterprises. Internationally, the market dominance of Japan has been maintained and its influence upon other producer nations continues (Womack et al. 1990; Oliver and Wilkinson 1992).

Nevertheless, other pressures are also emerging to confront established producer countries. Japan, along with Europe and America, is now facing a serious challenge from the recent emergence of 'Pacific Rim' countries whose import penetration into key markets is beginning to rise. Whilst the liberalization of Eastern Europe should herald the arrival of new market opportunities, it will also provide signals for inward investors attracted by the twin prospects of cheap labour and large unexploited consumer markets (Hare 1991). The completion of the Single European Market offering freedom of movement for goods and services throughout member states also represents a further stimulus for intra-European competition, leading to growing numbers of corporate mergers and acquisitions and hence larger and more remote management systems. The merger process has already seen an acceleration in the Community since 1983: in 1983–4 155 mergers were recorded, rising to 387 four years later. In 1988 the number was 753, a figure which had climbed to 1,190 by 1989 (reported in Ramsay 1991:544–5).

Markets internal to organizations have also been promoted through a combination of government policy and corporate restructuring by large organizations keen to maintain an international competitive advantage. At the policy level, the UK government has sponsored the development of internal markets in the health service (Spry 1991) and endeavoured to introduce competitive reform to different levels of education provision (see Flude and Hammer 1990).

Second, growing market uncertainty has been compounded by rapid technological advancements which have persuaded many organizations to scrutinize the skills profiles of their labour forces. Frequently, these appraisals have resulted in a diminishing number of employees and the restructuring of work arrangements and work content, with corresponding changes to terms and conditions of employment (Fogarty and Brooks 1986).

A major potential implication of technologically driven change is that there may also be consequences for management style resulting from the change, in that some employees may gain broader discretion over their jobs and become more valuable to their employer, whilst others may be confronted by control loss as previously 'skilled' tasks become redundant through technological innovation. These points will be covered in more depth in forthcoming chapters.

Third, at national level, global market and technological influences have been supplemented by a broadening of the political ideology which strongly upholds the merits of free market liberalism. Translated into policy terms, these ideologies have been reflected in initiatives such as privatization programmes (a policy which has been extending throughout Europe), compulsory tendering for public services in the UK and encouragement of small firms as the prime generator and motor of an 'enterprise economy' which also advocates removal of state support from unprofitable and uncompetitive undertakings. In practice, the release of free market forces has also given strength to protectionist employer activity through merger. Generally, market competition for the supply of 'factors of production' has also been injected into the labour market with phased relaxing of employee protections through tightening restrictions against union activity, removing low-pay controls and continuing campaigning against trade union influence in the public sector.

### The impact of industrial change in the UK

In the early 1980s, as part of a strategy for economic regeneration, government economic policy in the UK combined high rates of interest with high sterling exchange rates as part of the means deployed to tackle inflation, which continues to be regarded as the main constraint upon economic growth. These policies, administered in the face of vigorous market challenges from both developed and developing countries, as well as rationalization following privatization and changing consumer demands in areas such as agriculture, helped to accelerate employment decline in the primary and heavy manufacturing sectors in the UK.

In consequence of these fiscal policies, the most visible sectoral change to manifest itself throughout the 1980s was the shift from manufacturing industry to the service sector. Between 1980 and 1990 employment in the manufacturing sector fell by about 2 million, from around 7 million to 5 million. Over the same period, manufacturing's share of employment declined from 31 to 24 per cent (Millward et al. 1992:17). But between 1983 and 1990, employment growth in the service sectors amounted to about 2.7 million jobs (Employment Department 1991:26–7). Not surprisingly, this industrial reordering was accompanied by substantial occupational shifts. In 1979, the proportion of employees in the non-manufacturing workforce stood at 68.6 per cent: by 1989, the figure had risen to 77.6 per cent (Mayhew 1991:10). Between 1984 and 1990, the number of manual labourers dropped by more than half, from 302,000 to 148,000 (Employment Department 1991:29). Between 1975 and 1985, 70,000 full-time agricultural jobs were lost (Hill 1988:8). Employment in the coal industry has been in continuous decline during the post-war period, and this process is accelerating in the 1990s through competition from other coal producing countries and access by customers to alternative fuel sources (Thomas 1988) and through the government's commitment to reduce dependence upon domestic fossil fuels.

In contrast to manufacturing, employment growth in business services was spectacular, with over 1.25 million jobs created in the 1980s in banking and insurance following the abolition of exchange controls and deregulation of financial services. Substantial growth also occurred in hotels and catering (325,000 during the 1980s) and miscellaneous services which include leisure, tourism and cultural activities, with 1.25 million jobs established in the 1970s and 1980s (Employment Department 1991:27–8). Under the stimulus of government encouragement, the numbers of small businesses also boomed during the 1980s. It was estimated that by the late 1980s there were three-quarters of a million independent companies employing fewer than 50 people, and of these, one-third had been established between 1982 and 1988 (Hakim 1989).

One consequence of this restructuring is that industry has experienced difficulties in finding the advanced skills and professional expertise required to staff these changes. Results from the government's Skills Monitoring Survey of 4,200 establishments conducted in 1990 found that 22 per cent of all establishments claimed to have encountered recruitment difficulties and 42 per cent of these establishments reported that their business activities had been hampered as a consequence. Professional, engineering, managerial and skilled occupations were the most difficult positions to fill (Employment Department

1990:Chapter 4). The engineering consultancy group, EGOR, estimated that the supply of qualified engineering graduates trailed demand by some 8,000 a year in the UK (EGOR Group 1990).

There seems little doubt that current patterns of industrial restructuring will continue. Manufacturing, mining and engineering are all expected to continue to contract the scale of their operations. The implications for employment in these areas are clear, for whilst employment overall in the UK is expected to grow by an aggregated 2.6 per cent between 1990 and 2000, there is an anticipated employment decline for these industries as shown in Table 3.2.

Table 3.2    *Forecast employment decline for selected industries, 1990–2000*

|  | Decline (%) |
| --- | --- |
| Agriculture | 25 |
| Mining, etc. | 25 |
| Utilities | 24 |
| Metals, minerals, etc. | 33 |
| Engineering | 10 |
| Textiles and clothing | 30 |

*Source*: Institute for Employment Research, in Employment Department 1991:27

Over the same period, major increases are projected for employment in health and education (17 per cent), hotels and catering (17 per cent), and 'miscellaneous services', concentrated upon leisure and tourism (25 per cent). Business services, which include banking, insurance and other commercial activities, are also expected to continue to expand, albeit at a slower rate (12 per cent) than was experienced during the 1980s (Employment Department 1991:27). In consequence, the composition of employment is predicted to continue its progressive shift from manual to non-manual work, with demand increasing for higher-level professional and managerial skills. Table 3.3 charts the projected changes in occupational composition for the years 1990–2000 for selected occupations.

A similar trend in the demand for highly qualified personnel is apparent throughout the industrialized world. It has been predicted that: 'By the end of the century, 70 per cent of all jobs in the [European] Community will be carried out by so called brain workers, and of these activities, no less than 35 per cent will require a university degree' (*Times Higher Education Supplement* 2 March 1990).

## Restructuring and manpower shortages

There is little doubt that demands for labour in the competitive markets opened in the European Union will reinforce the pressures for highly skilled personnel. Recognition of industry's problems in finding qualified staff coupled

Table 3.3   *Projected employment changes for selected occupations,*
*1990–2000*

|  | Change (%) |
|---|---|
| Corporate managers and administrators | +13 |
| Professional occupations: |  |
|    Science and engineering professions | +27 |
|    Health professions | +14 |
|    Teaching professions | +18 |
|    Other professional occupations | +26 |
| Skilled construction trades | +7 |
| Industrial plant and machine operatives | −17 |
| Drivers and mobile machine operatives | −7 |
| Other occupations in agriculture | −19 |
| Other elementary occupations | −6 |

*Source*: Institute for Employment Research, in Employment Department 1991:31

with acknowledgement of the contribution which education and training can make to economic performance have stimulated educational reforms geared to raise the supply of skills through enhancing rates of advanced educational participation. The UK government expects that by the end of the present decade, nearly one in three of all 18–19 year olds will participate in higher education (HMSO, 1991a:10) and is actively encouraging more young people to continue with vocational education by offering support to employer proposals to set targets for half of 16–19 year olds to achieve two GCSE A levels or their vocational equivalent by the year 2000 (HMSO 1991b:55).

Industry therefore is facing both a transitional and a chronic problem of skill shortages. The short-term problem will be exacerbated by the downturn in the number of young people available for employment through the twin effects of demographic change and higher post-compulsory educational continuation rates. Participation in education by 16–18 year olds has increased from 52 per cent in 1980–1 to 58 per cent in 1989–90. In higher education, the full-time student population expanded by 48 per cent in (the then) polytechnics and by 14 per cent in universities over the same period (*Labour Market Quarterly Report* 1992:5). The increase in demand for people with formal educational and skill-based qualifications, coupled with current shortages and fuelled by continuing changes in industrial and employment structure, mean that the workforce will need to become more educated. The signs are that this trend is already under way (see HMSO 1991b:Chapter 2). Moreover, whilst the skill shortage problem is compounded by the notorious and continuing failure of British employers to train and develop their staff (Finegold and Soskice 1988) or managers (Handy et al. 1988), pressures for people to continue with their education and training at work are also growing. For example, there is a body of evidence that performance appraisal is increasing in usage (Long 1986) and one of the functions of appraisal is to offer employees scope for occupational advancement and personal development (James 1988).

These twin developments, of chronic shortages of key personnel and a growing dependence upon a workforce with high qualifications which are readily transferable across different workplaces, have put pressures upon employers to take positive steps to attract and retain their scarce employees whilst securing high levels of commitment from them. These pressures complement a further, quality-based, requirement which emerges from the changing nature of competition.

### The pursuit of quality

In a competitive economy, price of product or output has traditionally been treated as the key determinant of consumer choice. In circumstances where products are simple in design, where there is little product differentiation, where skill inputs are limited and where customer quality expectations are low or indifferent, price remains a key criterion – and the main objective for management is to deploy its labour resources in order to produce optimum output at minimum cost. Under these conditions, workers are likely to be seen in 'cost' terms and treated as a factor of production: in consequence, sub-managerial work is likely to be repetitive, fragmented, undemanding in terms of skill, discretion and decision-making, closely monitored through human or technological supervision and rewarded by output-based remuneration such as piece work or incentive schemes. In other words, demand for labour by an employer can be seen as a demand *derived* from the nature of the product or service offered by the employer. Elementary products are likely to require elementary standards of labour and relatively unsophisticated processes of labour management geared to optimizing output. Clearly, alterations of the broad industrial environment such as those described in the preceding paragraphs help to structure employer demands for labour, and the pressures generated are partly responsible for mismatches between supply and demand and hence the skill shortages noted above. In similar ways, changes in customer requirements, production methods and technological advance can influence demands for labour.

In contemporary developed societies, increasingly sophisticated and demanding consumer requirements may be noted. Quality standards introduced and aggressively promoted by Japanese and American companies have helped to stimulate organizational responses at both domestic and European levels. A European Foundation for Quality Management has recently been established which aims to 'develop and implement comprehensive quality strategies, which cover the whole industrial educational system, and will become embedded in Europe's industrial culture and values. These strategies create quality advantages in the market by providing value for the customer' (Burke and Moss 1990:15). Other EU initiatives include Europe-wide co-operation on quality projects in a number of high-technology industries and a movement for EU-wide specified quality standards.

Domestically, sustained interest in quality assurance is maintained through the system of British Standard BS 5750, which seeks to 'lay down the requirements for a cost effective quality system, and how to establish, document and maintain it with a view to demonstrating to customers that the organization is committed to quality' (*Personnel Management* 1990). Quality management, described as 'a total philosophy involving the focused attention of everyone' (Giles and Williams 1991:30), concerns satisfaction of the needs of both 'internal and external' customers through an integrated approach to quality control and enhancement, involving the entire workforce. This approach is visible in many Japanese companies and is increasingly being discussed and indeed adopted in American and British enterprises (Giles and Williams 1991; Wickens 1987:Chapter 5).

It is not surprising that for many products and services the key is not price alone but price combined with a range of other criteria which help to structure patterns of consumption choice. Quality, strict adherence to delivery times, variety of models or of services, extended periods of warranty and after-sales facilities have all become common attractions of a modern competitive economy. An early 1990s survey of over 200 large manufacturing concerns located throughout the European Union confirms that: 'Broadly speaking, the average European manufacturer's sequence of priorities is: quality, delivery, dependability, price and flexibility' (*Financial Times* 21 January 1991). Consumer expectations of service standards in sectors where market disciplines cannot easily penetrate have also led to public utility experiments in setting performance targets through various 'customer charters' and documented declarations by corporations of their obligations to the public and the ways in which these will be met. According to one commentator:

> The old-style public services, each a monolith with a single organizational structure, ethos and rigid set of pay and conditions, are withering fast. Choice, standard and quality are the catchwords: flexibility, performance and local management the tools; the private sector the model. The Citizen's Charter unveiled by the Government . . . reverberates to them all. (reported in Beaumont 1992:113)

Whilst technical innovation is undoubtedly a key feature in ensuring high and consistent standards of quality, choice and output, technology must be combined with the required human inputs along the entire chain of production. Again, this suggests that employers are required to recruit and develop staff who are capable of meeting ever more stringent quality standards. Satisfying these criteria not only requires a level of technical competence but, in the view of many management writers, also demands employee commitment and loyalty as expressed in positive work orientations and willingness to remain with the employer. Managers also need to develop the social skills required in order to sustain employee commitment over time. Hence, the Director of Personnel at Nissan UK lists the key responsibilities of supervisors at the company as involvement in personnel selection, formal communication with team members, having total responsibility for quality, ensuring continuous improvement in quality and output, and training team members in pursuit of maximum adaptability (Wickens 1987:184–5). Moreover, in the process of developing skills for quality, 'management have to learn to lose a little power, employees to take empowerment' (Giles and Williams 1991:29).

In consequence, it is arguable that managers are seeking (or need to seek) ways to gain more than mere compliance from their subordinates. As part of this process, a social as well as a contractual dimension to the employment relationship can be identified; and if the social element is geared instrumentally to soften the harshness inherent in contractual relations, it also serves to establish a working environment aimed at securing organizational objectives through meeting the needs of employees as identified by management. One approach employed in the development of 'social' employment relations is to foster a style of management which offers involvement opportunities to employees reinforced by paying attention to satisfying their purported motivational needs. It is against this background that a 'human resource management' approach to staff control is said to have emerged, and which is discussed in the following chapter.

## Technology and the demand for labour

One factor that can influence the demand for labour by employers is the impact of technology. Many commentators assert that technological innovation is facilitated or promoted by an appropriately educationally equipped workforce and cite the examples of Japan and Germany as countries demonstrating technical competence acquired through a combination of preliminary education and subsequent workplace development programmes. Studies have indicated that the growth of UK manufacturing productivity has progressively lagged behind that of comparable industrialized countries and that technological drift has been a major contributor to the UK's productivity problems. The relative performance of the UK is shown in Table 3.4.

Table 3.4   *Index of output for all manufacturing, 1970–1987 (1970=100)*

| Year | UK | W. Germany | USA | Japan |
|------|------|------|------|------|
| 1970 | 100 | 100 | 100 | 100 |
| 1975 | 96.8 | 103.2 | 109.3 | 110.7 |
| 1980 | 96.7 | 122.5 | 137.9 | 150.4 |
| 1985 | 100.3 | 126.2 | 159.8 | 183.5 |
| 1987 | 107.1 | 129.5 | 170.3 | 190.3 |

*Source:* Cox and Kriegbaum 1989: Table 52

Differences in productivity between the UK and other countries can be attributed to three main interlocking weaknesses: (i) failure to invest in new technology (ii) insufficient numbers of skilled workers able to utilize new technology (iii) managers unskilled in the management and application of new technology. These problems were identified in comparative studies conducted in the early 1980s which concluded that 'Britain was falling behind other countries in the industrial application of microprocessors', again, for three main reasons (Fogarty and Brooks 1986:9):

1   Too many managements were ignorant of the potential scope of new technology applications.
2   Companies faced practical difficulties in recruiting skilled staff.
3   Depressed market conditions constrained employers from investing in new technology as a return on the investment might be difficult to achieve.

Despite these shortcomings there is evidence of widespread adoption of new technology in the UK. The latest WIRS shows that by 1990 computing facilities of some kind were to be found in 75 per cent of establishments compared with 47 per cent in 1984 (Millward et al. 1992:Table 1.3). The main problem is that other countries appear to be adopting a faster pace of change than the UK, based on a better prepared workforce. Researchers from the National Institute of Economic and Social Research have conducted a series of comparative studies of specified industries. In all of these, the higher technical abilities of employees and management in neighbouring countries was apparent. For example: 'the broad net of craft training in Germany has provided a basis for the rapid mastery of modern "high technology" skills. In this country [i.e. Britain], the numbers of craft and technician trainees in the engineering industries . . . have fallen drastically' (Steedman and Wagner 1987). Further evidence of recent disparities in technical qualifications between the UK and other countries is provided by details of numbers qualifying in relevant areas at different levels. Table 3.5 details these differences.

Table 3.5   *Numbers qualifying in engineering and technology, 1985*

|  | UK | France | Germany |
|---|---|---|---|
| Craft | 35,000 | 92,000 | 120,000 |
| Technician | 29,000 | 35,000 | 44,000 |
| Graduate | 14,000 | 15,000 | 21,000 |

*Source:* based on Cassels 1990:43

These figures help to fuel continuing doubts about the UK's capacity to mount an effective and sustained productivity campaign (e.g. see Mayhew 1991) and are leading to calls for the labour force to become more technologically literate. Competitive pressures are leading to an upscaling in the skills and qualifications profile of potential and existing labour force and management. However, it is for the same reasons that *all* industrial (and industrializing) countries are taking urgent steps to increase levels of qualified manpower. In France, for instance, though the proportion of school leavers taking the *baccalaureat* has grown from 11 per cent in 1970 to 45 per cent in 1990, it is still the government's intention that four-fifths of school leavers should pass the examination or one of its vocational or technological variants by the end of the century (*Human Resources Europe* 1991). In Germany, the proportion of young people taking the *Abitur* examinations (equivalent to GCSE A levels but broader in range) has almost trebled since 1970 from 10 per cent of the relevant population to 29 per cent in 1987 (West 1992:47). Both major political parties in the UK have pledged to double the number of graduates by the end of the century.

Employees empowered with advanced academic and occupational qualifications will hold expectations for progress and fulfilment from work which, if not adequately realized, could set in motion a spiral of demotivation, leading ultimately to withdrawal and loss of expertise to the company. Recent UK research has indicated that at present most young graduates who leave their first employment positions after less than two years' service do so through lack of fulfilment and opportunities for advancement. One survey disclosed that over one-quarter of graduate recruits considered that their organizations failed to show interest in their careers. More than one-third said that their managers had not been trained to look after graduates and a further 55 per cent were not able to say whether their managers had received this training or not (*Personnel Management Plus* 1990).

In an information-based advanced economy, people can be expected to want greater control over the directions taken in their own lives, and in the employment context these pressures are certain to lead to growing demands for information and involvement in issues which affect people at work. Employees will wish to make their occupational decisions as fully informed as possible and in this regard will expect their employers to provide a comprehensive and regular flow of information on which to base their decisions. Well-educated employees will also possess adequate background knowledge, capabilities and confidence to understand, question and perhaps challenge the directions taken by their organizations and the effects these might have on their working lives. Secrecy could increasingly be seen as detrimental to corporate performance.

## Organizational responses: restructuring and rationalization

From the 1980s, tightening competitive forces meant that managers of corporations were among the first to feel the effects of market pressures; often they were expected to streamline or even contract ('downsize') their commercial activities in order to maintain efficient and competitive systems of production under tight financial controls (see Ferner and Colling 1991). Many organizations sought ways to move closer to their customers, in some cases literally through geographical location or relocation: some became 'flatter' and less pyramidal as burdensome tiers of authority were shed, to be replaced by responsive, more 'organic' and less bureaucratic structures. The M form of organization, with operational autonomy delegated to functional, product or geographical divisions in order to facilitate product diversity and penetration into new markets, leaving corporate planning and overall strategy to be formulated and monitored by head office, has also grown over recent years (Marginson et al. 1988:6; Brown and Walsh 1991:49–51).

Heightened levels of internal structuring by multinational corporations seeking to make employee savings and to maintain their grip on existing markets or expand into new ones are now apparent. In the aftermath of 1992, when the internal European Union was formally completed, it has been anticipated that intensive merger activity and restructuring will be complemented by exercises designed to improve efficiency through job shedding and/or skills enhancement. There will be inevitable casualties leading to the raised possibility of corporate fatalities (Rajan 1990: 56–8). Inter-organizational co-operation, intended to avoid costly duplication of mutual benefit activities, such as sectoral research, will ultimately also be inspired by the 1992 project (Ramsay 1991:543).

Companies operating across national boundaries can create an internal market by setting up parallel operations and then use comparative performance data to discipline domestic managements and workforces. Hence, car assembly at Ford's Dagenham plant in England was threatened with closure unless it met the higher quality and cost standards set by Ford's other European operations. As a consequence of these pressures, improvements have been forthcoming, according to Ford of Europe Manufacturing Director Albert Caspers:

> I think that the whole environment is improving, there is a different attitude in the plant. We have created an environment of teamwork. It is not like them and us . . .The changes have been brought about by a combination of actions ranging from a more open management style, a willingness to involve all personnel in the changes. (*Financial Times* 26 June 1990)

Part of the emphasis has also been on upgrading workforce skills to achieve greater functional flexibility, in combined actions which are 'central to the company's attempt to develop a system of employee involvement in its UK plants' (*Financial Times* 30 August 1990). This interpretation and the objective of involvement, operating within the context of tight internal and external market disciplines, conform to the management orientation of employee involvement offered in the previous chapter. A further dimension to Ford's response to its flexibility problem is demonstrated by the job losses announced by the company early in 1992 in which over 2,000 jobs were to be shed across the company's UK operations, both in an attempt to compete with Japanese car manufacturers and as part of Ford's European restructuring exercise. Similar pressures have induced other major European car producers to announce prospective heavy job losses (*The Guardian* 2 February 1992).

## The impact of inward investment

In Chapter 2 we noted that all recent major studies have confirmed a proliferation of employee involvement practices over the past few years. In the present chapter we have indicated that there are very good reasons why employers should have turned toward innovative employee management techniques which aim at employee integration in order to cope with the demands of enhanced competition along technical and quality-based dimensions. Pressures are also building up to educate and develop at least key elements of the workforce to manage and work with these technological and qualitative developments. We have argued that education and development go hand in hand with employers' attempts to raise employees' awareness through information disclosure, to retain their loyalty through devices such as share schemes and to secure their interest and commitment through task- and group-related involvement projects. It may also be the case that involvement eases the way for managers to undertake changes in organizational structure which may be needed in order to meet these competitive demands.

Abundant involvement practices are also found in plants owned and run by overseas companies operating in the UK. Numerically, these plants are becoming more significant: the number of Japanese companies establishing manufacturing operations in the UK and America has mushroomed in recent years, from 20 in the UK in 1980 to about 160 in 1991 (Oliver and Wilkinson 1992:244). In America this process is even more advanced, with 10 major automobile plants established there by Japanese companies in the past 10 years, a period which also saw the closure of 12 domestic factories. If the pace of inward investment experienced during the 1980s continued through the 1990s (see comments in Chapter 9 on why Japanese investment may slow down), Japan's automobiles could become responsible for a quarter of USA motor vehicle sales (see Womack et al. 1990:254) and estimates of a 30 per cent market penetration in the UK by the year 2000 have been offered following the establishment and consolidation of production arrangements by Nissan, Toyota and Honda (*The Guardian* 2 February 1992).

The proportion of British workers employed in foreign owned companies has grown from 7 to 9 per cent in the space of 10 years. Moreover, the involvement culture associated with Japanese companies has generated much media and practitioner interest. Oliver and Wilkinson examined the policies and practices of 31 companies in 1987 and of 52 in 1991 and their findings attested to the high profile afforded to quality and the linked involvement methods applied in its attainment in these companies. A similar picture has been presented by Nissan's Director of Personnel in his account of the 'Nissan approach' to obtaining quality through teamwork and the lessons for the UK contained within these practices (Oliver and Wilkinson 1992:251–2; Wickens 1987). We consider these issues in greater depth in Chapter 9.

### Conditions for participation

The same pressures facing companies and the environment in which they are operating are not, however, conducive to extensions in employee participation. If anything, participative initiatives have taken a backward step, even in once favourable contexts, as we shall see with regard to collective share schemes in Scandinavia, where concerted political and industrial opposition to the concept has weakened its popular appeal and its political potency for social democrats.

In the UK and America, participation has found its most lasting and substantial expression in the form of collective bargaining conducted between employers and unions. However, for a complex of reasons, collective bargaining has lost ground in recent years in terms of overall coverage of employees and in terms of the range of employment areas subject to the coverage of collective negotiations (see Millward 1994; Deutsch 1993).

The main environmental constraint arises from the political climate, which has swung heavily against collectivist ideology in all areas of life but especially in industrial affairs. In both America (at least, pre-Clinton) and the UK expressions of political antagonism have been located in a series of statutes aimed to constrain union activity or to reduce employee protective safeguards on grounds of labour market efficiency. In the UK, the strategy has been clear: the government as policy-maker has also altered its role as employer. Where once it would regard union recognition and substantial bargaining rights as expressions of its status as model employer, it now treats unions in the public sector as impediments to the market freedoms which its policies promulgate; in consequence, bargaining rights in the cases of teachers and nurses in the UK have been narrowed (Millward et al. 1992:94) and a series of controls designed to encourage market competition for labour in other areas of the public sector have been established. In one notorious case, at the government's information gathering centre, GCHQ, union recognition has actually been withdrawn by the government. Tripartite national bodies involving policy consultations between government and representatives of employers and trade unions have been abolished, prime examples being the Manpower Services Commission in 1988 and the National Economic Development Council in 1992.

A second trend, which also partly derives from government policy, has been the dramatic downturn in UK union membership since its peak levels in the late 1970s when more than half of the nation's workforce were union members. Now, the density figure is estimated at about 35 per cent. This decline can be attributed largely to the worsening fortunes of manufacturing industry during the early 1980s as shown earlier in this chapter, exacerbated in more recent years by the rise in (typically non-union) small companies (see Beaumont 1988), the growth in the service sector and the occupation compositional shifts which accompany these changes. In one growth area, electronics, it has been suggested that smaller plant size, low age of establishment and harmonization of employee status are major determinants of non-recognition (Sproull and MacInnes 1989; Findlay 1993). Trends to decentralization (Towers 1992; Millward et al. 1992:355) and an increasing number of cases of derecognition by employers (*Labour Research* 1992) have also helped to restrict the scope for trade union representation.

In this climate, there have been no new participative initiatives by the government, whose self-appointed task has been to encourage the wider spread of involvement in order to enhance labour utilization. At the same time, no new participative initiatives have received employer encouragement or endorsement and, more significantly, few if any have been forthcoming from a somewhat demoralized and reactive union movement. In consequence, collective bargaining, the traditional instrument for participation in the UK, has narrowed in scope and in its coverage of workplaces. In Poole and Mansfield's British Institute of Management study, management experiences of formal collective bargaining and especially informal joint meetings between management and union representatives showed marked decline between 1980 and 1990 (1992:Table 12.3). These changes were paralleled by constriction in bargaining areas, as Millward et al. reported in conclusion of their nation-wide survey: 'Broadly speaking, fewer issues were subject to joint regulation in 1990 than in 1980, although most of the change appears to have occurred in the early part of the decade. Given the contraction of the unionized sector, the reduction in bargaining activity overall has been sub-stantial' (1992:353).

The United States, like the UK, has tended to eschew legalized forms of participation (Hallock 1993; Deutsch and Schurman 1993); worker influence derives from its negotiating capability and this has been undermined in recent years by confrontational employer strategies or by their attempts to avoid unions altogether (Deutsch and Schurman 1993; Meyer and Cooke 1993). Decline in union density, especially in the private sector, has been sharp and continuous (Meyer and Cooke 1993:532) and attempts to maintain or secure a participative foothold in company decisions have also been jeopardized (see Rose and Chaison 1993).

In Europe, though the prevalent forms of participation differ from UK and American experience, the vitality of its development has also been adversely affected by the reactions of employers to the prevailing economic climate, as we shall see in Chapters 6 and 7. In addition, many employers appear to be seeking more individualistic relationships through the adoption of human resource management practices, a consideration of which is presented in the next chapter.

# 4

# Employee Involvement and Human Resource Management

We have proposed that a defining feature of employee involvement is that company management acts as the prime source for the genesis, implementation and deployment of work-based involvement projects. We have seen too that under combined pressures from competitive markets, changing technology and restricted availability of skills, management is seeking to direct efficiently the performance of resources under its authority to ensure that high-quality output co-exists with consistent production flows. These changes find expression in the enhanced profile given to performance criteria in defining management objectives and tasks and in the growth of performance-related reward schemes applied both to managers and to their subordinates (Bevan and Thompson 1991; Fletcher and Williams 1992; Millward et al. 1992:361). In the light of these developments, we need to consider whether there exists a direct link between broader environmental pressures and the overall state of employment relations and the growth and directions of involvement projects.

Of particular interest for managers pressed to secure and maintain competitive performance standards is the organizational need to monitor and harness the efforts and abilities of its 'human resources' particularly as, with the growing specialization and wider dispersion of knowledge and skills, the work of these employees may be relatively resistant or inaccessible to direct forms of measurement, supervision and disciplinary procedures. High-discretion occupations such as those involving computer technology and financial control, research and the creative and labour intensive activities found in the high-profile private services sector provide growing numbers of employees with specific 'expert authority' and hence with considerable potential to influence aspects of organizational performance. Shortages of skills in certain areas, both geographical and occupational, can compound the dependence of management upon segments of its workforce.

The broad theme of this chapter is to review general patterns in the management of employees under changing conditions, and in particular to examine the extent to which EI may be associated with (or conditional upon) moves toward a distinctive human resource management emphasis in employment relations which closely integrates with broader operational objectives sought by the organization. The potential implications of the adoption of such an approach upon collective relations will also be considered in a concluding section. We first look at the main approaches which have been adopted in the management of employee relations and the role of personnel management in discharging the responsibilities associated with these approaches.

## Employee relations in a changing world

In the opening chapters we observed that one stimulus for the establishment of employee decision-making initiatives derives from managerial needs to motivate employees and direct their efforts in pursuit of organizational goals to ensure that tasks are performed in cost-effective and market-effective ways. Indeed, since the earliest days of industrialization, management control over the labour process has been treated as an essential condition for successful organizational performance, and this has provided the inspirational core for the fields of motivational studies and organizational analysis (Rose 1988:51). But competitive pressures and tighter market conditions have added several twists to the management dilemma of effectively controlling work within complex and dynamic organizational settings.

The main foundational changes which affect the nature of employee relations arise from contraction of heavy industry and manufacturing, matched by expansion in service sector activity and employment; increased flexibility of information technology; organizational rationalization (including divisionalization); trends towards flatter organizational structures; decentralization and, associated with all of these, job losses. Linked with these changes have been continuing decline in trade union numbers and density and correspondingly lower profiles for collective bargaining and union influence at work. Together, these shifts have presented both challenges and opportunities for systems of employee relations. The challenges are clear: with active and strong trade unions, management priorities incline toward conflict containment and toward maintaining stability through collective regulation, and consequently, employee relations management largely focuses on relations with trade unions (Tyson and Fell 1986:25). Looser union links mean restricted specialized joint regulatory activities which may have particular implications for personnel practitioners whose claims to specialization are largely founded upon their expertise in dealing with trade unions.

The opportunistic side of industrial and organizational restructuring is represented by prescriptions to shift from traditional modes of employee management to approaches which pay more attention to consolidating employee relations within a coherent corporate philosophy and within policy-making networks which aim to integrate workforce control with other areas of management control systems. In practical terms this reorientation involves combined action over two areas: first, a shift from a collectively oriented 'industrial relations' frame of reference to a more individualistic employee relations framework; and second, moving from a 'personnel' approach to a designated 'human resource management' style of management.

## Models of employee relations management

Repeated attempts have been made to classify management styles of employee relations, with the Fox (1974) dichotomy of unitarism and pluralism providing the foundations for a number of later derivations. It is Fox's unitarism/pluralism dichotomy which forms the platform for Purcell and Sisson's model of four 'ideal-typical' styles of employee relations management (1983:113–18) which has become a widely accepted basis for classification. Hence, unitarism might be associated both with 'traditionalists', forceful opponents of collectivism and avid defenders of managerial prerogative, and with 'sophisticated paternalists', who deploy more subtle measures to achieve the same objectives. The third group, 'sophisticated moderns', could also be designated 'reluctant pluralists', for they recognize unions but attempt to limit their influence either by constitutional or by consultative means. The fourth group is termed 'standard moderns', who have an essentially pragmatic fire-fighting approach to employee relations, underpinned by no dominant managerial ideology; and as a result, employee relations in these concerns would be highly sensitive to environmental changes impacting upon the organization. The role of personnel in this group has consisted essentially of trouble-shooting and fire-fighting negotiations with workforce representatives.

During the 1980s there were initial and well-publicized signs of a shift towards a more aggressive traditionalist orientation by managers on both sides of the Atlantic. Labelled as 'macho management' in the UK, vivid demonstrations were offered by the union confrontational approaches of Michael Edwardes at vehicle manufacturers BL, Rupert Murdoch at global publishers News International and Ian McGregor in both the national steel and coal industries. Subsequent evidence suggests, however, that this management style has not achieved common purchase (at least in larger organizations) despite the acknowledged decline in union power during the past decade (see Poole and Mansfield 1992:207). Explanations for this pattern can be found in the nature of contemporary markets for both products and labour as discussed in Chapter 3: quality, co-operation, and wider staff responsibilities co-existing with skilled manpower shortages are not consistent with overtly aggressive assertions of managerial power.

Nevertheless, union weaknesses at political, industrial and organizational levels do provide employers with opportunities to contemplate alternative arrangements for employee relations, especially at so-called green-field sites, where 'strategic choice' in the adoption of a desired employee relations system is uninhibited by existing industrial relations traditions or precedents. Some commentators suggest that increasing numbers of established enterprises are now also in a position to exercise elements of strategic choice in their relations with employees, and that a strong feature of this might involve an attempt to shift toward the 'humane' unitarist styles displayed by sophisticated paternalists such as IBM, Hewlett Packard and Marks and Spencer. Purcell and Sisson noted that the standard moderns comprised the largest private sector grouping within their classification (Sisson 1989:11), and under conditions supportive of management ascendancy, it is arguable that pragmatic and opportunistic managers might be drawn towards employee relations policies and practices less reliant upon joint regulation for maintaining control over labour resources.

Evidence from numerous sources does indeed confirm that in the UK and in America, industrial relations practices are moving towards a more unitarist stance. At the same time personnel attention seems also to be shifting from a hitherto somewhat restricted, fragmented perspective towards broader and more strategic horizons.

## The traditions of personnel management

An obvious approach to analyse and classify personnel management is to examine what personnel managers actually do and from this perspective construct appropriate models of personnel practice within organizations. Unfortunately, though, there are problems with this approach. At the outset, we must accept that because of variations in national contextual and organizational circumstances, comparisons between dimensions of personnel practice across international borders may not be particularly helpful. An additional complication, as Sisson acknowledges, is that 'not enough is known about the detailed practice to make a definitive judgement' (1989:15) about comparative personnel systems. Indeed, because of the variability of *domestic* personnel practice it is highly questionable whether a single uniform and systematic approach to personnel is identifiable in any one country. For example, in North America, personnel practice in some large organizations is highly unitarist in its formidable safeguarding of undiluted managerial prerogative, its denial of union presence, and its sophisticated paternalistic personnel processes (Kochan et al. 1986; Sisson 1989:14). Conversely, other large American concerns recognize and negotiate extensively with unions and appear willing to consolidate their bargaining relationships in order to facilitate change and maintain stability in turbulent market circumstances (see Walton 1985). To take another example, in Japan, it was only in the 1960s that sophisticated personnel processes associated with large corporations emerged alongside changed manufacturing practices (Oliver and Wilkinson 1992:53) and these have rarely extended to the mass of smaller producers where the bulk of employment is located; for more than three-quarters of employees in the private sector in Japan can be found in establishments with fewer than 100 employees (Hyman 1992:81; Eccleston 1989).

Nevertheless, we can point to some factors which are common to personnel practice and which tend to emphasize its potential vulnerability as a management discipline. As we saw above, the first common factor is, paradoxically, its variability according to environmental and organizational contexts. Further, the principles of personnel management have never been drawn from a coherent ideology or unified body of stable and independent knowledge, with the consequence that the contents and scope of personnel practice have tended to fluctuate both over time and in accordance with variables internal to the organization such as size, industrial sector, economic activity and internal management ideology. External factors, too, such as political ideology, associated legislation and national culture, impinge upon personnel's scope.

Second, personnel activities have tended to be detached or even marginal to the central or strategic directions of organizational endeavour. Arguably these personnel activities, such as employee engagement, discipline, welfare and training, have frequently been undertaken by personnel specialists as distinct activities with little or no integration between them or with core organizational strategies. Indeed, in order to maintain a position as a discrete management activity, personnel has often sought alliances with more influential management colleagues by undertaking a range of marginal tasks delegated by senior executives (and in the process enhancing personnel's 'trashcan' reputation as strikingly visualized by Drucker), or has adopted those attractive occupational objectives (i.e. results oriented, short term, easily measurable) considered by personnel to be most associated with dominant managerial behaviour (see MacKay and Torrington 1986). At best, the position of personnel has been an advisory rather than executive one. The combined result of these factors has been to reconfirm personnel dependency status and even to reinforce its subordinate position through association with ponderous bureaucratic procedures and reliance upon administrative paperwork prised from reluctant 'doers'. Also, the advisory emphasis has tended to be subordinated to the requirements of production management and to financial controls, such that policies (for example, developmental systems of appraisal or equal opportunities) formally 'espoused' by the organization and delegated to personnel for execution may not be fully operationalized if these impede more pressing production requirements or conflict with short-term cost reduction exercises (see Brewster et al. 1981 for a full discussion of the tensions existing between 'operational' and 'espoused' employee relations policies).

A related dependency problem for personnel specialists has been their somewhat deferential role to the imperatives of financial accountancy, especially in the UK, where the position has been exacerbated by shareholder pressures for companies to operate in accordance with short-term profitability criteria. According to Armstrong, there has been 'increasing domination of business organization by management accountancy' (1989:164), a profession which has the means and access to both influence and control key aspects of personnel work. A relevant example is provided by the introduction of employee share schemes in which company financial specialists are frequently closely involved, with the personnel department relegated to the comparatively minor role of administration and monitoring (see Baddon et al. 1989:249).[1]

It appears that few personnel specialists are adequately equipped to understand or challenge the ascendancy of financial controls. An associated weakness from the personnel specialist's viewpoint has been the unwillingness or inability of accountants to include human investments as part of the organization's capital assets (Armstrong 1989:160–1). Occupational subservience to 'harder' management activities such as production and finance has been reflected in the traditional hierarchical under-representation of personnel management at senior levels within the organization. To survive, personnel specialists would often take on a miscellany of roles and even neglect those longer-term activities which might develop their employees but would receive little support (or long-term finance) from their more influential managerial peers (see McKay and Torrington 1986). Under these conditions it is not surprising that, until recently, main board representation for personnel was a comparative rarity in UK companies, reflecting the typical personnel function of location alongside employees to act as the management watchdog or as provider of liaison services.

Third, personnel management has been associated since its earliest days with an inclination toward enhancing the welfare of employees rather than that of the employing organization. This association has helped to reinforce its subordinate status as a management activity. Even when it became clear that a concern for welfare need not preclude (and may even enhance) an interest in pursuing broader organizational goals, front-line production managers might not regard such 'soft-centred' approaches as compatible with good management practice, where firmness and fairness applied to close adherence to the terms of the employment contract might provide more visible means of ensuring employee compliance.

Personnel has continuously struggled with its welfare image of employee centrality. Even in recent years when institutions of collective bargaining have come under threat, personnel has been seen by some senior managers as the protector of joint procedures and defenders of pluralistic privilege in a period when unitarist principles and manifestations of managerial prerogative are increasingly being articulated.

Fourth, the management of people can be seen as a 'common-sense' activity requiring little formal preparation or specialist qualifications, unlike clearly identifiable professions such as engineering or accountancy, for example. In consequence, it is frequently maintained that personnel responsibilities could (or should) be undertaken by any competent manager. Indeed, in both the USA and the UK, the value of personnel as a distinctive management function has been subject to considerable scepticism (see Skinner 1981; Tyson 1987; for a more practical account, see Drucker 1968, who has commended the total abolition of personnel and its absorption into mainstream line management).

Fifth, until fairly recently, personnel managers have not been well qualified technically or occupationally (Millward et al. 1992:37). In consequence personnel management has not achieved the same level of 'expert authority' as that enjoyed by other technical or professional services, and has rarely enjoyed sufficient organizational status to impose its occupational authority upon sceptical line and senior managers.

Observers are agreed that these underlying weaknesses were exacerbated by broader environmental developments in the 1980s and 1990s. The rise in global competitiveness helped to push efficiency and cost saving concerns to the forefront of management priorities. In well-publicized cases, senior personnel managers were forced to abandon or modify their commitment to pluralistic bargaining and participative processes. Elsewhere, staff have been informed that company management can no longer afford the luxury of time consuming and costly bargaining encounters. Under the weight of these pressures, it seems clear that personnel practice would also be under pressure to change. But this is nothing new, for personnel has always been elastic in its breadth of coverage and plastic in relations with management peers and supervisors. The dynamics of industrial and economic development have continuously helped to mould different personnel traditions and produce different models of personnel practice.

**Models of personnel management**

The first and to some extent abiding model of personnel was provided by its welfare and charitable origins in which paternalistic employers would offer facilities to welfare visitors on a quasi-independent basis with the aim of raising health and hygiene awareness among workers (Niven 1967). This 'social reform' model gained later support from the prescriptions of industrial psychologists (see Rose 1988:Chapter 6) and from various human relations formulations. Echoes of this tradition can be found in the range of counselling services offered by personnel (Hyman and Beaumont 1985) and from its ascribed role as the guardian of the employer's conscience.

As organizations became larger and more complex in the early years of the present century, the requirements of the personnel role changed. One strand became more administrative as bureaucratic procedures were employed to ensure good employee habits of time-keeping and low levels of absenteeism. Another strand emerged in the form of the 'labour relations' function to shield employers from the emergence and eventual consolidation of trade unions by deterring union membership and activity. Subsequently, in many industries, the role adapted to include union recognition and bargaining procedures which offered limited rights of joint regulation of terms and conditions of employment to unions. In the USA, however, the union-oppositional role of personnel has never really disappeared from the management agenda (see Troy 1992; Wheeler 1993).

Other expressions of personnel activity emerged from the function's lack of organizational or occupational coherence. In the post-war years personnel management would often be defined according to a shopping list of unrelated employment activities. Manpower planning enjoyed a brief but unfruitful vogue in the 1960s (Sisson and Timperley 1994:153), after which many personnel activities fell into collective bargaining and administrative services functions.

From these different styles Tyson and Fell (1986) have attempted to construct a more sophisticated typology of personnel which embraces contemporary approaches to labour management. These writers identify three dominant strands of personnel practice. The first is as clerk of works, in which personnel practitioners undertake routine or junior clerical responsibilities, whilst employee relations policy and practice are pursued through the management line. The second model is designated as contracts manager, which corresponds to the dominant peace-keeping responsibilities allocated to personnel in union-organized concerns, especially during buoyant trading conditions, when union demands may require sensitive handling. The third approach is deemed as the architect model in which personnel takes a leading and strategic role in executive decision-making. This model emphasizes long-term policy-making and planning of 'human resources' which are treated as core contributors to organizational success (Tyson and Fell 1986:29).

### The transformation of personnel management?

In the light of the above it is surprising, perhaps, that throughout the 1980s and the 1990s there were signs that personnel not only retained its identity as a distinct organizational function but actually consolidated its place within management. This consolidation has been expressed in the following ways.

First, numbers of personnel practitioners not only remained stable but actually began to increase, in the UK (Millward et al. 1992:27), in the USA (Strauss 1992:28) and throughout Europe (see Brewster and Smith 1990; Besse 1992:40).

Second, the status of personnel, in terms of seniority remained buoyant, and according to some accounts even rose. In the UK, about 70 per cent of all establishments have personnel representation at board or director level (Millward et al. 1992:49), though throughout Europe these proportions are consistently higher (Brewster and Smith 1990). In America, too, 'the status and perhaps the clout of the newly named HR departments seemed to grow' (Strauss 1992:28). Also, there has been greater attention to occupational qualifications within the personnel specialism (Millward et al. 1992:35).

Third, there was greater appreciation of the value of people in organizational success, stimulated by growing awareness that scarce skills need special handling, especially in otherwise contracting organizations operating under intense competitive conditions. Isolation of personnel policies from business strategy becomes increasingly dysfunctional in such circumstances. It was in the United States that executive recognition of this latter requirement began to take shape, initially and perhaps significantly through the inclusion of previously optional personnel classes into the core curriculum of the highly influential Harvard MBA programme (Guest 1991; Sisson 1994:9).

Observers of the management scene began to report that a strategic manifestation of personnel management, corresponding closely to Tyson and Fell's architect model, had emerged from the competitive environment of the 1980s, and this approach of 'human resource management' (HRM) became identified with particular characteristics which differentiated it from the older fragmented, disparate activities which were said to comprise the traditional formats of people management.

### Distinctions between HRM and personnel management

Recent attempts have been made to draw distinctions between the practice of personnel management and HRM. Whilst there is no consensus as yet on all the prime characteristics of HRM, the following would represent the main distinctions between the two approaches (see Beer and Spector 1985; Sisson 1990:5; Blyton and Turnbull 1992:3; contributions to Storey [ed.] 1989).

First, the employer is unequivocally treated as the focus of HRM attention, in contrast to the employee-centred approach alleged for personnel management. In the words of one observer, 'the human resource manager starts not from the organization's employees, but from the organization's need for human resources: with the demand rather than the supply' (Torrington 1989:60).

Second, there is a strategic dimension to HRM which integrates manpower utilization within a coherent and dominant element of mainstream corporate planning and activity. Virtually all accounts of HRM stress that its proactive nature distinguishes it from the more passive and reactive traditions of personnel management (see e.g. Legge 1989).

Third, an individualistic, rather than collective, orientation is given to HRM systems of employee management, in which unitarist values are upheld. Responsibility for operating HRM policies is devolved to line management (Kirkpatrick et al. 1992:131).

Fourth, core employees are seen as assets, or social capital, whose value to the organization can be enhanced through appropriate systems of communication, employee involvement and development. It is useful to expand on this point, as it provides a key distinguishing feature for HRM.

The main departure in concept between established approaches toward employee management and HRM is that traditionally employees have been perceived and treated (if not necessarily viewed by personnel practitioners in this light) primarily as *variable costs*, and as such, much of management attention on employee relations has focused on maintaining minimal aggregate employment costs. Confirmation of this emphasis is not difficult to find: one expression of responding to the 'capital' content of employee inputs would be management attention to investment in training and development for employees, an area where UK employers consistently, and American employers less routinely, have lagged well behind their European and Japanese counterparts (see, for example, National Institute for Economic and Social Research 1989; Dore and Sako 1989). Similarly, HRM approaches would concentrate upon employee retention, whereas much of recent employment practice has been oriented toward loosening employment security (see

Blyton 1992). Moreover, efforts made by managers to enhance organizational productivity have concentrated almost exclusively on reducing employment costs rather than on long-term development of employee capability (Hyman 1992:14).

In contrast, an investment-based approach should offer employees the opportunities to enhance their 'human capital' through access to regular and continuous training and development opportunities, based upon systematic appraisals, programmes of communication to employees and quality-driven employment practices, all initiatives which 'are consistent with moves towards human resource management' (Guest 1989:51). Similar human capital characteristics dominate the profile of HRM offered by Beaumont, whose typology of HRM consists of:

1   relatively well-developed labour market arrangements (in matters of promotion, training and individual career development)
2   flexible work organization systems
3   contingent compensation practices and/or skills- or knowledge-based pay structures
4   relatively high levels of individual employee and workgroup participation in task-related decisions
5   extensive internal communications (1992:11).

The fifth distinction between personnel management and HRM is the development of the strong corporate values and culture within which systems of HRM operate. It is perhaps not surprising that two key influences upon the emergence and development of HRM have been Japanese and American approaches to people management. In their contrasting ways both Japanese industry and key American commentators stress the values of employee identification with quality directed production of goods and services within a corporate framework which emphasizes mutual responsibility between employer and employee or the pursuit of 'excellence' along a range of performance parameters: 'Such "strong" corporate cultures emphasized the values of "being the best", of flexibility, initiative and innovation, of superior quality and service, of open participative communication and, above all, of the organization's employees being its most important asset' (Legge 1994:402).

### Human resource management and employee involvement

From the above it is clear that at the very least the presence of employee involvement projects would be indicative of a move towards an HRM approach by management. We could go further and state that EI is an essential component of any move towards HRM. Sisson, for example, cites as one feature associated with HRM the 'stress on commitment and the exercise of initiative' by employees (1994:7), with managers adopting a supportive role towards these objectives. This so-called 'empowerment' approach towards

EI ostensibly aims to enhance individual discretion and has become particularly associated with the development of quality consciousness among employees. It is also apparent that an individualistic focus with regard to managerial treatment of their employees is common to both EI and HRM.

Though they do not employ specific HRM terminology in their classification of 'new industrial relations' techniques, Kelly and Kelly do include implementing performance-linked reward mechanisms such as share schemes, restructuring the organization of work by introducing quality circles and autonomous working groups, and deploying employee communications and joint consultative committees as managerial attempts to change employee behaviour and attitudes and consequently to raise productivity performance (1991:25–6). Again, use of these EI techniques is consistent with the adoption of an HRM management style.

## Hard and soft versions of HRM

We mentioned earlier that there is considerable doubt as to whether 'traditional' or authoritarian approaches to employee management have become more evident in recent years. However, a more subtle expression of traditionalist thinking might be discerned in consideration of the flexible firm where numerical, skill and financial flexibility have been identified by management researchers as the means available to employers to cope with fluctuations in product market activity (Atkinson 1985; Hunter and MacInnes 1991). This flexible deployment of manpower forms one 'hard' (in Storey's terminology) strand of an HRM approach to employee relations, typified by emphasizing the 'qualitative, calculative and business strategic aspects of managing the headcount resource in as "rational" a way as for any other economic factor' (Storey 1989:8; see also Keep 1989:110).

In terms of the three dimensions of flexibility identified above, numerical flexibility would entail a reduction in the core workforce strength, to be supplemented by expendable unconventional work patterns, such as subcontracted labour, term contracts and part-time employment. Functional flexibility might be sought through work intensification by enlarging the range of tasks to be performed by groups of employees such as craft workers. Finally, financial flexibility might be expressed by tying an element of remuneration to workgroup, unit or enterprise performance, such as through profit-related pay.

Though aspects of employee involvement might be associated with this hard dimension to HRM, it is unlikely to form a core feature of its deployment. Conversely, strategic and operational considerations might also induce managers to adopt humanistic philosophies which aim to mobilize enterprise resources toward securing coherent and possibly long-term organizational objectives. It is in this sense that an alternative formulation to hard HRM and one which has generated most interest as a presumed departure from traditional patterns of personnel management has emerged in recent years. This approach to HRM has been described by Storey as 'soft' in that it emphasizes the role of employees in establishing competitive advantage through building up the social and human dimensions to the employment relationship. This it does by emphasizing the value of employee involvement in treating employees as strategic and valuable resources, by concentrating on EI factors like 'communication, motivation and leadership' (Storey 1989:8). With the soft manifestation of HRM, there is an assumption that 'employees give of their best when they are treated as responsible adults' (Fowler 1987:3).

**Weaknesses of the HRM model**

Already, doubts about the meaning and practice of HRM are beginning to emerge; in Storey's words 'the very idea of HRM is controversial' (1992:23). The reasons for this controversy are also beginning to unfold. The first doubt is a conceptual one: observers are not yet agreed as to the meaning and significance of HRM (see Singh 1992:128), reflected in the variety of forms which personnel practice is taking in different countries with different or even contradictory characteristics emerging (Pieper 1990; see Singh 1992:127). According to some accounts, HRM can be regarded simply as a reformulation of personnel management which derives from earlier 'human relations' thinking.

Second, a practical difficulty is encountered: if HRM implies a more strategic approach to the employment of people, and if it is being implemented, we would expect to find evidence of changes, either extensive or profound or both, in patterns of employee management and in the consequences of this management. However, a number of commentators have argued that despite the putative adoption of HRM by a growing number of companies, the same companies have done little to raise their training expenditures, despite the fact that training can be regarded as the prime means of undertaking investments in 'human capital' (see, for example, Woodhall 1987). Moreover, many of the changes associated with HRM/EI, such as the introduction of quality circles, would necessitate attention to both employee and managerial training for successful implementation, but again there is little evidence that training activity or expenditure have been seriously or consistently located in this direction. A recent study by the consultancy group MORI, for example, revealed that whilst transfer of a range of employee relations responsibilities from personnel to line management is now common practice, preparation for these new tasks is afforded comparatively minor attention (S. Walker 1992:99).

Other doubts have been raised about the operational purposes, incidence of application and impact of performance appraisal, which should aim to provide the linking pin between individual and organizational performance (Townley 1989; Gellerman and Hodgson 1988). Further, though it is acknowledged that gaining genuine and enduring employee commitment is an integral part of HRM philosophy (Storey 1992:25), and there is little doubt that a whole raft of EI techniques have been launched in recent years, little is known about either management intentions for, or the effects of, these initiatives. A suspicion lurks that EI, rather than forming a distinctive strand to an integrated and long-term organizational strategy, simply represents an opportunistic attempt by management to take advantage of union vulnerability. Alternatively these techniques may be injected as a concomitant to other contemporary management practices, such as just-in-time (JIT), where it has been contended that involvement might be seen as the 'software' essential for the successful operation of the JIT 'hardware' (see Delbridge and Turnbull 1992).

A third problem with HRM is that little as yet is known about the effects upon organizations who have ostensibly adopted an HRM style of people management. Early published academic studies do not as yet provide convincing evidence for radically changed employee relations outcomes. A recent analysis of the British WIRS of over 2,000 workplaces concludes that:

> In broad terms HRM makes little or no contribution to good industrial relations. The climate of relations between management and employees and the quit rate are both worse in workplaces practising HRM than in other workplaces and the absenteeism rate is only the same as that in the average workplace. (Fernie et al. 1994b)

At this stage, however, there is insufficient evidence to conclude that there are contingent negative or minimal consequences arising from HRM practice, for there are immense problems involved in measuring both the inputs and outcomes of HRM implementation and isolating these from other potential influences on employee behaviour (see e.g. *Personnel Management Plus* 1994:9).

Nevertheless, as we have shown, EI is regarded by commentators as a prime input into HRM. If the impact of EI on employee behaviour, attitudes and performance fails to live up to the expectations of protagonists, further doubts about company conversion to a more strategic investment-centred approach to employee management would be raised. Similar conclusions would be expected if EI initiatives are introduced piecemeal with little evidence of their being part of a coherent policy of people management or of systematic integration into a wider HRM organizational strategy. These issues will be taken up in greater depth in the following chapters. Prior to this, a summary look at the relationship between HRM and participation will be made.

## HRM and participation

We initially referred to participation as those initiatives which aim to promote or reinforce collective employee influence in or over organizational decision-making. Participation practice derives from pluralist ideas which acknowledge the existence of divergent or sectional interests operating within a framework of unequal power relations between employees and employers. Recognizing the potential tensions inherent in this imbalance, pluralistic participation attempts to insert appropriate mechanisms by which the parties can resolve interest differences or make decisions in a way which takes account of the needs of both employers and employees in addressing the broader bene-fits (or in resolving negative consequences) to be derived from the undertaking. The principal European expressions of participation are found in works councils, board representation for employees and, to a much lesser (and continually diminishing) extent, collective share schemes. In the United States and the UK, the prime manifestation of pluralistic participative rela-tions has been through the machinery and operations of collective bargaining, described by Poole as 'the principal agency for workers' participation' in the UK (1986:131).

Notwithstanding the diversity of views with regard to HRM, the bulk of current writing locates HRM within an essentially unitarist context of rela-tions between employees and management for three reasons. First, work and reward practices are introduced either on the understanding that common interests exist between employees and their managers or with the intent to promulgate such commonality of interest. Second, under external competitive threat, management acts as a single locus of authority on behalf of all stake-holders in the enterprise, with the expectation that all organizational participants are likely to benefit from the unhindered exercise of that author-ity. Third, HRM has a primary individualistic orientation.

If these premises are accepted, the need for employees to be supported by externally directed protective institutions in the form of trade unions would be obviated. In this respect, Towers felt able to say that in the USA at least, 'non-unionism remains a significant characteristic of HRM companies' (1992:xvi). But whether non-unionism encourages HRM or whether HRM helps to shift employment patterns toward non-unionism is unclear. Nevertheless, UK managers display a continuing antipathy to forms of col-lective participation which are not located in traditional (and restricted) collective bargaining processes (Poole and Mansfield 1992:202). Derecognition of trade unions by employers and associated moves away from collective bargaining toward personal contracts have increased in the late 1980s and early 1990s (*Labour Research* 1992:7) and in the UK the overall extent of recognition has slumped from 66 per cent in 1984 for all work-places to 53 per cent in 1990. Decline has been most marked in manufacturing where unions were recognized in only 44 per cent of work-places in 1990 compared with 56 per cent in 1984 (Millward et al. 1992:70).

Potential danger signals to unions from HRM are demonstrated by the defining characteristics agreed by most observers of the HRM scene: a uni-fying corporate culture, individual treatment of employees through induction, appraisal and reward systems, and reinforcement through individual employee involvement and communication programmes (e.g. see Sisson 1990:5). Not surprisingly, then, we see precious little reference within HRM to anything which contributes to a collectively participative programme. In consequence and as we might expect, trade unions have generally indicated concern that HRM initiatives could represent a concerted effort by manage-ment to undermine union organization, workplace representation and bargaining influence at a time when political, economic and legal forces are already arraigned against collective activity (see Thomas 1988; Beaumont 1992; *Labour Research* 1994:5).

## Conclusions

In many countries a dominant expression of pluralistic employee relations activity is collective bargaining. If union fears of HRM intentions or effects are well founded, it would appear that among the aims of EI could be included an attempt to oppose or displace collectively based participative activity, especially in its bargaining format. Certainly, in the UK over the 1980s and 1990s, there have been few initiatives in participative activity to locate alongside the support given to involvement programmes. In the most recent WIRS, conducted in 1990, Millward and his colleagues reported that management activity over involvement practices 'increased substantially' between 1984 and 1990 (1992:175), whilst the proportion of workplaces with joint consultation declined from 34 per cent in 1984 to 29 per cent in 1990 (1992:153). During the same period, the coverage of collective bargaining extended to fewer employees, embraced a diminishing number of topics and was practised in fewer establishments (1992:Chapter 10). Even so, in those organizations where collective bargaining continued, there appeared to be few signs of it diminishing or of being superseded by other arrangements (1992:350).

It appears, therefore, that there have been substantial changes to participative procedures and outcomes. Whilst the framework of collective bargaining has not collapsed, it has certainly buckled; in addition, joint consultation, regarded generally as a management initiative, relies upon *collective* representative machinery and has declined in incidence, and there is continuing resistance by industry and government to participative proposals emanating from Europe. Also, as we shall see in Chapter 6, Scandinavian employers have introduced individual share-based programmes in a successful attempt to water down the effects of those provided by government endorsed collective shareholder funds. There may not be a fundamentally changed order in industrial relations, but change elements have been introduced through involvement projects and linked individualist practices; the extent to which these elements provide a platform for management to move against collective participation and trade unionism will be discussed in the following chapters.

## Notes

1 The problems of disassociation from core resource issues are not reserved just for personnel but apply also to personnel's bargaining partners, the trade unions. Baddon and her colleagues found that many companies intend to maintain a clear distinction between their share schemes and other elements of their remuneration practices (1989:249), thereby distancing the programme from routine pay negotiations. In consequence, union representatives would inevitably find

difficulties in gaining any influence over the operation of the scheme or over share allocations. Typically, the schemes are formally separated from other remuneration practices (and hence not the responsibility of personnel with whom employee representatives deal) or union representatives face considerable difficulties in interpreting and utilizing the profitability figures. The difficulties of attempting to negotiate from a profit base were well described by a case study workplace representative who commented: 'We talked about profit, but they lose us with the figures, so much spent on this plant, so much there – you haven't a clue where it's gone . . . they can do whatever they want with figures' (1989:194).

# 5

# Employee Involvement in Practice

Conceptually, employee involvement tends to be an amalgam of American human relations management techniques dating back to the 1920s and, as we saw in the previous chapter, the more recent development of human resource management. In practice, it is often the experience of Japanese management methods brought to the West (especially the United States and the UK) through growing inward investment that is seen as representing the working example of best practice involvement approaches (we explore this issue in more depth in Chapter 9).

Essentially unitaristic in philosophy, practical methods of EI tend to be largely focused on 'direct' forms of involvement, i.e. those approaches which involve each employee, either individually or in groups, in direct communication between management and employees without third-party intervention. In the US, Europe and the UK representational methods are normally associated with trade unionism, which by definition challenges managerial prerogatives over unilateral agenda setting. Hence, structurally, we deal with approaches such as joint consultation committees in Chapter 7, which focuses on participation.

## Employee involvement in the USA

Government policy towards the issue of EI has shifted over time in the USA and the UK, whilst in Europe there has been a more consistently participative approach adopted by governments in the post-war period. In America, the limited extent of employee influence on organizational decision-making became a 'political' issue in the 1960s, largely driven by the concept of worker alienation. The salience of this issue was highlighted by a significant deterioration both in workplace performance and in employee attitudes to work in strategically important companies and industries, such as General Motors in the automobile sector (see e.g. Harvard Business School 1981). Heightened awareness of the importance of employee motivation to the well-being of the economy inspired a large number of organizational-level EI initiatives during the 1970s and 1980s, under the rubric of the 'quality of working life' (QWL) movement.

At governmental level, however, during the 1980s, an ostensibly free market Republican government in America adopted a hands-off, voluntaristic approach to the issues of EI and participation, similar to that found in the UK in this period, and little was done to encourage the development of QWL initiatives taken at the grass-roots level. The situation changed again in the early 1990s, under the Clinton Democratic administration, with a number of new initiatives being launched by the government: first, in its role as a major employer itself, and second, to exhort the private sector business community to experiment with employee 'empowerment'.

In the context of the government being a major employer, in September 1993, Vice President Gore published a report (entitled *From Red Tape to Results*) aimed at minimizing bureaucracy in the public sector, primarily through a process of 'delayering' (i.e. eliminating middle and line managerial roles). Central to this policy document was the introduction of employee involvement methods, to encourage employees to increase productivity, partly by eliminating layers of supervisory control.

In July 1993, President Clinton's Cabinet organized a national conference on the *Future of the American Workplace*, to foster greater awareness amongst organizations of the centrality of EI and motivation, to enable American companies to regain a competitive edge in world markets. The conference advocated 'best practice employee relations', centring on: the philosophy of perceiving employees as strategic assets, investment in training and development of employees, and empowerment of employees to make decisions in the workplace. At the same time, the US government created a new section within the Department of Labor, called the Office of the American Workplace (OAW). Mirroring the UK Employment Department's early 1980s policy (see below), the OAW has been commissioned to collect and disseminate information on EI practices throughout the US (Schneider and Comfort 1993).

### Employee involvement in the UK: an overview

In the UK, to reiterate a point made in the introductory chapters of this book, much of the policy onus with regard to employment relations continues to be put on 'voluntarism'. Governmental agencies and management organizations argue strongly that companies should be allowed and encouraged to develop their own systems of involvement and communication to suit individual requirements and circumstances. This is counterposed against the European approach which is relatively more formal and legalized, and puts greater stress on those EP processes which involve consensus building collective forums. This latter approach has been most significantly expressed through various EU initiatives introduced since the early 1970s (which we explore in Chapter 7).

Within the framework of voluntarism, however, it is possible to distinguish different emphases between 'prescriptive' and 'open' approaches to EI. The UK government (Section One of the Employment Act 1982 notwithstanding[1]) has adopted what might be called an 'open voluntaristic' approach advocated principally through Employment Department publications, which in its words 'make[s] plain that British employers know best themselves how their businesses should be run and that their employees have nothing to gain from any fresh legislative constraints in this field' (Employment Department 1989:13).

Moreover, the Employment Department emphasizes the multifaceted ways in which organizations 'strive to promote the fullest participation of their people' (1989:5). In fact, legislation within the Employment Act 1982 simply requires organizations to report what initiatives they have taken in respect of EI under four very broad categories, and as we show below, offers no further guidelines on this matter.

In contrast, a more 'prescriptive voluntaristic' approach is favoured by some industrial organizations, such as the Involvement and Participation Association (IPA) and the former Institute of Personnel Management (IPM), which have jointly produced a code on EI and EP (IPM/IPA 1990). Whilst in principle supporting the UK government's anti-legalistic arguments, the IPM/IPA guidelines offer a prescriptive framework for organizations to follow that covers principles, standards of practice and application of what we would classify as both employee involvement and employee participation.

A growing body of evidence has been collected over recent years that clearly indicates the increasing utilization and importance of EI to the human resource management and 'total quality' movement in the West. In the following sections of this chapter, we turn our attention to an aggregate assessment of the incidence of involvement since the mid 1980s, then go on to a disaggregated exploration of some of the main forms and methods of EI.

Within this framework, we conclude that not only have distinct methods of EI experienced a high utilization across Western economies since the mid 1980s, but turnover in usage is high, and formalistic methods, such as quality circles (QCs), are increasingly being superseded by a more holistic 'total quality management' (TQM) concept. This latter approach, *inter alia*, entails a relative informality in the involvement of employees in decision-making processes, and less reliance upon formal, mechanistic structures. However, a mixed picture emerges regarding the implications for employee relations within the TQM trend. Some evidence points to a new strategic approach emerging for the management of human resources, whilst in other cases there appears to be a looser notion of 'open management' styles, with little impact on the maximization of employee performance in the organization.

### The focus of contemporary studies

Studies conducted since the mid 1980s have focused on three main aspects of EI. The first is the extent to which companies indicate that they utilize one or more *broad categories* of EI (UK Employment Department surveys; the Price Waterhouse/Cranfield European Project; and for the US, Osterman 1994). The second focus has been on *aggregated numbers and forms* of EI (i.e. WIRS, UK Employment Department and ACAS studies). In other words, surveys have set out to examine the total number of involvement methods utilized by individual companies, and the specific forms of involvement these take when disaggregated, such as quality circles, team briefing etc. These studies have produced a more complex picture of the trends towards open management. The third focus has been on the type of *issues* discussed in involvement forums (e.g. Millward et al. 1992). This latter aspect has produced critical insights into the rationales and expectations concerning open management, and allows us to go beyond the essentially quantitative and structural analysis offered by the first two foci. We deal with the first two aspects of EI in this chapter, leaving the nature of 'issues' to Chapter 8 where we explore more directly the question of managerial rationales.

### Aggregate surveys of EI initiatives

Across the Western economies, organizations have introduced EI initiatives as a central pillar of innovative work practices. In the US, for example, one study of just under 700 manufacturing establishments found that about a third of these had made substantial use of flexible work methods in 1992, including quality circles (QCs) and autonomous work groups (Osterman 1994:186). In Europe, the Price Waterhouse/Cranfield Project (PWCP), covering organizational communications in 12 countries, found that the most notable trend was in direct communication with employees, either verbally or in written forms (Brewster and Hegewisch 1993:14).

Section One of the UK Employment Act 1982 stipulates that companies employing over 250 workers are required in their annual reports to state the initiatives they have taken to promote EI. Under the provisions of this section, an explanation has to be given as to the steps taken in introducing, maintaining and developing arrangements for information and communication, consultation, financial participation and economic awareness. Much attention has been given to company responses to Section One by the Employment Department which concludes that companies have responded increasingly positively to the requirements of the 1982 Act.

Table 5.1 aggregates surveys conducted between 1985 and 1991 by longitudinal analysis and size of company. Clearly a very high level of companies report that they utilize one or more of the approaches categorized in Section One. By 1991 over 90 per cent of companies had introduced some form of involvement initiative. This very high proportion may not be truly reflective of actual practice, or seriousness of practice, however, as these figures include a 'simple reference' to any one initiative (i.e. denoting that the organization has raised involvement as an issue, without necessarily initiating a specific technique); nevertheless, the generally upward trend and absolute high level of involvement initiatives are clear.

In terms of size of organization, a linear trend is indicated, with larger companies (in any year) being more likely to utilize one or more Section One categories. For example, by 1991, whilst 93 per cent of companies employing 250–1,000 employees registered that they utilize one or more categories, 98

Table 5.1   *Proportion of companies responding to any Section One category of employee involvement, 1985–1991 (per cent)*

| Employees | 1985[1] | 1986[1] | 1988 | 1991 |
|---|---|---|---|---|
| 250–1,000 | 88 | 86 | 85 | 93 |
| 1,001–5,000 | 94 | 91 | 94 | 98 |
| 5,001 + | 99 | 95 | 98 | 100 |

[1]   Percentages for 1985 and 1986 calculated by dividing total numbers of reported categories (including 'simple reference' criterion) for each size of establishment, by the total number of reports analysed in each size of band.
*Source*: *Employment Gazette* 1987; 1991

per cent of companies employing between 1,001 and 5,000 responded similarly. Very large companies employing over 5,000 workers registered a 100 per cent response rate to this question (although the small sample size for companies over 5,000 employees should be treated cautiously). Overall, from the mid 1980s, Section One provisions had been taken on board by companies across the UK economy, and the majority of organizations in most size ranges responded positively that they were initiating one or other approaches to enhance communication and employee awareness of company position in the market-place.

Table 5.2 offers more insight into this question, by disaggregating the number of Section One categories initiated by companies. We have ordered this into three bands, namely those companies responding that they have not initiated any approaches; those companies who have initiated approaches to either one or two categories; and those who have initiated approaches to three or four categories.

Table 5.2   *Proportions of companies responding to numbers of Section One categories of employee involvement, 1985–1991 (per cent)*

| Year | Number of categories | | |
|---|---|---|---|
| | 0 | 1–2 | 3–4 |
| 1985[1] | 7 | 51 | 34 |
| 1986 | 9 | 28 | 55 |
| 1988 | 7 | 32 | 61 |
| 1991 | 5 | 23 | 73 |

[1]   Percentage for 1985 calculated by dividing the number of reports in 'All' column by total number of reports analysed (i.e. 751).
*Source*: *Employment Gazette* 1987; 1988; 1991

From the mid 1980s in the UK, only a very small fraction of surveyed companies appeared not to have responded to any Section One category: in 1985 only 7 per cent and by 1991 only 5 per cent. In other words Table 5.2 shows a very high level of response to this particular aspect of the 1982 Act, indicating a high incidence of EI initiatives responding to the Section One

Table 5.3 *Proportion of companies responding to Section One categories by company size, 1985–1991 (per cent)*[1]

| Company size and year | Number of Categories (%) | | |
|---|---|---|---|
| | 0 | 1–2 | 3–4 |
| **250–1,000** | | | |
| 1991 | 6 | 23 | 72 |
| 1988 | 8 | 25 | 56 |
| 1986[2] | 14 | 35 | 40 |
| 1985[2] | 12 | 63 | 15 |
| **1,001–5,000** | | | |
| 1991 | 0 | 30 | 70 |
| 1988 | 2 | 22 | 70 |
| 1986[2] | 7 | 38 | 43 |
| 1985[2] | 6 | 47 | 36 |
| **5,000 +** | | | |
| 1991 | 0 | 0 | 100 |
| 1988 | 1 | 10 | 87 |
| 1986[2] | 5 | 14 | 77 |
| 1985[2] | 1 | 38 | 58 |

[1]  Reading across the rows does not necessarily add up to 100 per cent, as the criterion of 'simple reference to EI' has not been included in this table. Also Employment Department figures have been rounded up to whole percentages.

[2]  Percentages for 1985 and 1986 calculated by dividing the number of reported categories for each size band by the total number of reports analysed in each size band.

*Source: Employment Gazette 1987; 1988; 1991*

categories. Only in 1985 did a higher percentage of companies indicate that they had responded to one or two categories (51 per cent) compared with companies which responded to three or four categories (34 per cent). In the second half of the 1980s and through the early 1990s an absolute majority of companies had responded to three or four categories. In 1991, for example, 73 per cent of companies claimed to have responded to three or four, whilst a further 23 per cent had responded to one or two categories.

In other words, as the 1980s progressed, companies were increasingly responding to the 1982 Act, with evidence that the breadth of initiatives had grown through this period, and that the majority of companies surveyed had attempted to address at least three categories with new EI initiatives and approaches.

Table 5.3 disaggregates the above figures according to company size and number of Section One categories. As in the previous two tables, a very high response level to Section One is indicated in Table 5.3. By 1991, all three size range organizations showed an absolute majority of companies responding to either three or four categories. This trend was most marked in companies employing over 5,000 workers, where there was a reported 100 per cent response rate to three or four categories. Companies employing 1,001–5,000 and 250–1,000 workers reported similar levels of response to three or four categories (70 per cent and 72 per cent respectively). Over the same time scale, the smaller companies employing between 250 and 1,000 workers showed the highest relative increase in response to three or four categories, growing from a level of 15 per cent of companies in 1985 to 72 per cent by 1991 (almost a fivefold increase). Middle-size companies showed a marginally less than two fold increase in percentage of companies responding to three or four categories, and large companies employing over 5,000 workers showed a 70 per cent increase in companies responding to three or four categories between 1985 and 1991. As the UK Employment Department concludes: 'it seems that the differences between smaller and larger companies are diminishing, and that a generally high level of employee involvement reporting is becoming more common' (*Employment Gazette* 1991:664).

The notable increase in response by smaller companies may have two inter-related explanations, both reflecting broader trends in EI. First, in the UK as well as across the USA and Europe, *informal* approaches seem to be sup-planting more formal and institutionalized methods of involvement, *inter alia*, favouring the small firm. Interrelated with the size factor, other studies have highlighted the strong correlation between informal styles of EI, and decentralized industrial relations approaches (European Foundation for the Improvement of Living and Working Conditions 1988:15); high skill levels of staff (Peters and Waterman 1982; Guest 1989); trade modes involving close staff/customer relationships (Marchington et al. 1992:45–8); and a volatile commodity market environment (European Foundation for the Improvement of Living and Working Conditions 1988:11). In other words, the trend towards informal approaches to EI can be seen to be reflective of a concomi-tant trend towards smaller, decentralized, high-skilled, customer-oriented and flexible organizations.

Second, the *unitarist* underpinnings of recent EI trends favour small firms. It is this size of company which has traditionally practised a more unitaristic style of management and contemporary involvement methods are located essentially within this framework. Moreover, smaller firms (perhaps those established in so-called green-field sites) are more able to instigate deliberately a unitaristic managerial approach to employee relations, partly reflected in the systematic utilization of EI methods.

Indeed, to an extent, the very concept of 'involvement' lends itself to a rel-atively informal expression compared with the ideas contained in 'participation', which as we have stressed are generally representative forms of employee influence, and must therefore be relatively more formalized (and perhaps institutionalized). This informality trend appears to have been devel-oping throughout the 1980s. In the UK the 1984 WIRS picked up on the same point, concluding that the overall increase in management initiatives in the early 1980s was due to more two-way communication channels being implanted (especially in relation to employee feedback) rather than to any structural innovation taking place (Millward and Stevens 1986:165). This is supported more generally by European evidence. The PWCP, covering 12 countries, for instance, found that rather than displacing collective channels, organizations are concentrating on supplementing them with more direct links with employees (Brewster and Hegewisch, 1993:14–15).

*Limitations of aggregate survey evidence*

Overall, it appears that a fairly consistent trend was noticeable throughout the second half of the 1980s, with increasingly more companies initiating multifarious EI approaches. With regard to the UK, a government Employment Department sponsored report concluded that: 'employee involvement arrangements have been consolidated and developed over recent years to suit individual companies, and . . . are now, even more than previously, an established part of working life' (*Employment Gazette* 1991:664). WIRS concurred with this view, noting in particular the growth of new involvement initiatives in the service sector (Millward et al. 1992:180). Clearly then significant developments have taken place in EI in the UK since the mid 1980s, continuing a trend established in the earlier 1980s (see Millward and Stevens 1986).

However, four caveats need to be made at this stage. First, Section One category responses give little indication of 'depth' of initiatives, for example, the organizational level of the specific method is not specified, nor indeed is the degree of employee influence on decision-making (we examine these two issues comprehensively below). Rather, these responses merely offer an overview of breadth of initiatives, under the four categories stipulated by the legislation.

Second, whilst information and communication, consultation and financial involvement tend to imply some degree of specific involvement method, the category of 'economic awareness' is relatively vague, requiring companies to indicate how they have achieved a common 'awareness' on the part of all employees of financial and economic factors affecting the performance of the company. Whilst this latter category is aggregated into Tables 5.1–5.3, it does not in itself imply, let alone explicitly indicate, that a particular method or form of EI is in place. In fact, there has been an apparent decline in the provision of strategic information concerning the financial position of the organization, according to the 1990 WIRS data.

Third, companies employing fewer than 250 employees do not need to respond to Section One, and are therefore excluded from the analysis. Therefore, we are dealing essentially with medium and large companies only, which may have a distorting effect in terms of what is happening in the UK economy overall. (Although at the same time, the trend toward informal approaches to EI is even more noteworthy given that small companies are excluded from this picture.)

Fourth, as noted in Chapter 2, UK Employment Department research and publications throughout the 1980s have reflected government policy regarding its attempt to 'improve the flexibility and efficiency of the labour market' (Employment Department 1989:5). Hence caution should be used in interpreting the findings of Employment Department surveys, in that both methodologically and interpretatively there may be a bias towards maximizing the apparent growth trends in EI, and in drawing 'positive' conclusions regarding the effect that 'voluntaristic' EI initiatives are having on employee, managerial and organizational behaviour.

## Multiple involvement practices

The above caveats notwithstanding, however, the surveys provide a valuable overview of broad trends in the UK during the 1980s. Again using UK survey evidence, Table 5.4 indicates that the growth patterns of EI presented above are also evident in the number of involvement exercises undertaken by organizations. For each organizational size band, between 1986 and 1988, there was an increase in the number of initiatives being utilized – most notably in companies employing between 1,001–5,000 workers, where the number of initiatives increased between 1986 and 1988 by 61 per cent. Over all companies, the average number of initiatives in 1986 was 4.8, growing to 6.2 by 1988, representing an increase of 29 per cent.

Table 5.4 *Average number of involvement practices by company size, 1986–1988*

|             | 1986 | 1988 | % increase 1986–8 |
|-------------|------|------|-------------------|
| 251–1,000   | 3.0  | 4.1  | 37                |
| 1,001–5,000 | 3.8  | 6.1  | 61                |
| 5,001+      | 6.9  | 8.1  | 17                |
| Total       | 4.8  | 6.2  | 29                |

*Source*: adapted from *Employment Gazette* 1988

Caution is needed in interpreting whether these figures in terms of rapid increase in numbers of EI initiatives are indicative of longer-term trends. First, the late 1980s were economic boom years for Western economies, and this phenomenon may have had some bearing on the increased utilization and attractiveness of certain EI methods, especially those that were aimed at lowering employee turnover during a period of labour shortages (an objective sometimes associated with financial EI for instance). Also, there is obviously a notional maximum in terms of the number of specific methods any one company is likely to initiate. Nevertheless, when viewed in an overall context, it is clear that multiple EI initiatives have been increasingly noticeable since the mid 1980s.

## Forms and methods of EI

In order to present a systematic exposition of the practice and rationales of both involvement and participation, the matrix in Figure 5.1 is utilized. We see involvement and participation focused on one of three employee categories: an employee representative (often a trade union workplace official), a specified group of employees (as with team briefings and quality circles) or the individual employee (such as with appraisal and development schemes). This focus entails a communication flow that is either downward (e.g. team briefing), upward (e.g. quality circles) or two-way (implied in the use of joint consultation committees for example). Two-way *representational* participation we deal with in Chapter 7: therefore the rest of this chapter focuses on group and individually oriented involvement forms, structured around upward, downward and two-way communication foci.

A multiplicity of methods are employed by enterprises for direct EI contact with individual employees (Table 5.5), such as chairman's forums, appraisal and development, counselling/mentoring and suggestion schemes, all of which attempt to involve individuals in improving their own performance and to create a satisfying working environment. Briefing groups, semi-autonomous workgroups and quality circles are examples of methods which allow for direct employee involvement, but which emphasize the importance of the workgroup or 'team' in improving the quality of production and group performance.

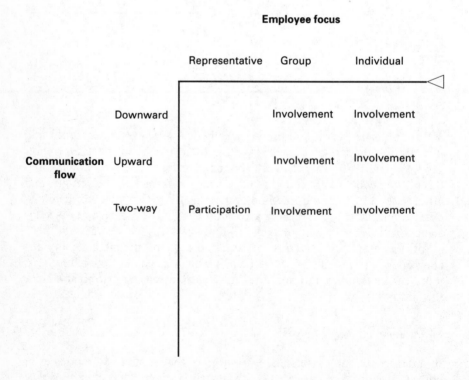

Figure 5.1   *Involvement and participation matrix*

Table 5.5 *Principles of involvement methods*

| Methods | Communication Flow | Goal |
|---|---|---|
| *Group* | | |
| Briefing groups | Downward | Team communication |
| Chairman's forums | Downward | Information dissemination |
| Semi-autonomous workgroups | Upward | Group responsibility |
| Quality circles | Upward | Quality ethos, diagnostic improvements |
| *Individual* | | |
| Counselling/ mentoring | Upward | Employee welfare/ development |
| Appraisal and development | Upward | Career development |
| Suggestion schemes | Upward | Diagnostic improvements |

## Downward communication EI

Involvement methods based on downward communication channels are aimed at transmitting information from the higher levels of the organization down to the bottom level, i.e. the shopfloor or office, and include *verbal systems*, which are often focused on the group or team of workers; and *written* forms, focused primarily on the individual employee. A key rationale for downward communication involvement methods is to enable the organization to focus employee attention more systematically on product market competition, with the aim of striving for a quality ethos across the organization. Potentially there is no technical reason for downward methods not to have a looping flowback upwards through the organization. This would mean that feedback could be obtained by higher-level management concerning responses to, and interpretations of, the original information and communication from the shopfloor. As Marchington (1990:258) reports, employees often value the consultation aspect of this type of communication, and initial managerial goals can be revised in the light of employee responses. Many organizations utilizing team briefings (the most common method of involvement in this context), however, typically argue against creating a two-way communication flow, for fear of turning this method into a consultation forum.

## Downward communication to individual employees

Written communication, often taking the form of company house journals, or newsletters, has become widespread across Europe. The PWCP found the highest incidence of written forms of communication in Finland, France, the Netherlands, Sweden and the UK, where around 60 per cent of organizations provided employees with information on 'major' employment-related issues. Approximately 40 per cent of organizations in Ireland, Portugal, Spain and Turkey provided employees with similar information. Interestingly, there appears to be little correlation between extent of unionization in the different countries and the utilization of this type of direct downward communication to employees, with companies in high union density Scandinavian countries just as likely to use written communication as low union density states such as France and Turkey (Brewster and Hegewisch 1993:16).

For the UK, a number of surveys largely support the PWCP findings as can be seen in Table 5.6. These figures are gathered from a number of diverse sources, ranging from an in-depth study of 25 companies (Marchington 1992) to the national Workplace Industrial Relations Surveys (Millward and Stevens 1986; Millward et al. 1992), and so should be viewed as reflective of general utilization and trends. But together they clearly point to the increasing popularity of this type of method for relaying basic company information to employees as each individual source shows an upward trend. WIRS offers the most reliable statistics, and shows, for example, that usage of newsletters grew from 34 per cent of companies in 1984 to 41 per cent by 1990.

Table 5.6  *Individual downward employee involvement, 1984–1991*

| Method | Companies (%) | Year | Sources |
| --- | --- | --- | --- |
| Newsletter/report | 76 | 1991 | 1 |
| Varied | 51 | 1991 | 2 |
| Newsletter | 41 | 1990 | 3 |
| Newsletter | 53 | 1990 | 4 |
| Varied | 47 | 1988 | 2 |
| Newsletter | 34 | 1984 | 3 |

*Source*: (1) Marchington 1992; (2) *Employment Gazette* 1991; 1988; (3) Millward et al. 1992; Millward and Stevens 1986; (4) ACAS 1991

However, it is unclear how well this approach achieves its informational goals, or indeed whether management have thought through the aims of written forms of communication, such as newsletters. A survey of 102 publications drawn from the UK's 1,000 largest companies found that of over 4,000 different news topics, only 24 items were contributed by employees; of this handful, five were on critical or industrial relations issues, with the rest consisting of general interest items (Spurr 1990:14–17).

This superficiality raises the conceptual issue of the extent to which written, essentially downward, communication methods might be considered a meaningful form of 'involvement'. The above survey concluded that 'a freer industrial press would provide employees with more credible news about their organisation and be a useful step to more informed employee participation' (1990:15), taking newsletters and publications out of management control.

## Downward communication to groups of employees

Group methods of downward communication have been popularized by team briefings, again reflecting the unitarist approach to employee involvement, placing great emphasis on 'cascading information down the line', from executive management through to the shopfloor. Such methods are used for informing employees of high-level or strategic decisions; for communicating general information on items such as company goals and performance; and for explaining rationales behind change decisions, for example in production technology, but with an emphasis on their effect at the local level (i.e. workgroup, department). This local orientation to briefing is reflected in the idea that teams should be made up of workgroup members, rather than based on occupational lines. Teams are typically composed of between four and 15 employees and a 'leader' (or 'coach'); briefings are held at regular intervals (about once a month) and, according to advocates, should last for no more than about 30 minutes. In order to minimize distortions in the line of communication, there should be no more than four levels in the cascade flow (Grummitt 1983). A case study of a long-standing briefing system saw the essence of this method consisting of: each manager/supervisor regularly meeting their teams face to face; information cascaded downwards; information directly relevant to performance indicators; identification of targets and progress reports; and developing 'points of action' (Employment Department 1989:40).

Team briefings have two organizational aims: first, to give line/supervisory management a greater role in day-to-day employee relations, and help make this level of management feel an integral and strategically important part of the organization; and second, to increase commitment at shopfloor level. This latter point has a number of distinct rationales: (i) to decrease misunderstandings between management and employees (this intention often stems from a managerial belief that trade union representatives may misinform the workforce); (ii) to increase acceptance of change, by explaining its rationale to the workforce; and (iii) to improve upward communication in the long term, by making the employees feel that they have the knowledge about the organization that allows them to contribute positively to its decision-making processes. A relatively long-standing example of a formal team briefing system can be seen at Peugeot Talbot, which in the late 1970s utilized an existing management committee as the vehicle in which executive management met monthly to decide on a 'core brief'. This brief overviewed all major company indicators, and was disseminated downwards through briefing groups to the entire workforce over a period of two to three days, picking up local information on the way (Employment Department 1989:41).

Again according to recent surveys, team briefings commonly feature in UK organizations. Even though the top figure in Table 5.7 of 76 per cent may be misleadingly high given the smallness of the sample of 25 organizations, larger-scale surveys indicated that by the beginning of the 1990s at least somewhere in the region of a third to a half of companies were utilizing this method.

Table 5.7     *Group downward employee involvement, 1990–1991*

| Method | Companies (%) | Year | Sources |
|---|---|---|---|
| Team briefings | 76 | 1991 | 1 |
| Team briefings | 35 | 1990 | 2 |
| Team briefings | 55 | 1990 | 3 |

*Source*: (1) Marchington 1992; (2) Millward et al. 1992; (3) ACAS 1991

Whilst in general team briefing is a common downward communication method, it is clear from a number of studies that this method varies enormously in practice (e.g. see Employment Department 1989; ACAS 1991; Marchington 1992). These surveys tend to indicate implicitly that the main contingent factor shaping the way in which team briefing is utilized appears to be the existing organizational structure and culture. In particular, the degree of formality, managerial goals and mechanics of this method vary greatly. Larger companies tend towards more formal briefing structures, whilst smaller organizations tend to favour a more informal approach (ACAS 1991:17), reflecting the comment made earlier that involvement in general has become increasingly deformalized in smaller organizations.

Also the frequency of meetings varies, often depending on the practicalities of work organization. Marchington et al., for instance, quote a food retailing company which utilized team briefings on a fairly informal and irregular basis, largely to fit into times when customer demand was less intense (1992:15).

At Peugeot Talbot 'all employees are briefed by and fed back their views to their immediate boss' (Employment Department 1989:40), and it is important to note that there is no third party or representative intervention in this information flow, so that team briefings constitute a direct line of communication within the hierarchy of the organization. Furthermore, as mentioned previously, there may well be a reluctance on the part of management to allow the system to become a vehicle for two-way communication flows, for fears that it could develop into a consultation forum. Indeed even general discussion of the information communicated (rather than specific questions) may well be discouraged because of this perceived problem.

Critically, the key to the success of team briefing lies in the hands of supervisory or line management, as it is at this level that the information reaches the whole workforce. Briefing systems place much reliance on a level of management that, at least in the US and the UK, is typically poorly equipped to deal with these new responsibilities and roles: they often necessitate a systematic training and monitoring policy for this tier of line management, but experience shows this to have been almost invariably lacking. In the Peugeot Talbot case mentioned above, all managers and supervisors were trained in both the techniques and philosophy of briefings (Employment Department 1989:41), but one suspects that in companies without a well-thought-out or adequately financed human resource management approach, this is unlikely to be the case, perhaps leading to a low success rate in team briefing schemes, which may well have been adopted for superficial or trendy reasons.

Nevertheless, there is evidence that briefings can have an effect on employee relations. Of one study in the food manufacturing sector, Marchington and Parker (1990:148) conclude that 'team briefings seems to have had a direct, if minor, effect on activity and also on attitudes to the company'. They also cite evidence that the company monitored the attitudinal impact of a number of involvement initiatives introduced in the late 1980s, consisting of an employee survey which produced generally positive feedback. In particular, team briefings were seen as the most favoured method for receiving communications (1990:151). This latter example raises the issue of evaluation and systematic managerial monitoring of new initiatives. In many studies, anecdote seems to be the main form of assessing the efficacy of involvement methods such as team briefings (see for example Employment Department 1989:41). But in organizations which approach information flows systematically, this delivery method may well constitute a genuine and important form of information provision, although again there is some conceptual doubt over its ability to act as a meaningful form of involvement beyond that.

### Upward communication EI

Whilst downward communication methods are underpinned by a quality ethos rationale, upward communication techniques stem from a striving to maximize a zero-defects standard in production. In other words, employees are encouraged to become involved in 'diagnostic' techniques, with the aim of utilizing employee knowledge of the production process and various aspects of organizational systems. This approach often focuses on technological issues within what are normally volatile product markets and environments. As one study commented: 'minimisation of uncertainty, the full utilisation of skills and the realisation of the full potentiality of the new technology often went hand in hand with the development of new forms of co-operation' (European Foundation for the Improvement of Living and Working Conditions 1988:13).

Upward, diagnostic involvement techniques focus on both the individual employee and the workgroup. Common examples of the former include suggestion schemes and attitudinal surveys; and of the latter, perhaps the best known group-oriented involvement technique is quality circles.

## Upward communication for individual employees

A number of studies have focused on suggestion schemes and attitude surveys (e.g. Marchington et al. 1992; *Employment Gazette* 1991:83) in the context of upward communication methods oriented towards the individual employee, with WIRS providing the most comprehensive overview of 1980s' trends. Table 5.8 indicates that the utilization of both these methods increased in the second half of the 1980s: suggestion schemes rose from 25 to 28 per cent between 1984 and 1990; and attitudinal surveys from 12 to 17 per cent during the same period.

Table 5.8   *Individual upward employee involvement, 1984–1990*

| Method | Companies (%) | Year | Sources |
|---|---|---|---|
| Suggestion scheme | 28 | 1990 | 1 |
| Attitude survey | 17 | 1990 | 1 |
| Suggestion scheme | 25 | 1984 | 2 |
| Attitude survey | 12 | 1984ß | 2 |

*Source:* (1) Millward et al. 1992; (2) Millward and Stevens 1986

Whilst both attitude surveys and suggestion schemes are upward and individualized forms of communication and involvement, their aims are rather different. Whilst the latter is utilized primarily as a diagnostic tool, focused on the technical and systems aspects of work organization and production methods, attitude surveys are usually conducted to ascertain employee feelings and opinions on employee relations issues.

### Attitude surveys

Attitude surveys can easily become a superficial aspect of employee involvement, unless the scheme adheres to two key principles. First, the organization must encourage this method to ascertain information and views on a broad range of company activities and policies, and not just wish to hear 'what it wants to hear', no matter how negative the opinions and attitudes appear to be. And second, the organization should respond positively to generalized feelings and views, rather than just collecting and collating data to be filed away in the personnel department. For example, spurred on by adverse publicity (internal as well as external) and impending technological changes, British Nuclear Fuels Ltd (BNFL) now employs attitude surveys as a normal part of its communication policy, especially during change processes (Othen 1990).

A more recent trend in the 'open management' context has been the use of attitude surveys as a method for employee appraisal of their managers. Little evidence exists about the spread of this trend, although a few case studies have been conducted. One such focused on the retailer W.H. Smith (Ainley 1992). The company introduced a management appraisal survey during the latter 1980s, largely in response to a period of relatively high employment and a general fear of the 'demographic downturn', which, as we show in Chapter 3, put companies under pressure to review their ability to attract and retain staff. W.H. Smith's attitude surveys have two goals: first, to ascertain employee perceptions of individual manager's performance; and second, to aggregate this information to build up a composite picture of the strengths and weaknesses of the whole management team (1992:11).

*Suggestion schemes*

Turning to suggestion schemes, the figures given in Table 5.8 are consistent with an Industrial Society and UK Association of Suggestion Schemes (UKASS) estimate of around 500 existing schemes in the UK (Balcombe 1988). Indeed the reemergence of this type of involvement method has led the UKASS to move from under the umbrella of the Industrial Society, in order to establish itself as a separate organization (Devine 1992:15).

Suggestion schemes have a long pedigree, and are one of the oldest forms of employee involvement. The UK's first formalized scheme was introduced in the Scottish shipbuilding industry in the 1880s. Traditionally Western organizations have used suggestion schemes as a cost saving mechanism, recognizing the important knowledge base of employees in this respect. However, Japanese companies have utilized suggestion schemes as one element in raising involvement levels with the aim of encouraging employee commitment to the organization, rather than as a cost saving mechanism *per se*. The Industrial Society sees suggestion schemes as a means to enhance productivity and employee relations. But for many UK companies, cost saving is still an important and more tangible outcome of the suggestion scheme method. One survey, for instance, found that among 61 organizations with available data, an aggregate figure of £16,146,352 was saved through employee ideas, representing an average of £1,250 saved per suggestion (Balcombe 1988:11–12). In contrast, Japanese organizations tend to play down the direct cost saving aspect of suggestion schemes, putting the onus on their integrative employee relations function. Cornell (1992) relates the story of one Japanese manager who, perplexed at being asked about the cost saving aspect of the organization's scheme, responded that: 'the modern improvement suggestion scheme can be summarized as a management system to elicit the self motivation of the workers. Workers become self motivated when they realize that their voluntary activity is indispensable to management and a vital element in the company's success' (cited in Devine 1992:23).

This dichotomy between broad employee relations benefits and sharply defined productivity and cost savings has become increasingly problematic in recent years for two reasons. The first is the debate over *motivating* factors, or what Herzberg (1968) classically defined as the 'hygiene' and 'motivators' dichotomy. In short, does financial gain constitute a key motivator, and if so, at what level should it be set? On the first issue, the Japanese approach clearly puts the onus on motivatory factors such as responsibility and recognition, whilst the UK approach tends to stress the motivatory impact of monetary reward. However, typically in the UK the financial reward is relatively small. In 1987, for example, one estimate put the figure at £118 on average for each implemented scheme (Balcome 1988:11–12). Given the average savings made of over £1,000 per scheme (see above), it is difficult to see this level of financial reward serving as a motivatory factor.

A second more critical issue concerns the recent trend toward 'total quality management' (TQM). An indication of the competing philosophies of motivation can be seen in the tendency in many organizations to either avoid or disband existing specific upward diagnostic methods, such as suggestion schemes, in favour of a more all-embracing 'total quality' ethos, an issue which is considered in-depth below. First, and in the same quality context, we broaden our examination of individual upward communication approaches with a look at employee appraisal and development.

*Appraisal and development*

An important reflection of the trend towards TQM is the revitalization of appraisal and development schemes, a practice which has undergone a number of important changes in recent years compared with its traditional utilization, which was restricted to managerial staff and focused largely on subjective (and often vague) assessments of past performance or, even more subjectively, the extent to which staff possessed desirable qualities. Underpinned by the assumption that the individual employee is a strategic resource to be systematically developed to his/her full potential, a small but perceptible trend in appraisal utilization amongst UK companies, and a more noticeable trend in American and Japanese companies and their UK subsidiaries, could be detected by the late 1980s (Townley 1989:92; Storey 1992:107). A more fundamental trend is also discernible in the extension of appraisals to cover both white- and blue-collar employees, as well as the more traditional coverage of managerial grades. One much quoted UK study found that between 1977 and 1986 the proportion of companies using appraisal for its blue-collar staff grew from 2 to 24 per cent; and for white-collar staff the increase over the same period was from 45 to 66 per cent (quoted in Townley 1989:98). Whilst Storey (1992:107) cautions against interpreting these findings too literally, in that a number of schemes were at an experimental stage in the mid 1980s, subsequent case study evidence tends to confirm the continued utilization of appraisal for all categories of employee, especially in American and Japanese owned companies (Incomes Data Services 1987; *Industrial Relations Review and Report* 1984; 1987b).

Essentially, appraisal and development consist of an appraisee and an appraiser (usually an immediate manager/supervisor) assessing an employee's past performance, setting goals for the employee in the coming period (e.g. two years), and monitoring how effectively these goals are achieved. In addition, the 'development' side of the equation stresses the need to put resources into helping the employee achieve these goals, i.e. through training and education. The UK government-backed Advisory, Conciliation and Arbitration Service (ACAS) sees appraisal and development schemes as mutually beneficial to employees and employers: 'They can improve employees' job performance and suitability for promotion while at the same time helping to use labour more effectively. In addition they can improve communications and the quality of working life and make employees feel that they are valued by the organisation' (ACAS 1988:32).

At IBM, a similar developmental approach is discernible in its long-standing appraisal scheme, but with the added function of linking appraisal to performance pay. An internal company booklet outlines the three main reasons for appraisal as: (i) a practical demonstration of concern for the individual; (ii) a basis for company merit pay; and (iii) to help employees make the most of their skills and realize their ambitions (Sapsed 1991:8). In short, this type of appraisal and development scheme is designed to make employees a key strategic resource in the organization, by treating them as active 'agents' in the process of organizational change rather than as passive objects of managerial decision-making. As Townley puts it in an overview of both selection and appraisal:

> rather than their being seen as 'technical' readjustments prompted by immediate concerns with competition and efficiency, selection and appraisal are integral to what has been identified as HRM . . . understood as being characterized by an increasing emphasis placed on the *attitudinal and behavioural characteristics of employees*, factors which readily lend themselves to monitoring through selection and performance review. (1989:92, original emphasis)

Emphasis here appears to be placed upon the 'soft' aspect of HRM, but the IBM case is instructive in that its approach has undergone continuous change since the 1950s when appraisal was first introduced. Emphasizing a 'desirable traits' focus in the 1950s, IBM's appraisal system at that stage was largely aimed at inducing greater company loyalty and employee dependability. The 1960s and 1970s saw a shift away from 'retrospective appraisal' towards next stage planning and assessment of performance. Perhaps as a sign of the increasing push in the 1970s for greater degrees of employee involvement, appraisal at IBM in this decade brought progressively more two-way interactive employee inputs in agreeing and setting performance criteria and goals. The 1980s again saw a shift in focus towards a more rigorous approach to measurement and standards of performance – partly because of the quality movement in the 1980s, and partly in an attempt to quantify intangibles such as relationships and creativity in work performance (Sapsed 1991:14).

Whilst traditionally 'traits' criteria have been used for non-managerial staff appraisal (Townley 1989:99), one might conclude from the above that appraisal may progressively function as a mechanism to enhance and measure the 'hard' side of the HRM equation, which emphasizes the economic/efficiency aspects of relating employee behaviour to organizational performance, rather than the 'soft' empowerment and self-actualization element. An interesting finding in this latter context in the IBM case study was that 30 per cent of employees apparently do not participate in objective setting (Sapsed 1991). However, in the early 1990s it appears that appraisal and development have evolved further, spurred on by the trend in 'delayering' in large companies (i.e. making redundant middle-level managerial posts). A number of large companies, including Unilever, British Petroleum, National Westminster Bank, GKN and IBM, have introduced the concept of 'management competencies' to assess their senior managers. Assessing qualities such as intellect, tenacity, vision, impact, skills in active and general management, are now seen as the way forward. To some extent, this may herald a return to the personality traits of an earlier period, although there is much controversy over the meaning of 'competencies' at top management level (see e.g. Storey 1994). Nevertheless, the intention of many organizations is to develop a more general type of manager, who can operate flexibly and who can be readily transferred within the company as a result of flattening structures and devolution of decision-making responsibilities downwards through the organization (see *Financial Times* 25 April 1991:12).

Although the multinational companies mentioned above may have practised long-standing and highly sophisticated appraisal systems, many organizations will need to develop appraisals with little experience of this method. As with most sophisticated involvement approaches, this may be problematic. The following prescriptive points are highlighted in an ACAS (1988) study:

1  Appraisals need the commitment and support of all levels of management.
2  Managers and trade union representatives should be consulted before appraisals are introduced.
3  Appraisals should not be seen in isolation but should be closely linked with policies and practices in other areas such as manpower planning, training and pay.
4  Those responsible for appraisals should receive adequate training to enable them to make objective assessments and to give them confidence in carrying out effective appraisal interviews.
5  The purpose of appraisals and how the system operates should be explained to those who are being appraised.
6  Paperwork should be kept to a minimum and appraisal forms should be simple and clearly designed.
7  Appraisal systems should be reviewed periodically to ensure that they meet changing needs.

Leaving aside the conceptual argument that individual appraisals are inappropriate in the 'total quality environment', as performance is largely determined by the 'organizational system' (argued most cogently by Deming

1982), appraisal and development schemes face three critical practical problems. First, the scheme must be properly resourced, in the sense of offering employees the opportunity (including funding) of improving their performance, for example through the provision of training and educational facilities. For many organizations, especially in the public sector, this can be problematic. In the UK university sector for example, although appraisal programmes are generally well designed, they tend to be undermined by limited resource provision. This is a critical weakness as employees will lose faith in the ability of an organization to 'meet its part of the bargain', and may over time increasingly see appraisal as a device to establish or reinforce managerial control over discretionary work patterns, whilst development, by its absence, is met with an increasingly cynical eye.

The second problem derives from the tendency for many organizations to link appraisals with performance-related pay, such as at IBM and British Rail for example (see IPA 1990:12–13 for an overview of the BR case). Whilst there is an obvious logic to this development, especially in reducing duplication of administrative and bureaucratic efforts related to this technique, the linking of pay with appraisal can put much strain on the development of high-trust relationships within the organization. This latter factor is crucial to the successful implementation of many involvement methods, but is particularly pertinent to appraisals, where there is a strong reliance on the appraisee being open and honest about his/her strengths and weaknesses and successes and failures. Again, to cite the IBM case study, not only financial remuneration but also promotion chances are highly dependent on the appraisal system. Once linked to pay levels, this open relationship may well become distorted, with the appraisee becoming reluctant to be open about weaknesses (see, for example, a case study of the UK National Health Service by George 1986).

A more obvious issue in linking appraisal with pay is that distribution of rewards might put limitations on managers' willingness to praise too highly. Moreover, if the aim of appraisal is the systematic raising of performance standards, a logical outcome if this goal is achieved will be upward pressure on performance pay awards – again causing difficulties especially during periods of market downturns (see e.g. Fowler 1988:34). Further, this issue highlights the need for appraisal systems to be periodically reviewed and updated, to minimize these problems (see Bowey and Thorpe 1986:Chapter 7). Finally, in the context of linking appraisal to pay, practitioners argue that performance appraisal needs to be simple, but this becomes harder to achieve when it is associated with performance-related pay – especially for managers whose performance might be judged according to a broad range of complex criteria (see Fowler 1988).

Third, appraisal and development schemes can fall between two stools, in that on the one hand, as argued above, they need to be fairly simple in design and operation, but on the other hand a degree of sophistication in technique will be necessary in order to tease out the goals and support requirements of the appraisee. This implies a complex system which necessitates careful training of both appraisers and appraisees. But whilst it is not unusual for organizations to provide some training for participants in involvement techniques such as quality circles, many appraisal and development schemes only facilitate appraiser training and often on a limited or initial basis only. At IBM, for example, new managers receive a five-day basic management course which includes training on appraisals and counselling. However, new IBM employees (either new entrants or transferees) appear only to enjoy a relatively brief initial discussion with their new manager on her/his approach to appraisal (Sapsed 1991:8). To some extent, this particular problem may be slightly offset in the longer term, as members of an organization learn through experience the ways and means of effectively handling this type of involvement method. Nevertheless, training in both the process and philosophy of appraisal will continue to be important.

The above problems may well help to explain reservations expressed by managers in studies of appraisal schemes. In one survey, for instance, conducted amongst almost 600 employers in the UK, it was found that only 20 per cent of personnel officers were happy with their company's appraisal scheme. In fact, echoing the second problem outlined above, only 11 per cent believed that they had a system that delivered performance-related pay effectively. Regarding the inherent complexity of appraisal schemes, 60 per cent of personnel managers found that performance ratings between different departments in their organizations were inconsistent, and 56 per cent thought the ratings were too subjective (Wyatt Company 1990).

These findings might indicate a need for a more systematic and strategically oriented approach to appraisal. In her study, however, Townley concludes on a pessimistic note that the systematic utilization of appraisal and selection techniques is more likely to lead to 'ritualization' than to 'creativity' in the individual's organizational behaviour (1989:108). The flexibility and adaptability sought by many contemporary organizations could be compromised by a too rigid adherence to an appraisal system, especially one founded upon job specifications as the source used to assess appraisee contributions.

## Upward communication for groups of employees

Whilst suggestion schemes, attitude surveys and appraisal are focused on the individual employee, an equally significant trend over the past 10 years or so has been the increasing emphasis placed upon teamwork and workgroup behaviour. The growing importance of 'quality' goods and services has already been noted in this book, and the idea behind upward group communication and involvement techniques is to enable workgroup teams to assess and implement improved methods of production and delivery of services.

### Quality circles

Perhaps the most often quoted of all direct involvement techniques is the quality circle (QC), which has been defined as:

a group of 4–12 people coming together from the same work area, performing similar work, who voluntarily meet on a regular basis to identify, investigate, analyse and solve their own work related problems. The circle presents solutions to management and is usually involved in implementing and later monitoring them. (Department of Trade and Industry, 1985)

The UK's ACAS stresses that the effectiveness of QCs depends on voluntary membership, a focus on problem solving, and an implied need for systematic training. These few key features combine to give QCs a special character quite different from other forms of group working such as 'task forces', which are normally brought together for one-off special projects, and disbanded after successful completion of the task.

In the mid 1980s, the UK Industrial Society surveyed the extent to which QCs had been introduced into British-based organizations. The results are reproduced in Table 5.9. Whilst this table illustrates the patchy utilization of QCs within the UK economy in the mid 1980s, this method was seen to be one of the key growth areas in the context of participative management and direct employee involvement. For example, the Industrial Society study found that more than 71 per cent of the QCs had been introduced within a three-year period prior to the survey, and whilst QCs were initially blue-collar oriented, over 40 per cent of schemes by the mid 1980s also covered white-collar groups. Reflecting the broader trend towards multi-involvement schemes, QCs tended to be located in organizations that utilized other forms of direct involvement; for instance, 40 per cent also used team briefings, and 60 per cent operated suggestion schemes. Similarly in the US, QCs tend to be associated with other forms of employee decision-making, such as autonomous workgroups and TQM programmes (see e.g. Osterman 1994).

Table 5.9   *Spread of quality circles by sector, 1986*

| Sector | Spread of QC in sector (%) | Total employees covered |
|---|---|---|
| Energy | 5 | 8,000 |
| Mineral extraction, metal manufacturing | 12 | 15,375 |
| Engineering, vehicles | 48 | 95,375 |
| Other manufacturing | 17 | 31,500 |
| Construction | – | – |
| Distribution, hotels | 1 | 750 |
| Transport, communication | 2 | 42,500 |
| Banking, finance | 8 | 10,250 |
| Other services | 6 | 9,125 |
| Total | | 212,875 |

*Source:* Industrial Society 1986

However, by the late 1980s opinion was divided concerning both the effectiveness and the likely trends in utilization of QCs. Whilst some saw QCs as an effective involvement technique appropriate for the 1990s, others noted a marked decline in the utilization of QCs, arguing that this reflected their lack of efficacy in raising quality standards.

Advocates of specific involvement methods still saw this method as central in the drive for quality and cultural change in UK organizations. ACAS's Work Research Unit reflected this approach, concluding in one study that, since their introduction in the early 1980s, QCs had evolved into a sophisticated organizational tool, and that 'the kind of changes described in this paper result more from an evolutionary learning process – out of experience- – than as a result of long-term planning . . . Quality Circles can become both an outward manifestation that participative processes are in operation and a sign that the business is working effectively' (Russell and Dale 1989:14).

An alternative view has been expressed, amongst others by Hill (1991), that QCs declined during the latter part of the 1980s, due to two main factors. First, QCs were often designed and introduced into organizations without adequate thought as to how they fitted into a broader quality change process. Second, QCs are inherently limited in practice and philosophy and have been largely surpassed by TQM programmes of change.

Although Hill's data were largely based on a small-scale study of 13 companies, recent larger-scale survey evidence confirms that the utilization of QCs is still fairly patchy. The figure of 27 per cent for 1990 in Table 5.10 is provided by the WIRS, which by its size and methodological soundness offers the most reliable estimate. Marchington et al. (1992) in their study of 25 organizations produced a similar figure of 25 per cent, whilst two Employment Department studies (which conflated QCs with suggestion schemes) found an even smaller percentage of companies utilizing this method, although noting an increase from 9 per cent in 1988 to 16 per cent in 1991. Given these figures, it is unclear if QC utilization increased at all during the 1980s. Marchington and Parker (1990:44) note that at most about 500 schemes exist in the UK, and compare this figure with an early 1980s' study by Batstone who found that QCs existed in under 20 per cent of establishments surveyed (1984:266).

Table 5.10   *Group upward employee involvement, 1988–1991*

| Method | Companies (%) | Year | Sources |
| --- | --- | --- | --- |
| Quality circles | 25 | 1991 | 1 |
| Quality circles | 16 | 1991 | 2 |
| Quality circles | 27 | 1990 | 3 |
| Quality circles | 9 | 1988 | 2 |

*Sources*: (1) Marchington et al. 1992; (2) *Employment Gazette* 1988; 1991; (3) Millward et al. 1992

In America and Japan, however, the picture is radically different. Japan has been estimated to have over a million QCs, and in the USA Osterman found an approximate 40 per cent spread of manufacturing establishments utilizing QCs in 1992. Just over a quarter of establishments involved at least half of their workforce in membership of a QC (1994:177). In large companies, utilization appears even higher with 90 per cent of the *Fortune* 500 companies reporting QC usage in the early 1980s (Lawler 1986). There is some evidence that suggests that foreign-owned establishments operating in the UK (and these are largely American or Japanese in origin) have a higher incidence of QCs; the ACAS 1990 survey, for example, found that 40 per cent of foreign-owned companies had QCs in place compared with 23 per cent of domestically owned organizations (ACAS 1991:14).

Whilst it is clear from surveys published since the mid 1980s that QCs *per se* are still utilized in a significant number of organizations, a more complex argument has arisen over the efficacy of this method of involvement. Whilst Hill (1991) argues that TQM programmes replaced QCs owing to the latter being too limited in scope and poorly thought out in implementation, an alternative explanation for the metamorphosis of quality approaches contends that QCs acted as an embryonic step in the direction of an organizational quality ethos, evolving into the later 1980s' and early 1990s' interest in TQM programmes (see e.g. Training Agency 1989). Whilst the jury seems to be out at this point in time in the QC debate, what is clear is that QCs have a high turnover. The 1990 ACAS survey for example found that 25 per cent of circles introduced in the previous three years had been discontinued, either totally abandoned or turned into new quality schemes (ACAS 1991:14).

In summarizing a number of recent studies of QCs, three main problems appear to be highlighted which might help to explain the rather unstable development of the practice noted above. First, QCs (similarly to other sophisticated involvement methods) are often seen as 'culture bound'. In other words, their underlining 'quality' ethos is not a concept readily accepted in Western organizations, unlike their Japanese counterparts, where the idea of QCs has been most developed. Kazuo Chiba, Japan's Ambassador in London in 1990, has argued that UK companies often lose contracts to supply Japanese companies because the former do not strive to achieve total quality production, but rather simply aim to meet the minimum requirements of a contract (reported in the *Financial Times* 26 October 1990). A more detailed analysis in this context is given by Watanabe (1991), who argues that there have been a number of serious misunderstandings of the Japanese approach to QCs in the West. Strongly advocating the efficacy of Japanese QCs, Watanabe maintains that this method has had a greater cumulative effect on industrial efficiency in his country than major forms of technological innovation, such as robotization. In the West, in his view, two fundamental mistakes have been made in the introduction and functioning of QCs: (i) basing circles on 'voluntary' membership; and (ii) the assumption that QCs both lead to and are underpinned by employee 'loyalty'. The reality in Japan, argues Watanabe, is that QCs are integrated into the organization as part of an all-embracing total quality programme, involving all workers from top management to the shopfloor. Moreover, Japanese employees are motivated not by devotion to the company but by instrumental factors such as lifetime employment, egalitarian remuneration and a promotion system based on seniority.

In many ways, QCs were designed precisely to meet this 'cultural' problem and, once this method had induced a 'quality culture' in the organization, were expected to become redundant. But at the very least, this type of profound philosophical change will take a long time to develop, as in essence, QCs are designed to move 'people from a state of dependence to a state of independence' (Russell and Dale 1989), at least in the context of production.

The second issue concerning the functioning of QCs has been their implementation into traditional unionized industrial relations environments. This latter point had raised questions over the attitudes and responses of both trade unions and management. In many ways, the problems surrounding QCs have encapsulated issues of more general relevance to human resource management trends, in particular the relationship between newer forms of consensual decision-making and older conflictual models of organizational behaviour. It has already been noted that some writers see an incompatibility between the essentially 'collective' nature of industrial relations, and the individualistic orientation of human resource management (e.g. Guest 1989). From this standpoint, it has often been assumed that QCs face a certain antipathy on the part of trade unions, who often believe that they are a method of bypassing traditional union representational structures. An interesting finding in the Industrial Society (1986) survey showed that of the 70 per cent of companies with QCs that used steering committees to introduce this method into the organization, only 11 per cent had union representatives on them.

In response to managerial attempts to introduce an HRM style of employee relations there seems to be an often made assumption that trade unions will only be able to respond defensively or negatively to the apparent threatening trend of individualizing employment relationships. However, Lucio and Weston (1992) suggest that the trade union response to HRM may well change from a 'reactive' to a 'proactive' approach, especially where the unions retain a reasonably strong organizational presence. Detailed studies have shown that the relationship between QCs and trade unions is in fact quite complex. In an American study Osterman (1994) found that unions had a neutral effect in the utilization of flexible working practices such as QCs, whilst Drago (1988) found that the most important factor in a circle's life chances (i.e. survivability) was union involvement in the scheme. Drago concluded: 'We might further conjecture that managers in unionized environments can reap the benefits of stronger circle programs by striving to involve unions or by ensuring that unions experience gains from circles' (1988:249).

This brings us to our third point, which concerns the responses of management to QC initiatives, and their fears of losing 'control' over what have been traditional areas of jurisdiction. We focus on managerial rationales comprehensively in Chapter 8, but suffice it to note here that these insecurities tend to reflect the inability or unwillingness of managers and supervisors to adapt to a more participative style demanded of them by QCs (and indeed other involvement methods). One managerial justification for their reservations over QCs is based on the belief that employees do not perceive QCs as meeting their involvement desires (e.g. Hill 1991:546–7). However some case studies on this question have found that employees generally are favourable towards specific quality programmes and schemes, even when they do not actually join a QC *per se* (Brossard 1990:15). We would speculate further that this way of articulating the problem may highlight managerial fears of exposure (for example in the *ad hoc* way decisions are often made), of loss of traditional methods of disciplining the workforce, and perhaps also of being made redundant through the radical implementation of open decision-making and subsequent 'delayering' of the management hierarchy.

This finally leads us to question the extent to which employees gain from either the existence of, or involvement in, QCs. As with other human resource oriented techniques, there is both a 'soft' and a 'hard' rationale behind QCs; in other words there can be both an empowerment/motivatory emphasis, and an economic/efficiency element. Bradley and Hill, from a small comparative study conducted in America and the UK in the early 1980s, argued that 'the most obvious and tangible benefits' were economic (1987:81). QWL factors such as positive attitudinal and relational changes in the workplace were much less in evidence, although the authors did point out health and safety and environmental improvements as underrated outcomes of the introduction of QCs.

Overall, QCs have represented a profound challenge in the context of traditional adversarial industrial relations to management, trade unions and employees. Whilst wariness and sometimes hostility to this method have clearly contributed to the high turnover of these schemes, rather than signalling the ineffectuality of this method of enhancing quality in the organization, QCs can be seen as a stepping-stone to a more holistic approach to the quality ethos, in part reflected in the growth of two-way, less formalized approaches in communication and involvement generally, which we now briefly focus on to conclude this chapter.

## Conclusion

The recent increase in relatively informal communication and involvement approaches is most marked in the UK, indicated in a number of surveys from the mid 1980s to the early 1990s. Marchington et al. (1992) found that a TQM or systematic change programme was in place in 84 per cent of surveyed companies. WIRS found that between 1984 and 1990, some means of direct two-way communication between an employee and a senior manager increased from 34 to 41 per cent; and similarly between an employee and a junior manager the increase was from 36 to 48 per cent. UK Employment Department surveys show a decline in this approach between 1988 and 1991, from 61 per cent of establishments to 53 per cent, but use a more generalized 'management' category to measure this (Table 5.11).

Table 5.11   *Face-to-face communication, 1984–1991*

| Method | Companies (%) | Year | Sources |
|---|---|---|---|
| Management/employee | 53 | 1991 | 1 |
| Senior management/employee | 41 | 1990 | 2 |
| Junior management/employee | 48 | 1990 | 2 |
| Management/employee | 61 | 1988 | 1 |
| Senior management/employee | 34 | 1984 | 3 |
| Junior management/employee | 36 | 1984 | 3 |

*Source:* (1) *Employment Gazette* 1988; 1991; (2) Millward et al. 1992 (3) Millward and Stevens 1986

Whilst direct two-way communication is an increasingly visible part of the involvement package for many organizations, it is difficult to know exactly what organizations mean by this type of approach. It could be argued that there are two extreme poles in a continuum concerning informal involvement approaches, from simply indicating that managers have an ostensible 'open door' policy, to a fully thought out strategic TQM programme.

The latter case might be reflected in Osterman's conclusion to his large-scale US study on employee involvement:

> the findings strongly confirm that a number of variables are positively associated with the adoption of flexible work practices: a market with international competition; a high skill technology; worker-oriented values; following a high-road strategy (emphasizing service, quality, and variety of products rather than low cost). (1994:186)

At the London Stock Exchange, in contrast, in the latter 1980s an informal network of divisional consultative groups and representatives was established. Facilitated through line management, this network was designed to enhance effective communication, develop an open managerial style, and offset problems of 'grapevine rumours'. Whilst more formalized team briefings were also utilized, especially for the dissemination of business information, one-to-one sessions were developed to deal specifically with staff issues (Dann 1992:2–3 and 20).

The Employment Department (1989) highlighted a range of large companies with an informal open management style, such as IBM, Pirelli, ICI, Nissan and CMG. Prestwick Circuits was publicized by the Training Agency (1989) as an example of how the quality circle movement evolved into a more all-embracing TQM approach, rendering the former method redundant. An Incomes Data Services study reviewed five 'leading-edge' companies that had developed a systematic approach to TQM: Johnson Matthey, Texas Instruments, Hewlett Packard, Rank Xerox and G-P Inveresk (1990b:11–21). These companies are underpinned by five essential TQM characteristics: (i) continuous problem solving activity; (ii) a quality structure to ensure a clear focus; (iii) statistical control and measurement of quality; (iv) identification of both internal and external customers; and (v) extensive training programmes

(1990b:1). However, this same study pointed out that in the UK economy as a whole, TQM companies are still 'few and far between', concluding that: 'In the vast majority of organizations, including those which may have adopted elements of TQM, there is a gulf between their practices and what is happening in the "advanced" companies' (1990b:1).

There is clearly some way to go in the creation of what some have called the 'fear free organization' (James 1991), which in part reflects much of the rhetoric in the move towards relatively informal involvement approaches. In a study of the QWL concept and TQM, James argued that 'The interlocking nature of real quality performance . . . requires each individual to understand concepts, tools and techniques of quality performance' (1991:11), but concluded that: 'The knowledge and ingenuity of the workers lies virtually untapped while managers generally are spending too much time "managing", i.e. working in systems firefighting' (1991:13).

Much seems to be happening on the surface, but when individual techniques are unwrapped the picture becomes more blurred in terms of what managements are doing and the effects of their actions on employee behaviour. We now turn to the issue of financial involvement to pursue these questions further.

### Note

1 Section One of the Employment Act 1982 (UK), later consolidated as Section 235 and Schedule 7 Part V of the Companies Act 1985, as amended by the Companies Act 1989, basically requires employers with over 250 employees to state annually in their company reports the initiatives taken to promote employee involvement.

# 6

# Financial Involvement
# and Participation

The subject of financial involvement and participation (FIP) merits a chapter to itself, for, in its generic form, the concept embraces a potentially rich variety of experiences. These extend from management determined monetary supplements to employee income, which involve no or minimal shifts in capital ownership or organizational control, to full economic democracy offering opportunities for plural ownership and social control of enterprise or industry. Also, following from this diversity, FIP has gathered support from across a broad political and industrial spectrum.

Nevertheless, very different ideologies inform financial involvement (FI) and financial participation (FP) and these raise highly contentious issues in current debates over the extent and application of employee influence. On the one hand, advocates of involvement argue that property ownership distributed broadly across the working population encourages self-independence among employees, distancing them especially from collective influences by establishing a nominal status equality between employees and their superiors on the platform that all work together as co-owners. The same ownership appeal is also assumed to serve as an incentive to work harder (Brannen 1983:129). The restrictions are also contentious in that only minority shareholdings are generally encouraged and that shares are issued on an individual basis to employees.

On a wider scale proselytizers for FI argue that the material sense of ownership which derives from property rights provides the key to employee integration with the market economy and acts as a catalyst to national economic success. Even wider claims have been made for property-based financial involvement: some critics of the divisive implications of capitalist dynamics contend that class conflict could be eradicated through making employees beneficiaries of a system which otherwise would be seen as opposed to worker interests (see Kelso and Adler 1958; Copeman et al. 1984). A similar line of argument flows through contemporary politically conservative claims for the 'property owning democracy' which advocates a broader spread of shareholdings throughout the population.

At the other end of the ideological spectrum the value of devolved property ownership is recognized as a necessary (though not sufficient) condition for employees to assert high-level influence within capitalist enterprises. Writing in 1986, Poole stated that: 'There is no question that, in the long march to industrial democracy, the issue of participation in ownership . . . is as far reaching in importance as involvement in decision-making processes them-selves' (1986:179).

Steps have therefore been advocated by social reformers to redress the obvious wealth and influence disparities which exist in market economies by promoting the aggregation of employee shareholders into trusts which can then influence company policy through these communal shareholdings. We term these social fund measures as financial participation. Not surprisingly, campaigns which offer employees countervailing powers to match those tra-ditionally enjoyed by company shareholders have met with widespread hostility from the business community as well as formidable political oppo-sition.

In the opening chapters, we argued that employee involvement and employee participation have rather different origins and objectives. Similar distinguishing features can be seen in remunerative initiatives to associate employees more closely to the management and progress of their companies. These initiatives can be allocated into financial involvement, embracing profit-sharing and individual employee share schemes, and financial partici-pation implemented typically in the form of collective share schemes. In both cases there has been considerable activity, and recent years have witnessed a number of notable experiments, developments and, in some countries, arrests in the momentum of FIP practice in line with shifts in political and industrial ascendancies.

Following from this activity, this chapter intends to review the ideas which inform and support different approaches to FIP, and to examine the reasons for their introduction and the main directions taken by FIP practice. Finally, claims made for financial involvement and participation by proponents and the extent to which experience matches these claims are scrutinized.

This chapter will pay particular attention to recent experience in the UK where government sponsorship allied to employer enthusiasm for innovative remuneration practices have meant that financial involvement developments have been especially marked. The government has strongly promoted both employee share schemes and profit-sharing, combined with an aggressive pri-vatization programme sweetened with offers of priority discounted shares for employees in the industries concerned. These initiatives have been moti-vated in part by the government's ambitions to increase the responsiveness of labour to market signals, which in turn have helped to stimulate reforms in employer remuneration policy toward flexible and results-based payment sys-tems.

## Types of financial involvement and participation

For the purposes of our examination, three generic forms of FIP can be iden-tified. These are profit-sharing, individual employee share schemes and collective employee share schemes. Located within each group can be found a diversity of approaches and techniques, summarized in Table 6.1.

Table 6.1 *Approaches to financial involvement and participation*

---

*Profit-sharing*
Profit-related pay
Profit- or revenue-linked remuneration
Some forms of performance-related pay

*Individual share schemes*
Shares distributed to employees according to predetermined formula (ADST)
Share options offered to employees (SAYE)
Employee share ownership plans (ESOPs)
Discretionary schemes in which shares are offered to selected employees
Employee buyouts

*Collective share schemes*
Wage-earner funds

---

## Distinctions between financial involvement and financial participation

The main defining features of employee involvement which help to distinguish it from employee participation were examined in Chapter 2. By applying the same criteria we are able to incorporate profit-sharing and both individual and collective variants of share schemes into the EI–EP framework. Table 6.2 shows the main features identified for employee involvement and how these relate to profit-sharing and to individual and collective share schemes. The table suggests strongly that whilst profit-sharing exhibits the features associated with EI, and individual share schemes display most of these, collective schemes barely meet any of the EI criteria and their features would appear to correspond more closely to an EP classification by providing tangible means for collective employee interests to be articulated within company decision-making frameworks. Therefore, the development of collective share schemes is considered later within an EP framework.

Table 6.2 *Profit-sharing and individual and collective share schemes*

| EI criterion | Profit-sharing | Individual share schemes | Collective share schemes |
|---|---|---|---|
| Management inspired | + | + | – |
| Stimulate individual employee contribution | + | indirectly | – |
| Enhance individual employee responsibilities | + | + | – |
| Management hierarchy undisturbed | + | + | partly |
| Employees passive recipients | + | partly | – |
| Task oriented | + | – | – |
| Common interests promoted | + | + | – |
| Concentrate influence among management | + | ? | – |

As explained below, this chapter focuses primarily upon individual share schemes as representative of EI, for it is in these areas that developments have advanced most rapidly. Individual share schemes have also enjoyed considerable government support in the form of repeated exhortation coupled with successive legislative reforms geared to encourage employers to adopt financial involvement programmes.

### Profit-sharing, involvement and individual share schemes

Using the defining characteristics of EI, there is a strong case for the inclusion of profit-sharing as a variant of EI. In this chapter, however, we concentrate our attention upon those forms of FIP which allow for and indeed rely upon an element of property ownership as the trigger for influencing employee and employer behaviours. The reasons for this emphasis arise from the perspective that though profit-sharing and individual schemes share important similarities, their anticipated links with employee behaviour originate from rather different analytical standpoints. Share schemes rely upon a premise that a community of interest can be forged between capital and labour; this assumption is made concrete through the property ownership nexus. A belief that property ownership will encourage positive employee orientations to the employing company, and possibly heighten support for the free market economic system, also helps to sustain employee share programmes. These favourable conjunctions are expected to feed directly into employee and subsequently organizational performance.

Profit-sharing, however, can be seen to have a rather more disciplinary or corrective character in that employee performance is emphasized as a key factor in determining a proportion of total employee income. No ownership link is appealed to in profit-sharing, which, conversely, might be viewed as a means to induce worker flexibility with regard to pay or performance under circumstances where it might otherwise be withheld. If company profits or revenue decline, then so does employee income. Thus there is the inescapable feeling that profit-sharing ascribes employees with being directly responsible for maintaining levels of personal income (see Bell and Hanson 1987:4).

Notwithstanding these differences, there is no practical reason why share schemes should not co-exist with profit-sharing arrangements in the same private sector companies, though public sector companies and other organizations which provide no share capital are, by definition, excluded from share allocation programmes. An interesting example of this 'dual' approach is offered by the vehicle components company Unipart, in which highly assessed individual performance will entitle employees to purchase a higher proportion of share options (*Financial Times* 7 August 1991). Nevertheless, despite common origins in managerial thinking and their joint promotion by conservative politicians, the beliefs which underlie the application of the two approaches are rather different. It is even arguable whether profit-sharing should be included as a genuine form of involvement as distinct from a complex and sophisticated form of incentive system. On the other hand, as property ownership indisputably provides the ideological stimulus to both individual and collective share programmes, we shall concentrate on these as representative of FIP.

## Individual share schemes

As with other EI initiatives, individual share schemes have received considerable political endorsement in a number of countries including Japan, where over 90 per cent of all enterprises listed on the stock market had introduced an employee share scheme following government endorsement (Jones and Kato 1993:355); America (Allen et al. 1991:133–5); Sweden (Bean 1994:182); and the UK. With financial involvement, government encouragement has frequently extended into active support through enabling legislation which offers tax concessions to companies and employees who partake in share programmes which receive approval from the relevant tax authorities.

In the UK, which has witnessed a major shift toward financial involvement, legislation passed in 1978 by a Labour government, in association with (and under pressure from) its then Liberal partners, introduced a Finance Act which provided tax concessions to companies who allocated shares to staff on an all-employee basis. Employee shareholdings are placed in a trust and distributed to beneficiaries exempt of income tax after five years. For this reason they are known as approved deferred share trusts (ADSTs). The change of government in 1979 resulted in a proliferation of FI initiatives starting with all-employee share option schemes gaining approved status under the Finance Act 1980; these schemes are also open to all full-time employees who satisfy service requirements and require participating employees to enter into a contract with a recognized savings institution to save regular amounts over a five-year period. At the end of this period, savers have the option to purchase company shares or to take accumulated cash and interest after five or seven years. These schemes are known as 'save as you earn' or SAYE.

In 1984 a second option scheme received legislative approval. This scheme provides for staff selected by their companies to purchase shares at favourable rates. Usually only a small number of senior managers are invited into this scheme, known for this reason as 'executive' or 'discretionary'. The Finance Act 1989 offered similar fiscal inducements to companies wishing to establish employee share ownership plans (ESOPs) which permit potentially higher employee concentrations of shareholdings than are associated with the earlier Acts. For this reason, ESOPs are considered in more detail later in this chapter.

Subsequent years have seen incremental improvements to each of these schemes through legislative amendments, though the principles underlying each remain undisturbed. The response by companies to these favourable environmental conditions appears to be positive, as Table 6.3 shows.

The increase in adoption of schemes has been matched by growth in their

Table 6.3   *Progress of approved[1] individual employee share schemes[2] introduced in the UK since 1978 (as at February 1993)[3]*

| Year | ADST | SAYE | Discretionary |
|------|------|------|---------------|
| March 1980 | 117 | – | – |
| March 1982 | 278 | 137 | – |
| March 1984 | 392 | 288 | 32 |
| March 1986 | 608 | 593 | 2,034 |
| June 1988 | 756 | 742 | 3,174 |
| January 1989 | 788 | 795 | 3,689 |
| September 1990 | 914 | 926 | 4,557 |
| December 1991 | 944 | 1,025 | 4,949 |
| February 1993 | 1,056 | 1,148 | 5,268 |

[1]  Approval is offered by the Inland Revenue to schemes which fulfil certain governmental requirements. In terms of ADST, SAYE and ESOPs, the principal requirement is that the schemes be offered on similar terms to all full-time employees who have served a minimum period of employment. Maximum annual allocations are also laid down.

[2]  Each scheme received approval under various Finance Acts in different years: ADST in 1978, SAYE in 1980, discretionary schemes in 1984 and ESOPs in 1989. The various Acts have subsequently been amended to provide monetary or administrative improvements.

[3]  These figures represent the number of schemes obtaining approval by the Inland Revenue. Approved schemes actually in operation may be fewer as schemes may cease to operate. No figures for ESOPs are published regularly, possibly because of the low numbers of cases involved.

*Sources:* Incomes Data Services 1989; Inland Revenue published data

coverage. In 1984, WIRS estimated that just under a quarter of all trading sector establishments had a share scheme. By 1990, this proportion had grown to 32 per cent. Moreover, the proportions of employees who participated in schemes rose by a similar figure, from 22 per cent to 34 per cent of employees in establishments where schemes were in place (Millward et al. 1992: 265–6). Other estimates have been made that approximately 2 million employees, representing about 8 per cent of the total workforce, are eligible to participate in ADST and SAYE programmes (Income Data Services 1990a). Roughly 870,000 employees are thought to participate in ADST schemes and a figure of 1.5 million SAYE savers has been suggested.

## Management objectives for individual employee share schemes

Individual share schemes are invariably management designed and initiated (Baddon et al. 1987). Whilst individual employers may have a complex of motives for introducing employee share schemes, these motives can be distilled into two main branches: an idealistic philosophy held by an employer to share equally the benefits and responsibilities of company ownership with employees; and instrumental management ambitions to enhance workforce performance through alteration of employee behaviour.

*Idealistic objectives*

Throughout industrial history industrialists have emerged whose ideological beliefs sit uneasily with the power and influence inequalities which derive from their concentrated capital ownership. On occasion, these beliefs have stimulated owners to initiate significant shifts in enterprise ownership through distribution of shares to employees. Classic examples would be the UK-based John Lewis Partnership which exists to 'bestow the benefits of ownership on all employees and to ensure the sharing of knowledge, gain and power' (Poole 1986:65). Similar motives inform the practices of the Industrial Common Ownership Movement established by Ernest Bader in 1958 (Brannen 1983:134). Whilst some commentators have reason to doubt the purity of effect, if not the motive, behind these projects, there is little doubt that similar, if diluted, sentiments of 'offering a stake in the company' have helped to motivate contemporary share-distributing companies. One-third of respondents in the Baddon et al. (1987) survey of 231 companies indicated that enabling and encouraging employees to become shareholders was an objective for management.

Nevertheless, judging from proportions of shares made available to employees, the numbers of employers that introduce share schemes with the intention of radically altering the ownership and influence structure of their enterprises appear to be very limited. One indication would be that ESOPs, which provide for majority employee shareholdings, have made very limited progress in the UK since the 1989 legislation facilitating their adoption (see below; also Allen et al. 1991:158–60). In the USA, the total value of ESOPs amounts to less than 3 per cent of company market values. In Japan an estimate of less than 1 per cent has been offered (Jones and Kato 1993:358). A convincing explanation of this lack of progress is that managers are fearful that concentrated employee ownership will increase labour force influence at work at the expense of hard-earned managerial prerogatives (Klein and Rosen 1986:398); an alternative view postulates that employee self-determination will sap managerial energies, degenerate into corporate apathy or display excessive short-term manifestations of employee self-interest; in either case there is expected to be negative consequences for organizational performance (see Maaløe 1993). Partly for these reasons, perhaps, barriers are erected to ensure that employee stockholdings are maintained at minority levels; in the UK the influential institutional investment protection committees recommend that no more than 10 per cent of shares be issued to employees, a guideline which is only rarely exceeded. In approved schemes, Baddon et al. found that less than 1 per cent of share capital was owned by employees in more than half of their sample of companies (1989:Table 5). In privatized British Telecom in 1989, employees held in trust a mere 1 per cent of the company's share capital (Nichols and O'Connell Davidson 1992:107).

It would seem that concentrated shareholdings are only rarely extended to employees in the UK, an outcome which would conform with the management defined profile of objectives normally associated with employee involvement. The more instrumental approach associated with limited share-holdings is the one which is more likely to attract company executives.

### Instrumental objectives

Many academic, political and management observers consider that share schemes are introduced in order to contribute to a more circumscribed range of objectives than that encompassed by the wider vision of the few employers who have initiated schemes aimed to radically alter the ownership profile of a company. The majority of employers are hoping to use employee share ownership in some way to enhance the performance of their enterprises. However, there is a problem, for it is well recognized in the literature that rewards and incentives, the attainment of which are not directly amenable to the immediate influence of employees, are unlikely to motivate employees to raise their levels of effort or performance. Share schemes, by their nature, are especially remote from employees according to dimensions of both time and effort; timing is relevant because shares are not immediately distributed and dividends are paid, if at all, at six-monthly intervals. Links with effort are tenuous because individual workers cannot see a direct association between the ways in which they perform their tasks and the number and value of shares made available to them, or in the prices of shares they hold. If the direct incentive and reward seeking properties are low, as appears likely, what do share schemes offer?

A look at the management, political and to some extent academic expectations for employee share ownership provides the clues. Though strongly identified with the Conservative Party, all the major political forces in the UK find some attraction in share allocation programmes. The Conservatives are concerned to encourage employee share schemes as part of their crusade to promote 'popular capitalism' and to lubricate their privatization programmes; Liberal Democrats have been traditional advocates for share schemes as a contribution toward the attainment of industrial partnership; and Labour, though somewhat divided in its stance, sees shareholder employees as a countervailing force to management, or more cynically, perhaps, gives support to share schemes because of their apparent attraction to workers. All political parties contend that economic benefits can accrue through share allocations. Similarly, many company executives visualize share ownership as acting as an *indirect* motivator. Hence one company's senior executive, responsible for steering through his company's share scheme, indicated that the programme formed part of an overall philosophy designed to embrace 'more people in the ownership of the company' in order to 'inspire their loyalty and commitment'.

### Property ownership and employee motivation

For proponents of individual share schemes, the effects of ownership upon behaviour provide the key to enhanced performance and, as the quote above indicates, a process involving two key elements occurs. The first step is that employees become part-owners of the companies in which they work. Second, this 'stake in the firm' leads to enhanced positive behaviour/attitudes by the employees concerned; and in consequence, corporate performance improves. Explanations for these effects vary; it is believed by some managers that behaviour changes might arise through the educative impact of share scheme ownership in making employees more aware of the 'economic facts of life' and how their labour contributes to these facts (Bougen et al. 1988). Managers may also believe that, through ownership, share schemes signal and confirm management assertions that they and their employees are on 'the same side' and hence help to encourage co-operation and foster positive attitudes toward work and management decision-making. These positive orientations can also be funnelled into greater employee flexibility, adaptability and loyalty. It might also be anticipated that attempts by the company to encourage individual employee share ownership will strengthen ties between individual employees and their workplace, and through development of the 'enterprise culture' loosen collective sentiments toward labour movement membership and activity. In that sense, share schemes might be seen, too, as an important potential element of an HRM management style.

Therefore, it seems that property ownership or the prospect of it, as the initial key requirement of this FI process, is the *sine qua non* behind the anticipated benefits of share ownership. It follows, then, that any attempt to evaluate the possible effects of share schemes should first examine the extent and depth of employee share ownership.

## Patterns of employee share ownership

Before exploring share ownership patterns in greater depth, we should note one area of ambiguity with regard to the property acquisition concept. As we saw above, concern has been expressed among management circles that concentrated shareholdings in employee hands might encourage employee gratification (in terms of earnings, security, discipline, etc.) to the detriment of overall corporate performance. One manifestation of this concern is that employers are generally hostile to collective employee shareholdings, as we shall see below. Yet, paradoxically, more diluted employee shareholdings are expected to exert a *positive* effect on employee attitudes and work performance. Clearly, this implies some invisible cross-over between a negative and a positive effect attributable to share ownership, a nonsensical proposition confirmed by the findings of researchers who have established that in small proportions, share allocations do little to influence employee expectations or orientations. In their American studies Klein and Rosen, for example, found a positive relationship between the size of the company ESOP contribution and levels of satisfaction and commitment expressed by employees (1986:402). Moreover, it appears from their study of 50 companies that 'employees are primarily motivated and inspired by the potential financial rewards of ESOP employee ownership' rather than by an intrinsic attraction of property ownership (1986:403).

The truth is that most schemes do provide for only small amounts of shares for distribution to employees, who tend to receive modest allocations of shares both in terms of aggregate shareholdings, as we saw above, and as a proportion of total remuneration. In reviewing the value of share scheme and profit-sharing bonuses together, Baddon et al. found that the modal proportion of pay received in the form of bonus from these programmes was between 2 and 4 per cent (1987:71). The 1990 IDS study arrived at a higher figure of 5 to 6 per cent bonuses, though again the value of shares in this proportion is not known (Incomes Data Services 1990a:11). In a four-year study of 21 companies with ADST and value-added schemes, bonuses accounted for 3 per cent of pay, though 'these bonuses varied significantly with the firm's economic situation over the trade cycle' (Blanchflower and Oswald 1986:12).

In addition to small share allocations, a number of factors can conspire to ensure that workforce employees do not fare as well from share programmes as do higher-status managers, an outcome that might help defeat the unifying intentions behind share schemes. In some cases, these differences can reach epic proportions. Nichols and O'Connell Davidson point out that whilst the average employee shareholding at the giant British Telecom company amounts to 270 shares, 1.3 million shares were accounted for by just five senior executives. A similarly skewed situation exists at recently privatized British Gas (1992:107). Even if we discount these extreme cases, managers have greater scope both to acquire shares and to retain them compared with other members of the workforce, whose lower incomes may require them to dispose of shareholdings in order to finance necessary expenditures (see Hyman et al. 1989). Discretionary schemes, which are highly exclusive and usually open only to senior managers, provide opportunities to accumulate very large amounts of company stock. Often, companies do not reveal to employees the existence of these programmes. Voluntary share saving schemes tend to attract managers and more highly paid employees; at most, only about 20 per cent of employees participate in these programmes (Millward et al. 1992:226; Ramsay et al. 1990:188), with participation skewed towards higher-status and higher-paid occupations. Baddon et al. found, for example, that in companies that operated these schemes, 8 per cent of manual employees participated in SAYE compared with 26 per cent of managers (1987:13). Not surprisingly, there is also a positive relationship between income and SAYE participation in terms both of proportions of SAYE participants earning higher incomes and of the amounts that they allocate for the purchase of shares (Ramsay et al. 1990:188). Similarly, Nichols and O'Connell Davidson found that their categories of 'superactive' and 'hyperactive' employee share acquirers in a privatized company were over-represented by managers and under-represented by manual workers (1992:114).

It is also relevant that although ADST and SAYE schemes are nominally open to all employees, the legislation permits important restrictions on membership, with part-time employees excluded along with those employees who have not served the required qualifying period of usually five years. Bearing in mind that part-time employment is on the increase and invariably involves women in low-paid occupations, these are important exclusions. The impact of these restrictions can be dramatic:

> At LeisureCo, there was a corporate-wide share scheme which employees at the site were eligible to join after four years' service: however, nobody at the site had that amount of service, and most of the workforce was employed on a temporary basis, so in effect share ownership was not an issue. (Marchington et al. 1992:17)

It is perhaps as a result of these factors that whilst the rhetoric emphasizes the property ownership dimension to share schemes, for employees, these same schemes serve rather more limited ambitions and may even be viewed with considerable scepticism (Baddon et al. 1989:204). Indeed, there is little doubt that share allocations, though generally welcomed by employees as a gratuity by management, are not strongly associated with feelings of ownership; in consequence, many employees see their shares in terms of 'just another bonus'. The Baddon study showed that just under half of all SAYE participants contended that to them their shareholdings represented just that (1989:263). In a study conducted by Bell and Hanson, 69 per cent of respondents in share scheme companies agreed that share schemes were popular because 'people like to have the bonus' (1987:24). In a major study of the views of 1,137 employees, carried out in four case study companies, the proportions of respondents who preferred a cash-based or combination scheme in preference to an exclusively share scheme were uncomfortably high at 45, 63, 47 and 72 per cent providing strong indications of employee bonus orientations (Fogarty and White 1988:38). A striking example of employee preferences is demonstrated by British Airways. Nearly 40,000 out of a total of 47,000 eligible employees opted to take *cash* in preference to ADST shares, leading one commentator to state that 'many more employees are eligible to take part in ADST than actually do, because they prefer the immediate cash incentive to waiting for at least two years for their shares' (Incomes Data Services 1990a:9).

There does seem, therefore, to be something of a disjuncture between management ambitions for shareholdings and employee expectations from them. On the one hand, through diverse routes, ownership is expected to lead to positive employee responses. But all the evidence suggests that the numbers of employees who actually receive a share of ownership, or take advantage of ownership opportunities, are limited. Moreover, the depth of ownership in terms of shares allocated to individual employees is shallow, and most employees evaluate their share allocations in terms of bonus. Bearing in mind these limitations, it is not surprising, perhaps, that the derived effect attributed to share schemes, that of changed employee behaviour or attitudes, has been difficult to identify.

## Problems in measuring the effects of financial involvement

Overall research findings indicate that change which is unambiguously attributable to the effects of employee share programmes is highly elusive. This is not to say that share programmes are not associated with positive outcomes; rather, it is to say that the effects are not easily attributable to share schemes. Neither has the direction of causality been satisfactorily resolved. The main problems are the following:

1   Share schemes are often established in association with or alongside other involvement practices (Smith 1993; Marchington et al. 1992:18) or systems of incentive payment (Casey et al. 1992:22). Often these programmes are introduced in companies with otherwise good human resource and performance records.

2   Profitable or successful enterprises are likely to introduce share schemes. Casey and his colleagues found that whereas 56 per cent of companies experiencing growing demand for outputs had profit-sharing arrangements, only 39 per cent of companies with declining or stable demand operated these arrangements (1992:22).

3   Employee attitudes and behaviour are difficult to assess, and attribution of these to a specific element of a company's complex and dynamic personnel programme is even more difficult to accomplish. Nevertheless, employees do not seem to regard share schemes in terms of property ownership.

4   Often, companies introduce and run more than one share scheme contemporaneously (Smith 1993).

5   As we have seen, participation rates are not high, especially among low-paid and low-status employees. Moreover, many employees are excluded from share schemes.

6   Numerous extrinsic as well as intrinsic factors influence company performance and profitability.

7   All advocates for share schemes recognize methodological difficulties in attributing positive outcomes to share schemes. The most empirically rigorous of these studies tend to signal the most severe doubts with regard to attitude change (Kelly and Kelly 1991:28).

8   In research studies, management reasons for scheme introduction have been non-specific. A company may well have a number of objectives, or simply operate a diffuse philosophy of 'involvement' in which share schemes are expected to play some, possibly unspecified, part (Baddon et al. 1989:100). It may well be that managers have articulated no coherent objective, especially if the scheme is introduced at the behest of an influential senior manager. For older established schemes, the original objectives or aspirations may not even be known.

It is possible that managerial attraction to share schemes may simply arise from opportunities to exploit tax favourable legislation as a means to supplement employee income and/or respond positively to political and social trends which stress the salience of property ownership for responsible behaviour. Indeed there is some evidence which suggests that employers have turned to share schemes as a result of tax favourable incentives. First, notwithstanding the putative benefits of share schemes, progress in the absence of governmental inducement has been patchy (Bell and Hanson 1987: Table 2.2) whilst, as Table 6.3 demonstrates, with legislative support the number of approved schemes has grown steadily since 1978. Nevertheless, managers do not necessarily respond positively to the stimulus of favourable legislation. Profit-related pay, for example, has failed to achieve widespread employer acceptance despite successive improvements in legislative support. Similarly, as we see below, ESOPs in the UK have yet to attain the momentum of earlier share programmes launched during the 1980s or that of the ESOP movement in the USA. Thus, it is questionable whether supportive legislation, on its own, provides sufficient stimulus to induce management action; the legislation must be compatible with other management aims.

Support for this proposition is provided by the results of the Baddon et al. survey in which managers were asked to nominate their objectives for 'profit-sharing and employee share ownership'. From a total of 679 choices given, only 43, a mere 6 per cent of the total, were for providing a 'a tax efficient way of improving the overall remuneration package' (1989:88). Perhaps, though, we should not be too surprised at this low ranking; companies are not likely to emphasize this aspect when offered a wide choice of more 'positive' alternatives. Even so, one-fifth of companies in the survey (i.e. 43 from 231 companies surveyed) did cite this choice as an objective for their schemes. Case study findings help to confirm, moreover, that legislation might be instrumental in converting favourable orientations into positive action. The Baddon et al. study examined share scheme operations of five companies in depth, and in two of these legislation was openly stated by senior management to have exerted a catalytic effect. Further, we shall see below that tax advantages appear to be a significant reason for American companies to introduce an ESOP.

## Financial involvement: a unitarist programme?

Not surprisingly, most companies introduce and publicize their share schemes on positive grounds of 'wanting to involve employees in the success' of their enterprises, or to 'give a stake in the company' to those who work in it. Publicists for share schemes comment unreservedly on the merits and rewards for employees to become 'owners' of the companies in which they work.

As with any management initiated involvement programme, however, we need also to consider other possible motivations, for there is evidence that other outcomes may be associated with the public proclamations. In particular, we mentioned that some share schemes launched during earlier peaks of interest were unequivocally aimed at suppressing or constraining collective employee organization or activity in what has sometimes been referred to as the 'deterrent' objective of financial involvement (see Creigh et al. 1981).

Arguably, then, behind the 'community of interest' façade may lurk an anti-collectivist ideology infiltrated within the contemporary practice of individual share schemes. A persuasive argument in this direction is to look at the practices and aspirations of the main UK sponsor of such schemes, the Conservative government, in office from 1979. Their enthusiasm for individual financial participation has been most ardent, whilst the same administration has launched a series of legalistic and practical assaults on trade union organization and activity ranging from laws designed to restrict union activity to banning union membership in specific governmental locations. The basis for this assault on collective organization has rested on the belief that a free market economy can only operate effectively if unhindered by the distorting effects of collective trade union behaviour (see e.g. Hayek 1985; Minford 1982). It is arguable that the hard approach of repression of collective interests synergizes comfortably with the softer one of attempting to establish or reinforce a feeling of community between employer and individual employee. Employers can feel at ease in acting upon a 'soft' unitarist option which poses no risk to their own influence or control, whilst leaving more overtly anti-collectivist sentiments to authoritarian managements or reserving them for possible emergency deployment.

Certainly, some recent events demonstrate how the nominally progressive benign image of individual share schemes can disguise employer determination to use the schemes to maintain their grip on workplace control. The recent débâcle of British Telecom management refusing to pay share dividends to striking engineers (and to all other eligible employees) provides a stark insight into a contemporary, if clumsy, management use of share schemes to 'structure the bargaining climate' in favourable directions. A more subtle illustration of this process is offered by a case study company investigated by one of the authors. The company, located in the hospitality industry, had introduced both an ADST scheme and a SAYE option scheme and had seen its share value rise steadily over the previous few years. At one of the biennial chairman's meetings attended by the researcher, to which all employees were invited, held shortly prior to annual wage negotiations, the chairman was quick to draw attention to the improved share price with the comment that it would be a pity for 'anything to happen' at the annual negotiations which might adversely affect profits or shareholder confidence in the company. 'If it does,' he added somewhat darkly, 'we all suffer.'

### ESOPs: involvement or participation?

We have noted that all the employee share schemes introduced and encouraged by the British government over the past few years have established rapid and growing support among employers, with the sole exception of employee share ownership plans, popularly known as ESOPs. This may be all the more surprising since ESOPs have attracted the attention of numerous participants to the industrial scene. They are of particular interest in the UK as they form the single current approach to FIP to be afforded broad support by the trade union movement. At the same time, but for different reasons, ESOPs have received moral and legislative endorsement from the Conservative government and the concept is given support by the other mainstream political parties. Employers in the UK, however, have been somewhat circumspect in their adoption of ESOPs.

In the USA, by contrast, employer responses have been markedly more enthusiastic. ESOPs have secured substantial and growing support among employers following their legislative recognition with the Employee Retirement and Income Security Act 1974: between 1975 and 1988 the number of ESOPs grew from 1,601 to 9,627. By the early 1990s the number of schemes exceeded 10,000. Of even greater significance is the massive expansion in employee coverage; over the same period the number of employees covered by ESOPs grew from a quarter of a million to more than 10 million (Allen et al. 1991:123). The size profile of ESOP companies has also changed; in 1975 the average ESOP company employed 155 employees, whereas by 1988 the figure was 1,028 (Allen et al. 1991:142). Nevertheless, the *median* ESOP is still small, consisting of 54 participating employees, each holding an average $5,226 worth of stock (Russell 1989:51). By contrast, in the UK, take-up of statutory ESOPs by employers has been extremely modest; by 1991, barely 50 schemes had been approved by the tax authorities. The huge difference between the American and UK experience of ESOPs can be attributable to important variations between ESOP philosophy and practical arrangements in the two countries, which in turn help to shed light on their different patterns of utilization by employers.

## ESOPs in the USA

In America, as their introduction under the 1974 'retirement' legislation indicates, ESOPs have largely been associated with company retirement plans and 'have never totally shaken off their image of being a poor substitute for a pension plan' (Stevens 1991/2:16). In their review of ESOP performance, Hanford and Grasso state unequivocally that 'ESOPs are retirement plans that . . . are required to invest primarily in the securities of the sponsoring employer' for which 'they are recognised as qualified for special tax treatment' (1991:221).

These tax advantages are well recognized by employers. In the US General Accounting Office (GAO) survey of ESOPs, three-quarters of respondent companies indicated that the tax advantage factor was a major reason for employers to introduce their ESOP (Russell 1989:52–3). Retirement plans which derive from the financial performance of the sponsoring companies also offer other advantages to these companies in terms of potential control over employees. However 'poor a substitute' they may be for a pension scheme, employees will be only too aware of their dependent status upon the employer's continued viability. Medium-service employees in particular may feel restricted in mobility if their accumulated retirement rights are jeopardized by moving to another employer. An employee leaving with, say, three years' service would only receive a fraction of his or her accumulated shares (Incomes Data Services 1989:9).

With regard to participation in decision-making, there is little evidence that ESOP status alters the decision-making structures or governance procedures in any strategic ways. For instance Jones and Kato point out that of the 'top 1,000 US ESOP firms, non-managerial employee involvement and influence via ESOPs is typically modest . . . fewer then 10 firms have non-managerial employees representing employee shareholders by serving on the board' (1993:359).

Moreover, a 'participatory' culture was identified in only 5 per cent of these same companies (Blasi and Kruse 1991). A number of reasons can be offered for this. First, employee ownership tends to be on a minority basis; according to GAO figures only 5 per cent of voting stock was owned by the median ESOP in 1985 (reported in Russell 1989:55). Second, the ESOP is governed by trustees appointed by the employer (1989:54). As Bryan Stevens, Director of the British Industrial Participation Association noted, following his study visit of American ESOPs: 'a fatal flaw in the legislation is the absence of any provision for employee representation' (1991/2:16). It seems that any increase in employee decision-making attributable to the ESOP has tended to occur at shopfloor level (Hanford and Grasso 1991:231) and to be of an informal nature (Russell 1989:55). These findings replicate the earlier studies of Klein and Rosen who found that ESOP employees tend not to consider that they enjoy more corporate influence or have an elevated say in company affairs as a consequence of ESOP participation (1986:401). Indeed, it is abundantly clear that ESOPs are not introduced in order to facilitate employee participation whether through employee voting rights or by board representation (Russell 1989; *Financial Times* 24 March 1992).

It appears then that American employers have few fears of loss of prerogative associated with ESOP provision, and the evidence confirms that they indeed have little to fear. ESOPs are identified as an employee benefit provided by the employer who in return can expect closer allegiance and, according to some accounts, raised employee morale and motivation and by association, productivity and performance (see Klein and Rosen 1986; Allen et al. 1991:141–5). By our definition, American ESOPs amply fulfil the requirements associated with employee involvement.

## ESOPs in the UK

But what about the UK, where uptake of employee involvement initiatives among employers, and of share schemes in particular, has been so pronounced over the past few years? How do we explain the apparent failure of ESOPs to take root despite their widespread endorsement in the UK and their obvious appeal in the United States? A number of reasons can be postulated for this situation.

First, in the UK ESOPs have largely been promoted as schemes designed to allow or even encourage employees to become shareholders in their company and, in contrast to American experience, they are not tied or related to company-based retirement schemes. Unlike other employee share schemes approved by the tax authorities, ESOPs can offer majority shareholdings to employees, a point which has proved attractive to the Unity Trust Bank (UTB), established in 1984 by trade unions in association with the Co-operative Bank. UTB has been involved in financing many of the ESOPs established in the UK over the past few years (Unity Trust Bank 1990:5). There is little doubt that concern over the possibility of majority employee shareholdings has acted as a disincentive to employer action over ESOPs in the UK.

Second, the statutory arrangements are complex, and ESOP advocates have suggested that this complexity, coupled with the associated fiscal and legal advisory costs, has proved a deterrent for employers. ESOPs received statutory backing with the Finance Act 1989 which offers tax concessions to companies which establish an approved ESOP. Further tax relief was offered to companies operating statutory schemes by successive Finance Acts in 1990 and 1991. Essentially, under the legislation, the ESOP is managed by a trust, which can borrow money in order to purchase company shares which in approved schemes are then distributed to employees through a second, profit-sharing trust.

Third, companies might also be deterred by the requirement (unlike in America) for the majority of the trust membership to be selected by employees, leading to employer fears of trade union domination of trust activities (see *Labour Research* 1990:21; Allen et al. 1991:167). Conversely, it is precisely the possibilities of assisting organized labour to organize capital (Unity Trust Bank 1990), to provide for collective participative influence over corporate affairs, that is attractive to the labour movement.

From these different perspectives, we can begin to see why ESOPs have not advanced in the UK even though they seem to command universal conceptual attraction, for whilst each political and economic interest group can envisage sectional gain as a consequence of an ESOP's introduction, individual employers can equally visualize potential loss of influence. Labour politicians can consider ESOPs in terms of advancing 'popular socialism', whilst Conservative supporters see them as an additional strand to their employee share initiative and as a means to lessen resistance to privatization moves. Employers, however ideologically inclined they may be toward employee share programmes, tend to be more pragmatic; statutory ESOPs are complex, costly to introduce, and might help to mobilize (or revive) collectivist activity at a time when manifestations of collectivist aspirations have been effectively subdued through a combination of economic circumstance, political action and employer initiative. In other words, ESOPs may well appear to be too closely oriented toward participation to attract the allegiance of British employers.

**Conclusions on individual share schemes**

We have seen that individual share schemes have been attributed with considerable powers of change by exponents, but examination of the evidence shows that few changes can be directly traced to the effects of share schemes alone. In particular, it appears that the quantities of shares on offer to employees are insufficient to trigger the ownership effect which, adherents claim, inclines employee orientations toward unitarist sympathies. Indeed, studies often show that employees attracted to share schemes already exhibit pre-existing unitarist tendencies, either as managers themselves or through positive identification with management ideals and objectives. Alternatively, share schemes can attract employees because they are free or offer little risk, but in line with their marginal status they make no noticeable impact upon broader employee perceptions or inclinations.

This is not to suggest that change cannot be associated with share schemes. As one element of an involvement approach adopted by management, they may contribute toward drawing employees into a closer management frame of reference; certainly, in one recent study of 700 employees it was clear that benefits to management do accrue from the aggregated effects of EI, rather than from the imposition of any one technique (Marchington et al. 1992:57).

Nevertheless, it does appear that, under favourable circumstances, share schemes can offer opportunities to employees to exert influence on corporate affairs. This may occur if sufficient shares are available to employees for them to influence executive decisions (as with some ESOPs), or if the shares of employees can be used in combination to allow employee interests to be expressed at corporate levels. It is interesting that in the first instance, ESOPs have made only patchy progress in the UK; and in America, where their progress has been faster, they are tightly enmeshed with company retirement plans, offering little scope for employee influence. Further, in most countries, the idea of collective share schemes has had a frosty reception from the business community and schemes in operation have faced continuing and debilitating opposition at both political and industrial levels. The next section examines the reasons for this situation and the effects of employer resistance upon the progress of collective schemes.

**Collective share schemes**

The diverse types of equity-based schemes considered above share one important characteristic; stock allocations are made or offered to *individual* employees by employers either as a gratuity or for purchase on preferential terms. An alternative approach to employee share ownership is offered by collective schemes in which stock is allocated to and administered by representative bodies on behalf of their members.

It should be clear at the outset that these two types of share schemes are unlikely to enjoy the same unitarist appeal. Share schemes introduced by employers extend ownership rights to individual employees but, even in aggregate, the proportion of shares allocated to the employees of a company at any one time can furnish only extremely limited ownership penetration. In consequence, there is no control contingent upon ownership and, other than normal individual shareholder rights, none is specifically offered by the schemes.[1] To some extent, influence by internal employee shareholders may be more constrained than for external equity holders. If the latter sell their shares in one company, it may make little impact upon their lives. For employee shareholders, if a company experiences difficulties or is subject to the attention of predators, selling shares may well undermine employment prospects of employees as well as contribute to their depreciating property rights.

Unions, in particular, are attracted by the prospect of greater corporate or industrial influence and will understandably be suspicious of, if not hostile towards, involvement projects promoted by otherwise unsympathetic governments which find expression in schemes subsequently launched by employers. History might serve to confirm that union suspicions are well founded, for earlier waves of employer interest in share schemes coincided with times of collective employee confidence during peak periods of economic activity, and at least some schemes were intended to undermine the emerging collective strength of employees (Ramsay 1977).

Suspecting that atomized employee share ownership offers few prospects of transferring control to members; that it also presents double risks to their accumulated earnings and livelihoods; and that it might serve to marginalize union activity as well as erode collective consciousness, union interests have tended to migrate (albeit with no great conviction or cohesion in the UK, as witnessed for example in the relatively low profile adopted by unions in the administration of occupational pension schemes) towards collective ownership, where individual risk is constrained and a measure of collective assertion of control over organizational assets is made feasible. Such support has been much more strongly articulated in countries where traditions of adversarial workplace relations are less firmly entrenched than in the UK and which have had a history of social democratic government (see Long 1986). The Scandinavian countries are generally held to share these characteristics (Kjellberg 1992). In these countries, supporters of the labour movement and unions have advocated and in some cases adopted programmes which provide for collective shareholdings.

Accepting the rather uncomfortable fact that share schemes *per se* have not been rejected by employees in the UK, and can be embraced by them, collective schemes have been proposed somewhat tentatively by the TUC and given even more tentative support by the Labour Party during its lengthy period of opposition (Baddon et al. 1989:53). Nevertheless, in countries such as Sweden, the original wage-earner plans have been progressively diluted following concerted political and employer opposition and many of the pioneering collective schemes have been abandoned under twin pressures of newly elected unsympathetic governments and tightening market pressures within industry.

In Denmark, too, there has been little progress. Labour movement demands followed a similar 'solidaristic' and economic democracy route as in Sweden, though the distance travelled has been somewhat less. A Bill for a wage-earner fund was introduced in 1973 but opposition from employers and conservative parties kept the proposals from the statute books. Modified versions were presented in 1979 and again in 1986 but without success and no collective schemes were actually implemented. Through the advocacy of employer associations, recent encouragement has been given to voluntary individual schemes (Bregn and Jeppesen 1991) and 'the debate on economic democracy is almost non-existent today' (Langeland 1993:217).

In Norway, until recently, the unions have shown little obvious enthusiasm for either individual or collective share plans, though pension fund partici-pation and company-based schemes are now under active consideration, largely as a consequence of 'the rapid increase in the number of financial transactions and extensive changes in the structure of industry and owner-ship' (Langeland 1991; 1993; see also Dølvik and Stockland 1992). Under these circumstances, protective legislation and collective agreements have provided inadequate safeguards for unions to influence strategic decisions; in consequence, they 'have found themselves as bystanders to take-overs and mergers' (Langeland 1991). A call has been made therefore for economic democracy to be established along collective wage-earner principles but, as with Sweden and Denmark, employer and politically conservative resistance to such ideas has been fierce: under aggressive promotion, company share schemes for employees have started to take a firm hold. By 1989, nearly a quarter (23 per cent) of companies with more than 100 workers had made stock offers to their employees (Langeland 1991).

The reality is that in the 1990s the prevailing individualistic political and economic ethos in Scandinavian countries has generated support for individ-ual employee share schemes whilst progress in collective programmes has faltered or even reversed. The outcome is described by Langeland in the fol-lowing terms: 'Today trade unions seem to be on the defensive as regards economic democracy, in all the Scandinavian countries' (1993:223). The Swedish experience in wage-earner funds provides an illuminating example of the difficulties faced by trade unions and their sympathizers in establishing and maintaining a participative initiative in the face of employer and politi-cal opposition.

### The Swedish experience

It has been one of the themes of this book that participative approaches to employment relations are highly contingent for progress and consolidation upon continued support from sympathetic governments who are prepared to face and resist opposition from a country's industrial and commercial com-munity, in order to erect a participative framework capable of withstanding the power and influence of that community. To accomplish this task requires that a government formulates an ideology sufficiently robust to confront or modify the model of competitive capitalist relations. It could be argued that the architects of Sweden's experiments in social democracy and employee participation, described by one writer as a 'socialist variant on market capitalism' (Ramsay 1992:37), had such a vision and were able, albeit temporarily, to make some of its participative elements concrete.

A number of factors contributed towards the evolution of the Swedish model. First, since the 1930s, there had been an almost unbroken sequence of social democratic governments with high concern for welfare policies and social justice. Second, this concern has been articulated among the country's political and industrial communities by adherence to 'progressive' industrial practices located within neo-human-relations and socio-technical systems theory promoting 'quality of working life' initiatives alongside attempts to democratize decision-making structures. The trade unions have endorsed a policy which gave 'industrial democracy . . . equal status with wage and employment conditions' (Lind 1979:12). With union density uniformly high across all industrial sectors and political governance favourable to the advance of industrial democracy, concern for industrial welfare has tended to remain ascendant on the political and industrial agenda. Moreover, an unusually high degree of accommodation between unions and employers (Kjellberg 1992) assisted the development of democratizing initiatives. The unions also had the support of influential thinkers capable of applying ideas of industrial social welfare within a planned economy as a route towards 'economic democracy' to supplement earlier phases of political and social democracy (Kjellberg 1992:97). Particularly influential in this regard in the labour movement have been the ideas of Gosta Rehn and Rudolf Meidner.

Rehn's initial concern in the early 1950s was to maintain high levels of employment but without contributing to excessive inflation (Martin 1984:203). To help achieve this objective, the 'solidaristic' pay policy approach was adopted in which restrictive fiscal policy was combined with an active manpower policy involving the provision of training and financial support to workers as protection against unemployment resulting from the failure of weaker firms to compete under equal pay conditions with the more effective ones. Against this background operated a form of national job evaluation in which common pay levels would be maintained for similar occupations by offering equal pay for work of equal value irrespective of company performance. Though the programme was implemented, an unresolved problem with the Rehn formula was whether sufficient funds could be generated under conditions of high taxation, in order to ensure adequate levels of investment to provide for continued profitability and growth among the more efficient firms and thereby maintain employment. One proposed solution to this problem was to ensure that sufficient equity capital be available for investment, and within this framework the economist Meidner, working on behalf of the Swedish Federation of Trade Unions (LO), formulated his proposal for wage-earner funds.[2]

The Meidner proposals involved the allocation of a proportion of company pre-tax profits to a central fund under the administration of the trade unions.

The shares would not be distributed to employees but would be retained by the fund in order to provide union influence over board decisions and to finance the development of union members to assist them to engage more fully in the participative arrangements passed by legislation in 1976 (Law of Co-Determination). Ultimately, and perhaps fatally, it was envisaged that through the wage-earner funds, 'private property would be progressively displaced not by state ownership, but by an alternative form of social ownership, transforming firms into something along the lines of . . . "social enterprises without owners"' (Martin 1984:278).

It was this commitment which contributed to the electoral defeat of the Social Democrats in September 1976, even though their original plans were amended under the combined criticisms of employers and the opposing liberal parties that the wage-earner funds represented a form of 'collective socialism', offering both an 'increased concentration of power' and 'a threat to freedom' (reported in Martin 1984:282–3). The subsequent Conservative period of office meant that the original Meidner plans were effectively shelved in the period between 1976 and 1982. Even when the Social Democrat partners were returned to power in 1982, it was without commitment to the original proposals, for, according to Martin, 'it was the massive campaign against wage earner funds from the right that made them a potential electoral liability' (Martin 1984:331), and thereby they were dismissed by all political interests with the exception of the Social Democrats (*Current Sweden* 1983).

Objections to collective funds were complemented and reinforced by alternative liberal plans to promote individual share programmes along the lines of those discussed in the first part of this chapter. Social Democrat concern at this attack on the Meidner proposals, coupled with the party's own growing doubts about the prospects for the radical elements contained within them, were sufficiently real for it to establish a commission to examine the question of wage-earner funds, the start of a retreat in the face of liberal scepticism and employer opposition which ultimately led to the adoption of a much diluted wage-earner arrangement (Long 1986). Almost 10 years after the LO call for wage-earner funds the modified version was put into place in 1984; the main departure from the original Meidner proposal was that regional funds, rather than a national scheme, were introduced, and whilst unions received majority status on the boards, other interests also received substantial representation. A level of maximum shareholdings in each company by the funds was also prescribed.

In the meantime, profound shifts in Swedish employment conditions were taking place as a result of the profitability crises of the 1980s. The centralized voluntarist doctrine began to give ground to a more legalistic and decentralized system in which one casualty has been the solidaristic pay principle to which the wage-earner funds were expected to contribute. Under employer pressure for flexibility and devolved decision-making within a market-oriented political framework (especially since September 1991 when the Social Democrats were replaced in office by a four-party coalition government leaning strongly to market principles: see *Current Sweden* 1991), the unions had to respond defensively to management pressures for more direct work-place 'bottom-up' employee involvement as a contributor to labour productivity, as opposed to concentration upon broader national participative reforms (Ramsay 1992). The collective wage-earner funds have since been abolished (EIRR 1991e) while individual schemes have proliferated at the instigation of employers; it is estimated that by the end of the 1980s in companies with schemes, 40 per cent of manual workers and 70 per cent of white-collar staff were shareholders in their companies (Kjellberg 1992:108). Under the new market offensives of the 1990s, it is certain that these proportions will grow.

### Conclusion: what future for collective share schemes?

In Sweden and other Scandinavian countries, it could be thought that conditions for participative reform of industry were solidly in place. A social democratic political and industrial consensus was prominent for many years. Union density was consistently high and in Sweden the main architects of the wage-earner funds, the LO, retained a dominant position in both industrial and political affairs. Further, these countries have long-standing traditions of social democracy which were able to provide crucial ideological support for the reforms.

Yet even under these apparently benign conditions, collective wage-earner plans with their far-reaching ambitions for reform of market relations foundered. The reasons for this failure are multiple and complex, but boil down to the fundamental issue that the plans met with the sustained opposition of the institutions at which reform was most directed; and equally importantly, these institutions were able to mobilize concerted power in defence of their interests at a time when economic circumstances assured that collective unity would be difficult to uphold.

In brief, the employers and their political and economic allies were always united in their opposition to collective funds and, despite the country's attraction to a moderated version of market relations, principles of managerial independence have always retained their attraction in Sweden as elsewhere. This independence of action is linked to access and control over property, the very issue which the wage-earner funds were designated to meet. Employer reaction to the prospect of diminished autonomy drew support from the increasingly market-driven policies which emerged from the economic and industrial relations crises which beset the country during the 1980s. These events even forced the Social Democrats to concede that :

> The period of Sweden's history which is characterised by a strong public sector expansion, centralised agreements on fundamental questions through an historical compromise between capital and labour, social engineering and central planning is at an end . . . The present change of times is characterised by individualisation and internationalisation. (reported in *Current Sweden* 1991:3)

The resulting industrial policies, which gave emphasis to decentralization and individualization in the private sector, also meant that the concept of distant and apparently unaccountable collective funds over which employees have no opportunity to exercise discretion appeared increasingly anomalous, and in comparison individual company schemes for employees gained in attractiveness. Perhaps for these reasons, by the end of the 1980s, other left-of-centre parties had abandoned the funds concept, leaving the Social Democrats isolated in their wavering support. It is doubtful whether collective wage-earner funds will again achieve the same profile as that they possessed in the middle years of the 1970s.

As with worker directors in the UK, when industry felt threatened by reformist participative arrangements, support was mobilized and maintained against any government measure which genuinely appeared to threaten employers and their prerogatives. Under this pressure, even when the Social Democrats were secure in office in the post-war years until the mid 1970s, the party felt unable to proceed with the wage-earner funds; there was 'a certain reluctance to push equalisation too far' (Rehn and Viklund 1990:304). This caution also raises an important and wider question as to whether any participative approach which ostensibly sets out to challenge the hegemony of capital can succeed in 'pushing equalization'. The only initiatives which will be tolerated are those which do not challenge employers in any meaningful way.

Poole's assertion, quoted at the beginning of this chapter, that ownership participation is equal in importance to executive participation in any move toward industrial democracy is clearly recognized by employers. By precluding collective employee interests from establishing a property base it could be argued that, even in friendly environmental conditions, the obstacles blocking the route of industrial democracy's 'long march' are rather more substantial than might have been anticipated before the ownership question was put seriously to the test through collective schemes.

## Notes

1    In practice, private shareholder influence is highly restricted, even though numbers of individual shareholders have grown considerably since the Conservative government's campaign to promote 'popular capitalism' as part of a universal property owning 'classless society'. However, the proportion of shares actually in private hands has declined considerably since the 1960s. In 1963 over half of all shares were owned privately; by 1990, this proportion had declined to 20 per cent. The bulk of shares are now owned and controlled by institutional fund managers, to such an extent that 'together the top 60 fund managers could determine the ownership of British companies' (*CBI News* 1990:8; see also *Labour Research*, 1987; 1991a).

2    There are two main union confederations in Sweden, of which the LO is the larger. The LO organizes over half the workforce, with membership drawn primarily from manual workers. The LO has historically established very close links with the Social Democratic Labour Party which meant that LO policy was usually translated into the policy formulations of that political party, until the relationship began to weaken in the 1980s under the stresses of lower economic growth, more open trade and a diversifying occupational structure which served to undermine the solidaristic pay principles.

# 7

# Employee Participation in Practice

Recent studies concerning employee participation have tended to have two main foci: trends in joint consultation, often included as a participative rather than an involvement exercise (e.g. Millward et al. 1992; Marchington 1987; Ramsay 1990; ACAS 1991); and European (largely EU) based studies of works councils, and to a lesser extent worker director schemes (*Bargaining Report* 1993; EIRR 1990a; 1993a; 1993b; Hall 1992; Gold and Hall 1990; European Trade Union Institute 1990). In this chapter, we look firstly at the broad trends in representative participation across the USA, Europe and the UK; and secondly at specific forms of participation, most notably works councils, worker directors and, in its borderline status between participation and involvement, joint consultation as a form of 'representational' involvement with the potential to enjoy informal participative status.

## Overview of participation trends

### UK

As was argued in Chapter 5, during the 1980s there was a strong trend towards direct forms of involvement in the USA and the UK, as pluralistic industrial relations practices (e.g. collective bargaining) came under pressure from an increasingly unitaristic managerial approach in many enterprises. This trend was reinforced by conservative government hostility to pluralist approaches to industrial relations, reflected in the UK by legislative attempts to alter the balance of power between management and labour in favour of the former. Moreover, indirect participation was perceived as a threat to the productivity and efficiency gains of UK industry in the 1980s, and therefore was not promoted by government agencies as part of their employee–management relations reforms (Employment Department 1989:3).

However, despite pluralistic underpinnings, a number of representational methods are still manifest in many contemporary organizations, often taking place through trade union and staff association structures. In the UK, WIRS indicate that whilst 9 per cent of establishments introduced new indirect schemes between 1980 and 1984, this rose to 13 per cent between 1984 and 1990 (Millward et al. 1992:178), representing an increase over the two periods of 69 per cent (albeit with the 1990 survey covering a longer period than the 1984 WIRS).

*Europe*

Across Europe, reliance on representational channels of communication remained strong throughout the 1980s and early 1990s. The Price Waterhouse/Cranfield Project (PWCP) found that in six of 12 surveyed countries, a third of organizations had increased their use of collective channels, whilst only a small minority of companies in the 12 states had actually reduced their reliance on this form of communication. Most marked, in the latter respect, was the UK, with a little under 20 per cent of organizations moving away from representative channels of communication (Brewster and Hegewisch 1993:14). Indeed, senior managers in about 75 per cent of organizations in the same survey felt that works councils and trade unions were the most important channel for upward communication, i.e. a form of participation that enables employee representatives to potentially influence managerial decision-making through either collective bargaining or joint consultation systems. Not surprisingly, with their high union density figures, managers in the Scandinavian countries felt especially prone to use collective channels for upward communication, which were present in around 90 per cent of organizations in Finland, Norway and Sweden; in France, Germany, Holland and Spain the figure was around 80 per cent; whilst in Ireland, Turkey and the UK it was approximately 70 per cent (1993:15–16).

*USA*

In the USA, a noticeable involvement trend was apparent during the 1980s, driven, in significant parts of the American economy, by an aggressive managerialism reasserting its authority in traditionally highly unionized sectors such as automobiles and the airline industry (see Cooke 1990). Where participation initiatives were introduced in this context, such as worker directors and industry-level consultation committees (see Kochan et al. 1986:182–7), they tended to stem from trade-offs between management and trade unions, in the broader context of industrial restructuring (usually involving 'downsizing') and concessionary bargaining on the part of the unions.

An alternative trend, however, was noted in the late 1980s and early 1990s, with a number of US organizations adhering or returning to the view that a positive-sum game can result through management/union mutual co-operation. Indeed, a number of American-based studies have argued that a positive link exists between productivity and unionization (see Eaton and Voos 1992; Kelley and Harrison 1992). Management in these organizations perceive EP and representative forums as integral elements of organizational success. Empirical observations on the relationship between improved organizational performance and union participation in decision-making are underpinned by the radical changes experienced in American industrial relations since the early 1980s. Most notably, a sea change in union attitudes towards both collective bargaining and direct involvement initiatives has led managers in many US organizations to reassess the implications of communicating through employee representatives. The old-style adversarial relationship previously characteristic of indirect/representational methods has been largely replaced by a more consensual approach by both union officials and managers, within the context of an increasingly management-driven agenda. Within this latter framework, the efficacy of dealing with collective groups of employees has surfaced in US employee relations, and is now seen to offer companies a potential competitive edge over their rivals.

This reappraisal of the role of unions in American organizations has counterbalanced the more extreme examples experienced in the 1980s towards individualizing the employment relationship, through such techniques as individual-based performance pay systems. Moreover, the 'new unionism' highlights the non-linear nature of the trends we are witnessing within contemporary industrial relations, not just in America but in the Western world more generally.

## Joint consultation committees

Within this diverse context across Europe, the USA and the UK, three main forms of participation have been practised in the 1980s and early 1990s: joint consultation committees; works councils; and worker director schemes. We now turn to an exploration of each in the following sections of this chapter.

### Forms and methods of employee participation

Joint consultation committees (JCCs) have perhaps been the most explored form of indirect involvement/participation in recent years. In the UK, for instance, WIRS largely concentrates on JCCs in its 'Consultation and communication' section, and the ACAS 1990 survey also devoted most attention to this approach.

The trends in the usage of JCCs and their character and structure have been a particularly popular topic for two reasons. First, they have a long history: JCCs have been utilized since the early twentieth century, and experienced an enhanced status during the two world wars, when consensual labour relations and the smooth running of industry were of critical importance to wartime economies. JCCs have an especially strong tradition in the public sector, and more recently have been a common practice in Japanese multinational companies operating in the UK and elsewhere. Despite changing trends, JCCs appear to have retained their attraction because management find them useful in distracting employees away from more important adversarial issues (Ramsay 1990), and/or because managers and employees value them as a meaningful form of involvement or participation (Marchington 1987). Rather than these two perspectives competing with each other, it is the flexibility of JCCs that enables the consultative approach to retain its place in contemporary industrial relations. Indeed, our second point about JCCs is that in practice they can either be managerially dominated forums, or act as a mechanism for enabling employee representatives to influence aspects of organizational decision-making.

In fact, JCCs highlight the tension between traditional forms of industrial relations (especially adversarial collective bargaining) and the less adversarial goals of joint consideration of management proposals and decisions. In this context, model JCCs are based on three principles:

1    There must be a clear separation between consultation and negotiation issues (i.e. those topics which usually fall under the remit of adversarial collective bargaining).
2    Management must show the workforce that JCCs are taken seriously (i.e. regular attendance at meetings of managers with the appropriate status to make decisions is essential).
3    Employee representatives must have legitimacy in the eyes of the workforce (i.e. often this will involve trade union representatives, although in multi-union and low-union-density plants this can cause problems).

In practice, however, a strict dichotomous model which places JCCs at one end of the spectrum of integrative (positive-sum) and distributive (zero-sum) issues, and collective bargaining at the other, can be misleading. Often negotiating issues can enter the remit of JCCs, either formally or informally. The 1990 ACAS survey conducted in the UK, for instance, focused on the private sector and found that almost half of these committees dealt with minor negotiating issues (ACAS 1991:9). Also there appears to be a problem concerning the issue of management status in JCCs. The ACAS survey found that managing directors and chief executives are only involved in about a third of JCCs surveyed (1991:10).

Conversely, a long-held criticism of JCCs from a pluralistic perspective is that they can be used by management to subvert the collective bargaining system, turning the latter effectively into a unitarist managerial decision-making process. A number of techniques can be utilized by managers, with varying degrees of subtlety, to minimize the influence of the employee perspective in joint committee meetings. Manipulating the discussion agenda, or allowing issues to be raised at joint committee meetings but having little intention of following up the points made at higher levels of decision-making, are just two examples of how managers might turn JCCs into ineffective 'letting-off steam' exercises. A less subtle approach might be found in managers simply refusing to discuss problematic or contentious issues raised by employee representatives in committee meetings, or by stating that the point raised, whilst valued, cannot be acted upon, for financial or other business-oriented reasons. As noted later in this chapter, irrespective of the type of participative forum, managerial/employer commercially oriented rationales can be difficult to counter with an employee perspective legitimized by democratic and equity arguments. Given this, adherence to the three principles outlined above become critical if JCCs are to retain their authority in the eyes of employees.

*Joint consultation: participation or involvement?*

The legitimacy problem outlined above concerning forums such as JCCs, has long been looked upon as critically undermining their efficacy as channels for pursuing employee interests within the organization. This argument, first expounded by Clegg in the 1950s, posits that collective bargaining, dealing with distributive (zero-sum) issues, is in practice the antithesis of those representational forums, such as JCCs, which essentially focus on integrative issues. Clegg, in a well-known passage, argued that 'The trade union [as the guardian of the collective bargaining function upon which this industrial governance model is established] is thus industry's opposition – an opposition that can never become a government' (Clegg 1985:84). Not only does this 'oppositional' role prevent the development of autocracy in industry, but in the absence of collective bargaining the trade unions would lose their voluntary character and be transformed into involuntary associations (1985:88). Collective bargaining, according to Clegg, should therefore remain the central role of trade unions, and its adversarial essence should not be diluted or confused by union involvement in forms of industrial democracy or employee involvement. In these circumstances JCCs can be best conceptualized as a form of representational involvement, as opposed to the participative approach of collective bargaining.

This argument has been analysed both historically and conceptually. Historically, collective bargaining has undergone significant change, and in a review of recent research, one study concluded that for the 1980s collective bargaining 'has less and less to say about employee participation in situations in which individually-oriented initiatives . . . are leading the way' (Allen et al. 1991:74). Conceptually, Clegg's thesis has left a lasting legacy, for good or ill. Marchington (1987), for instance, has argued that a misleading dichotomy has permeated the debate concerning the nature of the shifting trends in joint consultation. Marchington cites the work of Cressey et al. (1985) and MacInnes (1985) as representing examples of a *marginalization* thesis, in contrast to a *revitalization* perspective propounded by Batstone (1984) and Terry (1983). The marginalization thesis argues that JCCs have become a forum for increasingly trivial issues owing to the growing economic pressures which organizations have faced in recent years; whilst the revitalization thesis contends that JCCs have replaced collective bargaining as the key representative forum as unions declined in influence during the 1980s.

Marchington however argues that rather than the JCCs being seen as a competitor to collective bargaining (cf. Clegg), they could equally be seen as 'complementary'. In Marchington's words, 'consultation acts as an adjunct to the bargaining machinery, and to some extent fills in the gap left by the latter' (1987:340). In other words, a genuine commitment to JCCs on both sides, and clear demarcation lines between negotiation and consultation issues, may well yield a valuable dualistic approach for both employees (and their unions) and management, complementing rather than contradicting each other. Whilst all three models (marginalization, revitalization and complementarity) are useful conceptually, we have stressed in the current study the diverse character of changing trends in participation (and involvement), and the need to differentiate in terms of, for example, size of organization and sector. More critically, we would differentiate JCCs from collective bargaining, in that the former, even though offering a potentially important channel for employee representation and influence, are essentially managerially driven. Collective bargaining, we would contend, still retains a greater initial employee/trade-union impetus, which partly explains the inroads made into this traditional form of participation since the early 1980s (see Claydon 1989).

Outside the parameters of this conceptual debate, however, one can argue *a priori* that joint consultative forums are highly appropriate in the following contexts: (i) where collective bargaining tends to be centralized (i.e. taking place at industry or company level, and not at the plant/shopfloor level), hence creating a need for a discussion forum at local level; (ii) in large organizations where there is often a lack of communication channels between management and employees; and (iii) where companies are seeking to reduce the importance of collective bargaining, and JCCs offer a valuable alternative.

### Joint consultation in practice: the UK

In the UK, between the 1950s and 1980s, the use of JCCs declined largely owing to the growth of company/plant-level collective bargaining. However, since the 1980s a more stable picture has emerged. The 1990 ACAS survey produced the picture of the utilization of JCCs in the private sector, shown in Table 7.1. As can be seen, 40 per cent of all establishments responded that they utilized JCCs, with large plants in manufacturing in particular registering highly in this context (58 per cent). At the other end of the spectrum, only 17 per cent of small service-based establishments used JCCs. According to the ACAS findings, sectoral difference was more important than size of establishment in determining the likelihood of JCCs. Manufacturing was twice as likely as services to utilize JCCs (47 per cent and 23 per cent respectively), whilst large companies were one and a half times as likely to use JCCs compared with small plants (54 per cent and 35 per cent respectively).

Table 7.1  *Proportion of establishments utilizing JCCs, by sector and size, 1990 (per cent)*

|  | Small[1] | Large[2] | All |
|---|---|---|---|
| Manufacturing | 43 | 58 | 47 |
| Services | 17 | 42 | 23 |
| Total | 35 | 54 | 40 |

[1]  Establishments employing between 50 and 300.
[2]  Establishments employing 301 or more.
*Source:* ACAS 1991:10

ACAS felt that it could not offer any conclusions regarding trends in the utilization of JCCs, although its findings corresponded roughly with a number of other surveys conducted during the post-war period. However the survey did show that compared with experience from the earlier 1980s, the frequency of meetings of JCCs seems to have increased significantly, with nearly half (48 per cent) meeting at least once a month, and a further 25 per cent meeting at least bimonthly (1991:11).

In terms of incidence trends during the 1980s, the evidence is fairly consistent. In the private sector for instance, as noted above, ACAS found an incidence rate of about 40 per cent in 1990. This mirrored a CBI survey conducted in 1989 which also found 40 per cent of responding companies utilizing JCCs (*CBI News* 1990). Ramsay, utilizing data gathered in 1985 in a larger study (principally focused on financial involvement but including questions on JCCs), found that 33 per cent of companies in the private sector used JCCs (1990:15; a similar finding to WIRS 1980–4 in Millward and Stevens 1986). In Ramsay's disaggregation of the private sector, there is a stark contrast in incidence of JCCs between services and manufacturing, with construction, distribution, transport and banking all registering below 20 per cent in usage of JCCs, whilst energy, metals, engineering and other manufacturing recorded a 50 per cent plus response in the use of JCCs (see Ramsay 1990: Appendix A1).

WIRS concluded in its 1990 survey (Millward et al. 1992) that at establishment level JCCs declined in number during the second half of the 1980s, although noting that the number of higher-level company JCCs (i.e. multi-establishment committee structures) had remained fairly constant, and indeed, these increased in structural complexity. According to WIRS, the decline in workplace JCCs between 1984 and 1990 was most marked in private manufacturing, falling from 30 per cent of establishments in 1984 to 23 per cent by 1990, following a similar decline in the 1980–4 period (1992:153). In the public and private service sectors utilization of JCCs was fairly constant. Overall the aggregate decline in JCCs at establishment level was from 34 per cent in 1984 to 29 per cent in 1990. The size of establishment was significant in the relative decline of JCCs, with the overall structural shifts in the economy towards smaller establishments exacerbating this trend (1992:153). Indeed, the later WIRS concluded that rather than marking a sea change in managerial industrial relations policies within existing companies, the falling incidence of JCCs was primarily due to structural changes in the economy in the second half of the 1980s (1992:154).

This conclusion was further supported by evidence that in larger companies, the utilization of higher-level JCCs had remained constant since 1984 (43 per cent of companies in 1990 compared with 45 per cent in 1984). There was however a large sectoral difference, with 60 per cent of public sector companies and 25 per cent of private sector companies operating higher-level JCCs. Moreover, higher-level JCCs appear to have undergone a growing complexity during the latter 1980s, in terms of increase in the proportion of companies operating with a multiple committee structure. By 1990, 10 per cent of respondents indicated that they had four or more committees compared with 6 per cent in 1984, thereby continuing a trend apparent since 1980, when only 4 per cent of companies utilized this number of committees (1992:155).

Overall, the following conclusions can be drawn in the UK context. First, JCCs are an important part of the surface industrial relations context of many companies and establishments in the early years of the 1990s, although there has been no clear overall trend in their utilization over the past decade. Second, sector and size of establishment are critical variants, with an apparent trend towards, on the one hand, a growing complexity (and importance) in larger manufacturing and public sector industries, whilst on the other hand, a continuing reduction in usage in smaller, service-based companies. Therefore in respect of the representational involvement approach of JCCs, the UK is experiencing a dual trend in its industrial relations: a growing informality and loosening of structures in the expanding, relatively smaller service-based sectors; and an increasingly sophisticated, formalized approach in the shrinking, relatively larger manufacturing and public sectors. This duality is underpinned by a number of factors, such as the continuing presence of trade unions in the latter sectors, and the need for larger companies to operate with formalized structures of communication and participation. In the multinational sector, EU policies and potential legislation further increase the utilization of formalistic procedures. In contrast, smaller organizations, often in the service sector, with a particular need to respond rapidly to changing market conditions and customer requirements, tend to involve employees in a more fluid, often amorphous fashion, without the seeming rigidities of more formalistic methods of EI/EP (see Peters 1992 for some interesting case studies of the informal approach).

*Joint consultation in practice: the USA*

This dual nature of involvement through joint consultation in the UK bears comparison with developments in the USA, where, as noted above, two main trends are emerging. Aggressive anti-union and anti-representation attitudes, which are prevalent across a wide range of American organizations, can be contrasted with a growing recognition in other enterprises of the centrality of management–labour co-operation in enhancing organizational performance and international competitiveness. In this latter context, Deutsch and Schurman (1993) note the development of JCCs, largely at the establishment level, which deal with potentially strategic issues, such as changing technology, health and safety, and training requirements.

Few national or industry-level forums exist in the US, however, and where they do they have tended to evolve from crisis restructuring situations stemming from the early 1980s recession. Kochan et al. (1986), for example, note that by the mid 1980s a number of industry-level participative arrangements had sprung up in the US, typically in highly competitive, decentralized sectors such as food retailing. The Joint Labour–Management Committee of the retail food industry, established in the early 1970s, is an early example of this approach. These initiatives were intended primarily to create industry level representative forums to discuss non-bargaining issues, such as changes in technology; and more generally, they opened up a consensual framework for the discussion of long-term, strategic changes facing the particular industries (1986:182–7).

Whilst these initiatives have rarely led to meaningful union input into strategic decision-making, they have yielded some successes for both employers and unions. In the retail food industry, for example, three achievements have been noted. First, lines of communication have been opened up at national level between union leaders and executive management; in a highly decentralized industry this is a notable achievement. Second, a number of major long-term research projects have been initiated in these forums, for example examining the impact of changing technology. And third, committee members have engaged in arbitration and mediation of conflict situations in the industry. Another good example of industry-level participation has been in the clothing industry, where a Tailored Clothing Technology Corporation was set up, which gave the union involved unique influence at an early stage of technological change in the industry (Kochan et al. 1986:182–7).

These industry-wide initiatives reflect, and in turn have helped to shape, those changes noted earlier in US industrial relations and the role of trade unions in that country. This is a particularly noteworthy development in the context of North America, given the absence of a legal framework determining the nature of involvement and participative initiatives. In contrast, European practices of participation have been largely shaped by a legalistic context in which works councils have been prominent, and it is to these that we now turn.

## Works councils

Works councils offer an integrative mechanism for management to consult with employee representatives on a wide range of issues, mostly in the areas of production, personnel and employee relations matters. Moreover, councils may offer an alternative for potentially divisive negotiation structures; they can also provide a forum for the dissemination and discussion of issues which might otherwise not find a form of expression; and they can allow management and employees to increase the scope of consultation issues.

On the surface, works councils can be viewed as offering a representative forum similar to JCCs in terms of structure, levels and coverage of issues. But on closer examination, a number of key differences can be seen between typical continental European works councils and USA/UK forums for consultation. In particular, European councils usually have some statutory backing, are formal organizations (e.g. they often have written constitutions regarding membership elections), and are based either *de jure* or *de facto* on union participation. These characteristics are largely a reflection of the degree of employee and union influence in much of continental Europe since the Second World War, operating within a bargained corporatist political-economic context (see e.g. Baglioni and Crouch 1991) which gives support to participative initiatives.

In the USA and the UK, on the other hand, until the 1980s few organizations had works councils in the strict European sense, although many joint employee/management councils operated in the form of health and safety committees. Resistance towards a works council approach in both the US and the UK reflected a historical wariness of relatively strategic forms of participation among employers and trade unions. The former resisted councils because of the perceived inroads into managerial authority represented by this method, the latter owing to the traditional wariness on the part of unions of becoming implicated in 'negative' organizational decisions, such as job losses through relocation or restructured work organization. However, modified forms of works councils which have the effect of steering these bodies more closely toward 'representative involvement' began to be increasingly utilized in the UK and the USA in the 1980s, a trend which continued into the 1990s. These bodies are often referred to as company, employee or advisory councils. In the UK, this employer led initiative has stemmed from three main factors: the derecognition of trade unions during the 1980s (Claydon 1989); Japanese multinational companies which have spearheaded moves toward single-union deals (see e.g. *Industrial Relations Review and Report* 1993a); and a proactive attempt by employers to address pressures from the European Union (see e.g. Hurly 1992; *Bargaining Report* 1993).

Derecognition and single unionism can be incorporated in the term 'the new industrial relations' in the UK. For example, the then newly privatized Northumbrian Water company set up a two-tier representative participation system in 1990 for its 1,300 workforce, after derecognizing its individual unions for negotiating purposes. Local-level employee councils operate in the company's operational areas, customer accounts department and headquarters. Members are elected from distinct constituencies, together with several local management members. There is no direct trade union representation at this level. A higher-level company council brings representatives of the employee councils together with four appointed management members, one trade union representative (drawn from all the eight unions formerly recognized by the pre-privatized company), and an employees' staff association representative. The local-level councils deal with employee relations issues, but they are excluded from discussing pay and conditions. The company council meets at least four times a year to discuss and negotiate pay and conditions of employment, but decisions are reached through 'consensus' building rather than by voting (reported in *Bargaining Report* 1993:11).

The influence of Japanese management practices on much of US and UK industry has been extensively debated (see e.g. Oliver and Wilkinson 1992; Wood 1991; Womack et al. 1990; Wickens 1987). Whilst the concept of 'Japanization' is contested on both empirical and conceptual grounds over the extent of the spread of Japanese practices in Western economies, and the nature of Japanese working practices domestically (see Chapter 9 for a fuller discussion of these issues), Japanese multinationals have certainly paralleled, if not contributed towards, the council trend in UK industrial relations. Nissan Motor Manufacturer (UK), employing 4,600 workers, established a company council in 1989 as part of its single-union deal with the Amalgamated Engineering Union. Pay and conditions of employment are

discussed at special meetings of the company council, though it is more regularly used for consultation and information purposes, and the constitution
of the council makes its non-adversarial philosophy clear: 'The prime responsibility of all members of the Council is to ensure the prosperity of the
Company and by so doing promote the prosperity and security of all staff'
(reported in *Bargaining Report* 1993:12).

The approaches by Nissan, Northumbrian Water and other similar council systems have produced mixed feelings amongst UK trade unions. Some
unions, such as the large and influential National and Local Government
Officers Association (NALGO), have been openly hostile to the works council practised by Northumbrian Water, seeing it as initiated, driven and
controlled by management, with the prime purpose of marginalizing trade
unionism in the company (NALGO 1993). Other unions, however, have
engaged with the works council trend in a more collaborative way. One
grouping of major UK unions (which included engineering, finance, communications and general workers), for example, signed a 'Document towards
industrial partnership' in 1992, which *inter alia* noted that works councils are
an important and necessary innovation in contemporary industrial
relations, allowing for a wide range of issues to be discussed between
management and employees. Moreover, the document stated that membership of councils should not be confined to trade union representatives, but
should cover all of the workforce, thereby accepting the right of non-union-
ists to be involved in a key decision making forum (reported in *Bargaining
Report* 1993).

## The European Union and works councils

The influence of the EU on works councils has had a long history, characterized initially by the determination of the Commission of the European
Community (CEC) to establish a universalistic European-wide model of participation, only to encounter strong opposition from the European business
lobby (represented principally by the European Employers' Federation
UNICE) and from the UK government. Peppered by political in-fighting and
eventual compromise, the EU produced three main strands of participation
initiatives in the 1970s and 1980s: the so-called Fifth Directive, focusing on
participation models; the Vredeling Directive, concentrating on information
provision; and the European Company Statute, which created the concept of
a legally recognized and registered European company, within which
European-level representational participative forums would be compulsory.

The initial move made by the EU was based on the 1972 Fifth Directive,
which proposed a two-tier board structure for companies with 500 or more
employees, in which representatives from the latter were elected to membership
of a supervisory board. As a consequence of a combination of UK government opposition, employer lobbying, and differences in trade union attitudes
across the EU, a 1983 amendment put into place a more flexible approach,
whereby member states could select one of three participation models:

1   minority employee representation (between one-third and a half) of the members of a supervisory board, or through a one-tier board of directors with a minority of non-executive directors
2   employee consultation rights through representation on a works council
3   employee consultation rights to be incorporated into existing collective bargaining machinery (Wedderburn, 1990:58).

The Vredeling Directive first put forward in 1980 focused on the issue of strategic information disclosure, aiming at companies with 100 or more employees. Again, an amendment in 1983 watered down the initial proposal, both quantitatively and qualitatively. In the quantitative context, the amendment simply raised the organizational size criterion from those employing 100 or more employees to those employing 1,000 or more, thus allowing a broad swathe of smaller European companies to escape the net of the Vredeling proposal. More significantly, the concept of strategic information provision was blurred by the introduction of a clause which stipulated that disclosure to employee representatives should only include 'non-confidential' information, thus allowing organizations considerable scope for interpreting which information could be commercially sensitive. Differentiating between confidential and non-confidential information is highly problematic. Information given to shareholders, predicted future staffing levels, current profit margins, advances in technology through research and development, can all ultimately be seen as commercially sensitive, but at the same time could well be regarded as essential information to enable trade unions to discuss and negotiate with management on a range of issues of concern to employees. It is difficult to escape the conclusion that the evasion over defining what constitutes 'commercially sensitive' information was precisely the point of the 1983 amendment, underpinned by a political trade-off between the CEC and the European business lobby.

By the second half of the 1980s, despite EU compromises and 'dilution' amendments to directives on EP, both the Fifth and Vredeling directives had run into the ground, largely owing to UK government opposition, and new initiatives were introduced to revive the process of implementing a Euro-wide system of participation.

In 1976, the original European Company Statute proposed that European-wide conglomerated companies should have both works councils at the European level, and employee representation on supervisory boards. In other words, 'European companies' were to employ best practice employee participation schemes largely following the (West) German approach. However, after a series of amendments in 1989 and 1992, the current proposals (1989, draft Article 2) follow the 'menu' approach of the 1983 amended Fifth Directive with the CEC continuing to argue:

> that the Directive on employee involvement is 'an indispensable complement' to the proposed Regulation on the *Societus Europaea* [European] company structure and that employees must play a part, not in the day-to-day running of the business, but 'in the supervision and in the definition of strategy'. (Wedderburn 1990:59)

At the beginning of the 1990s, in the run-up to the introduction of the so-called Single Market in 1992, the CEC introduced a new version of the above initiatives (which had to a large extent lost momentum) with the directive on European works councils (EWCs) in September 1991. The EWC Directive was aimed at large multinational companies, employing at least 1,000 workers, and operating in at least two EU states (and employing a minimum of 100 people in each country).

This particular initiative suffered the same switchback history in the early 1990s as its predecessor Directives had done during the 1980s. Between 1991 and 1994, much leeway was given to the main European industrial relations parties, the European Trade Union Congress (ETUC) and UNICE, to reach a voluntary agreement on the most appropriate model of participation in each individual country. However, in April 1994 these discussions broke down, and the EU decided to return to a universalistic approach, planning to pass a Directive on European works councils in October 1994, from which date European-based multinationals would have two years to implement a European-level works council. It has been estimated that about 1,000 multinational companies will be affected, and the draft Directive stipulates that councils should meet at least once a year, with subcommittees meeting more regularly to deal with matters of immediate importance, such as an impending redundancy or merger situation (reported in *Financial Times* 20 April 1994).

Reflecting a more general sense of urgency in implementing 'social welfare' initiatives, to complement, and to some extent soften, the essentially economic and business-driven aspects of '1992', an Action Programme was put in place by the CEC in 1989. Covering 49 separate initiatives, including 'social partners and collective bargaining', 'information provision' and 'consultation and participation', this Action Programme is designed to accompany and act as a driving force for the Social Chapter. Each initiative has a time-scale for introduction, with the information and the consultation and participation initiatives originally planned for implementation in 1990, although the proposals here are largely contained within the European Company Statute. By the end of 1992, some 60 per cent of the 49 action proposals had been implemented, although the future of some of the remaining, but more contentious proposals, such as the European works councils Directive, have met with stronger employer led resistance.

The upsurge in the 'social dimension' issue, which reached a peak in the concept of the Social Chapter in the late 1980s, ebbed in the early 1990s in the face of European-wide economic recession, continued opposition from the UK government, and the loss of momentum after the initial Danish referendum in 1992 which rejected the Maastricht European Union Treaty. Furthermore, the economic costs faced by Germany in the process of reunification has at least slowed down the German drive for harmonization of labour costs across Europe. Despite this apparent brake on the progress of the move towards harmonization, much continues to happen in Europe in the context of works councils, promoted by an EU specified fund of some ECU

31 million to support the development of contacts between employee representatives in European-based multinational companies (see Roberts 1993 and Ramsay 1994 for an analysis of the post-Maastricht situation facing organized labour).

## Works councils in practice

In EU countries where works councils are universally operated (with legal backing in 11 of the 15 member states), the main function is usually to serve as a channel for information disclosure and consultation on non-bargaining issues, although, as noted with JCCs, in practice a strict dichotomy between integrative and distributive issues can be difficult to identify. In Spain, for example, works councils are fully integrated into the collective bargaining system (see below). Moreover, as one recent study of European works councils points out, information provision and consultation – terms often used interchangeably – can entail a very different degree of employee participation, with information provision often being one-way, i.e. from management to employees, involving no real employee influence, and very much resembling the involvement initiatives detailed in earlier chapters (EIRR 1993a:13). Reflecting this problem, Gold and Hall (1990) define works councils as those that exist or are introduced on the basis of the European works councils (EWCs) draft Directive, which gives works councils a legal basis and structure in Community undertakings.

The EWC draft Directive envisages works councils being *consulted* prior to important initiatives being taken by management, most notably over employment security and job conditions, with an emphasis on the more strategically important aspects such as training, technological change and relocation plans. The term 'consulted' implies a meaningful ability for the body of employee representatives to give 'its opinion with the aim of influencing the decision with the employer subsequently responding to the points raised' (EIRR 1993a:13). Apart from these general characteristics, the structure and functions of works councils vary between countries, for example over the minimum number of employees necessary before a works council can be set up by statute. In Germany, five employees is the minimum number, whilst in France and Spain it is 50, and in Belgium 100. In some countries such as Denmark and France the employer is represented within the works council, whilst in most other countries only employees have representation. The size of the councils can vary enormously, up to 31 members in Germany for example, although a notional maximum of 30 members is recommended in the EWC draft Directive.

A number of multinational company case studies undertaken since the early 1990s yield some insight into how works councils operate in practice. In the French-based information technology organization, Bull, the consultation procedure moves away from simply allowing for 'downward' information given to the council representatives towards a system where employee members are able to make recommendations to management within two weeks of the initial meeting, after which management must respond within a further two weeks. The management team is also obliged to inform the council secretary about issues of potential importance as soon as possible prior to the meetings, of which there are two each year. This provision enables the employee representatives to consider their position on important matters before the forthcoming meeting.

At another French multinational company, Elf Aquitaine, council members receive written notification of the annual meeting's agenda at least 20 days beforehand, along with any additional material, such as background briefing papers on proposed changes in company production plans. With management's agreement, expert consultants can be called upon by employee representatives if they need more knowledge of a particular issue, such as over financial or accounting technicalities. Council secretaries are usually elected by all committee members, together with a council bureau (composed of representatives from each country of operation), which draws up the agenda for the meeting alongside management, prepares plenary meetings, and ensures that the committee members liaise between formal meetings. The secretary ensures liaison with management, and is responsible for the annual works council budget, which amongst other things is used for written translation and foreign language interpreter fees. As in most European multinational companies, it is usual for committee members to receive adequate time off from work to pursue their works council duties (see EIRR 1993a; 1991c).

*The UK and the Social Chapter*

There is little doubt that the UK's future approach to employee participation will be influenced either directly or indirectly by European initiatives. In a direct context, the current arguments over the Social Chapter conceal a number of deep-seated political differences within the EU and its member states – especially in the case of the UK. The amendments of 1983 provide clear evidence of the resistance to the EU's proposals on employee participation from federations representing business, and from the UK government. The progressiveness of the universalistic approach of the 1970s was largely replaced by a more cautious 'menu' approach in the 1980s which offered member states 'best-fit' alternatives consistent with the peculiarities and traditions of each member state. Even so, this watered-down approach by the EU still finds little favour with the UK government or UNICE. Should the principle of 'majority voting' on social issues be adopted by the EU, however, the UK will have to adapt itself to some form of systematic European-wide participation mechanism (Roberts 1993).

The UK's refusal to ratify the Social Chapter at the Maastricht summit in December 1991 has meant that, for the foreseeable future, it will have no involvement in the design or implementation of European social legislation. This stance has, paradoxically, allowed the rest of the EU to push initiatives of this type much quicker than would have otherwise been the case. With the (re)introduction of the universally applied EWC Directive in 1994, indirect pressure has emerged as UK multinational companies (and European multi-nationals operating in the UK) come under pressure to move towards a relatively harmonized European-wide system of employee relations and per-sonnel policies. Harmonization would ultimately include not only communication and participation in its remit, through the introduction of a works council system across all member EU states, but also a similar legal basis for employment, such as rights for 'atypically' employed workers (in part-time jobs for example) equal to those enjoyed by full-time employees.

## Multinational companies and EWCs

The potential impact of the European Social Chapter has been addressed by a number of UK-based multinationals who have initiated discussions on the setting up of European-wide councils. However, a survey conducted in the early 1990s found no UK-based company operating in Europe with a for-malized works council agreement, and indeed identified only 18 European-based multinational companies with this type of approach, with German- and French-based companies accounting for all but one of these (the exception being the Swiss company Nestlé). Of these 18 multinationals, only three – Volkswagen (German), Bull (French) and Europipe (German/French) – have gone beyond the level of 'information committees', providing a Euro-wide consultation forum; at Europipe this has taken the form of employee representatives on a supervisory board (EIRR 1993a; 1992a; 1991d).

A study of European-wide participation initiatives conducted by the European Trade Union Confederation found that Elf Aquitaine had set up a consultation (as well as information) body in July 1991. However, the appar-ent disparity between this study and that of the EIRR may be due to a blurring of definitions over exactly what 'consultation' means. Another case study of Elf Aquitaine also stresses the consultation aspect of the agreement, although at the same time noting that the agreement contains the provision that this European-level forum is complementary to any national-level forums rather than a substitute for them (EIRR 1991c:11).

This provision in the formal agreement illustrates the complex nature of consultation and decision-making influence in multinational organizations. Indeed the establishment of this type of forum should not be viewed as a once-and-for-all agreement. For example, the basis of the French, German, British, Spanish transnational Airbus Industrie works council was legally challenged by French and German trade unions in 1992 in the French courts, on the grounds that except for the French Aerospatiale member of the con-sortium, election to membership of the council can be through both recognized union and non-union channels. This provision in particular upset the French union confederation CFDT, who see it as undermining French law, which gives recognized trade unions a monopoly in nominating candi-dates for works councils during the first stage of elections (EIRR 1992a).

A further 31 multinationals identified by EIRR in a follow-up survey had some form of informal participatory arrangements where trade unions or local unions had developed links on a European level but had little formal contact with management. Of these, only two involved joint UK/European-based organizations – Rothmans and Unilever (the former ultimately Swiss owned) (EIRR 1993c). When one places this total of 50 or so companies in the context of an estimated 900 multinational groupings with an EU head-quarters operating in at least two EU states (Sisson et al. 1992), it is clear that whilst the symbolic importance of companies like Volkswagen should not be ignored, the trends so far towards European-level participatory forums are still extremely limited. Moreover, on examining the substantive nature of most agreements, the following summary seems apt: 'It clearly emerges from the analysis of the existing agreements on workers' rights in multinational companies that employees' rights relate more exclusively to information and, to a more limited extent, to basic forms of consultation' (European Trade Union Institute 1991:11). Hence, it seems that even in ostensibly participative forums, pressures are emerging to restrict the scope and influence of these bodies to an involvement-aligned agenda.

*Case studies: Germany and Spain*

For different reasons, Germany and Spain provide useful examples of European participation and it is worthwhile to explore these in slightly more depth. The former is a core EU member state, with acknowledged 'best prac-tice' employee participation in Europe, and indeed a number of EU member states have argued that the Social Chapter is basically a German trade-union/employer joint stratagem, to ensure that German industry is not undercut by cheaper production areas elsewhere in Europe, particularly in the south.[1] Employee participation practices in Spain date back to Franco's time, but they were generally regarded as undemocratic forums. Since the return of liberal democracy to Spain in the mid 1970s, several pieces of legislation have underpinned new forms of participation, especially works councils. Spain is interestingly in the same context as the UK, since it represents a 'peripheral' EU state, whose geographical location and economic structure bear compar-ison with the UK.

There are two levels of participation in (West) Germany which are associ-ated with the concept of co-determination; first at plant level through works councils (*Betriebsrate*), and second at company level through the form of worker directors. Works councils are mandatory (Works Constitution Act 1972, amended 1988) for companies with five or more employees. Works councils range in size up to 31 members (in companies employing in excess of 9,000 workers), and are open to all employees (including part-time and tem-porary workers) over the age of 18. In practice, however, union activists tend to permeate these councils; for example 72.5 per cent of works councillors were union sponsored in 1987 (see EIRR 1990a:26). Both blue- and white-collar employees are represented on works councils.

In Spanish enterprises employing between 11 and 50 workers, the Workers'

Statute of 1980 originally provided for employee delegates (*delegados de personal*) – a type of shop steward – to air worker grievances. But a 1984 amendment gave these delegates similar powers and duties as are found in works councils, which were given legal status by the 1980 Act. On the initiative of employees, works councils may be set up in enterprises of over 50 workers. In multi-plant establishments, plant-based councils (*comites de centro*) may elect a maximum of 15 members onto a central council (*comite intercentro*). All employees over 16 years of age, including part-time and casual workers, are eligible to stand for election. Membership of works councils varies between five (in enterprises employing 50–100) and 21 (enterprises employing 750–1,000). In larger companies, membership can increase by two employee representatives for every 1,000 workers (see EIRR 1990a for an overview of the Spanish system).

It is normal in Europe for a works council to be restricted in its duties to consider workplace problems, and rarely to have full co-determination rights (even in Germany) apart from over matters concerning social and welfare issues. Section 80 of the German Works Council Act stipulates their responsibilities as follows:

1    to ensure the implementation of legislation, safety regulations, agreements and other measure to benefit the employees
2    to make recommendations to the employer on issues benefiting both enterprise and staff
3    to channel staff suggestions to management and to negotiate with management on their implementation, and to keep the staff informed of progress
4    to promote and defend the interests of disabled, young and elderly workers
5    to promote integration of foreign workers into the workplace.

To ensure the successful performance of these duties, the employer must provide the works councils with 'comprehensive information in good time', and in companies employing 100 or more workers, financial information must be given to a 'finance committee' of the council. Moreover, the employer must consult works councils over issues such as work reorganization, technical change, redundancies and training.

In Spain works council members have certain rights, including protection against dismissal from the enterprise, priority retention in times of redundancy, office space in the workplace, and paid time off for council activities. Whilst Spanish works councils enjoy a broad range of information and consultative rights (such as receiving all financial and other documentation given to shareholders), much emphasis is placed upon their negotiating role. Unlike in Germany, and indeed in Francoist Spain, councils are not exclusively devoted to the promotion of industrial co-operation, and in recent years have tended to put increasing emphasis on collective bargaining (EIRR 1990a).

Finally, it is worth pointing out that although co-determination is in theory the basis for works councils, one overview of the German system concluded that participation rights are strongest on social issues, relatively weaker regarding personnel issues, and weakest still on economic and financial matters: 'In other words, the potential for works council intervention in managerial decision making decreases the more closely it impinges on business policy' (Jacobi et al. 1992:243). Hence even EU best practice models do not necessarily reach their full potential in offering employees influence in strategic decision-making in their organizations, an issue we shall return to in Chapter 8, when we explore managerial rationales towards involvement and participation, and consider the European business lobby's hostility towards the EWC Directive in greater depth.

## Worker directors

If works councils often fail to live up to their potential, what of worker director schemes, which should, in theory, allow employee representatives immediate access to, and influence over, strategic decision-making processes in the organization?

The idea of worker directors has stemmed largely from Europe and especially Germany, where they were introduced in key industries in the aftermath of The SecondWorld War. The initiative to establish a European-wide system of worker directors was taken by the CEC in the 1972 Fifth Directive (amended in 1983), which proposed a two-tier board structure for companies with 500 or more employees, with employee representation on a supervisory board. As we have seen, the 1983 amendment put in place a more flexible approach, whereby member states could select one of three participation models, only one of which stipulated employee representation on a supervisory board.

### Worker directors: the European experience

As in the case of works councils, worker director practice varies greatly, depending on, in particular, company size, capital stock and economic sector. The framework which supports worker directors is, however, consistent: EU countries tend to advocate a two-tier structure, such as in Germany, Holland and Denmark (in the case of larger companies), allowing for employee representatives to sit on supervisory boards. These boards effectively act as an intermediary between the shareholders' annual meeting and the management, and have the following powers: appointment/dismissal of the management board; overseeing the work of the management board; and a veto on strategic issues, such as large-scale investments, employment of high-level managers, and financial transactions. Whilst these rights are extensive, they are not often used restrictively, possibly because employee representatives are normally in a minority on supervisory boards. A further organizational limitation on the radical use of such powers by worker directors is that it is normal for shareholders to be involved in sanctioning the appointment of a chairperson of the supervisory board where employees have equal voting rights (as in Germany and Austria for example). The chairperson would have an effective veto on decisions, should there be a stalemate between management and employee representatives on the supervisory board (see EIRR 1991a). However, in a less tangible way, the existence of a supervisory board should, *a priori*, have the effect of modifying the behaviour of all parties involved in organizational decision-making, thus making controversial matters less likely; for example in the appointment of a senior manager.

The German 1976 Co-Determination Act (*Mitbestimmungsgesetz*) regulates participation in large private sector companies employing 2,000 or more people, and stipulates that supervisory boards should have between 12 and 20 members, depending on the exact size of the company. Although employee representatives constitute 50 per cent of board membership, about one-third of this percentage is elected from outside the workforce (normally trade union officials). (A useful overview of the German system can be found in EIRR 1990a). A single-tier board representation system is the norm for smaller companies in France and Denmark, and a unitary board is the only option in the Irish and Spanish state sectors and in Luxembourg (EIRR 1991a:21).

Whilst this concept of co-determination allows for employee representation at board level, full parity representation (in which half the seats are occupied by employee representatives) is rare in any European state; for example, the norm in France is 33 per cent employee representation. Even in Germany, the concept of co-determination has often been misinterpreted. In terms of worker directors, several levels of employee influence are practised in Germany, from full parity representation in the coal and steel industries, through to a one-third seats system for medium-size companies employing between 500 and 2,000 workers. In the smaller sector (with five or more employees), legislation only allows for works councils (see e.g. Fuerstenberg 1987:175).

In most cases, worker directorship systems offer all board members identical rights (as in Germany, Holland, Luxembourg, Greece, Ireland, and in the French and Danish public sectors). However it is also the norm for restrictions to be placed on the appointment of key members of boards. In Germany for example, whilst employee representatives constitute half of the board of larger (2,000+ employees) companies, the shareholders appoint the chair, who has a deciding vote. Also, it is not uncommon to differentiate on what employee representatives can discuss between integrative and distributive issues. In Denmark for instance, worker directors cannot participate at board level in discussions on industrial disputes. In the French private sector, employee representatives are particularly restricted in that their role is purely consultative, and they have no voting rights (see EIRR 1991a).

*Worker directors: the UK experience*

Worker directors are far more common in continental Europe than in the UK, which generally has manifested negative attitudes towards this type of participation. The high point of institutionalized attempts to develop worker directors in the UK came in 1977, with the publication of the Bullock Report

(1977), emanating out of the Bullock Committee of Inquiry on Industrial Democracy. This report advocated the setting up of a system of worker directors in large enterprises in the private sector. The Bullock proposals advocated worker directors sitting on single-tier executive managerial boards, rather than on supervisory boards, which, as noted above, is the common practice in continental Europe. The formula $2x + y$ was devised, meaning parity representation of workers and shareholders $(2x)$ plus one or more neutral members of the board $(y)$ recommended by such bodies as ACAS. However, the few companies that took up the Bullock recommendations often did so opportunistically in an attempt to use worker directors to reassert managerial control. Generally UK companies were openly hostile to the ideas contained in the majority Bullock Report,[2] condemning what they regarded as unnecessary and divisive intervention in company affairs, an attitude reflected in a contemporary CBI booklet. After arguing that worker directors were impractical, and positively damaging to sensible long-term decision-making in organizations, the CBI concluded bluntly that: 'it is quite clear that no Government should contemplate bringing in legislation based on the majority Bullock Report. Surveys of public opinion show there is no popular support for it; the unions are divided; the owners and managers of industry are united in opposition' (CBI 1977:18).

It was in the public sector that honourably intentioned approaches were made to introduce worker director schemes, in British Steel and the Post Office (see e.g. Batstone et al. 1985). Even here, a number of critical problems were found within the schemes, most notably that worker board members tended to act as 'directors' first and 'worker representatives' second, and that their contribution was primarily in the area of industrial relations issues, rather than for example over investment decisions and other more strategically long-term areas of organizational decision-making. Company management also often endeavoured to marginalize the impact of worker directors, for example by discussing key issues, such as financial and accounting matters, outside the formal board meeting. This approach enabled the management team to develop a unified approach and a set of rational arguments, to effectively manipulate the employee representatives at the time of the actual board meeting. Despite the fact that the Bullock initiative stemmed largely from a desire to respond to the EC's Fifth Directive drafted in 1972, the Bullock Report failed to achieve legal status, and was largely overtaken by political changes post 1979.

*Worker directors: the American experience*

As noted in Chapter 5, involvement and participation in the USA has had a long history, and since the early 1980s, changes in EI/EP have been seen at both workplace and higher decision-making levels. The early 1980s recession was the spur towards consideration of greater degrees of employee influence on organizational decision-making, and one form that this took was in employee representation on the board of directors. These experiments in employee participation were usually conducted through trade union channels, where the latter represented a significant proportion of the workforce. However, the American experience of worker directors since the early 1980s has been mixed, born as they were out of economic crises.

The Chrysler car company was the first organization to experiment with employee/union (United Auto Workers) directors, as part of a federal government aid package to the company in 1980. Others to follow suit included trucking and manufacturing companies, and most notably several airlines (all of which faced severe financial crises).

As in Europe and the UK, there has been a tendency for union board members to be perceived amongst the workforce as representing managerial interests, rather than as advocates of a distinct 'worker' voice. One notable example concerned the Rath Meatpacking company, where a former union officer became the chief executive, but failed to convince the workforce of the continuing need for concessionary bargaining, or in other words, for cuts in wages and conditions. The Rath Meatpacking case is also interesting in that it illustrates a typical scenario in America (unlike Europe and the UK) of board-level representation being linked to an ESOP, with employees gaining 60 per cent of the company stock. This particular experiment in worker directors also failed to deliver a more consensual industrial relations climate, and eventually the company went bankrupt (see Hammer and Stern 1986).

Worker directors in the airline industry were also born out of crisis situations, and, as with the case of Eastern Airlines, failed to prevent companies from going bust. Kochan et al.'s (1986) seminal study of US industrial relations in transition reports on the case of Western Airlines, which, the authors argue, illustrated two generalized aspects of the American experience of worker directors. First, union attitudes towards this form of EP were mixed, partly, as indicated in the Rath case, because of fear of being entwined in 'negative' decision-making. In fact, one of the five unions involved in the Western Airlines case – the Teamsters – decided to nominate an 'outsider' to represent its interests, so as to 'minimize potential conflict of interest'. Second, employees in the organization tended to be lukewarm to the idea of worker directors, and felt that in general, it did not offer them a meaningful influence on managerial decision-making (1986:192).

## Conclusions

The limitations illustrated in the American case reflect broader experiences of participation in Europe and the UK. Whilst in theory representative forums of participation offer employees and their unions access to important, potentially strategic decision-making processes, in practice they tend to be inhibited by two main factors. First, following Clegg's view, it is often felt that formal representative forums which are not based on collective bargaining blur the distinction between the roles of trade unions and management. In particular, employees often see union representatives as gradually taking on a 'manage-rial rationale', and losing their distinctive worker perspective.

A second, related point concerns the broader environment, which so often will determine outcomes but which is beyond the control of either management or workforce. Particularly in the US and the UK, this problem has been exac-erbated by the introduction of schemes, such as worker directors, during crisis situations. In continental Europe, a longer-standing and more firmly estab-lished system of EP has been practised, enabling this type of decision-making process to gain greater acceptability and legitimacy within the respective coun-tries' systems of industrial relations. Even in these cases, however, the 'best practice' approach of the German model of EP is seen to have its limitations. The so-called co-determination concept challenges the distinction between ownership and control; it blurs demarcation with collective bargaining issues; and it does not allow for lower-level management representation. Trade unions also fear the evasion tactics often adopted by management, especially the hold-ing back of strategic information (see Fuerstenberg 1987 and Jacobi et al. 1992 for useful overviews of the former West German system).

Despite these limitations, representational forums, such as JCCs, works councils and worker directors, can offer employees and unions an important access point to organization decision-making. As one review of European works councils concluded: 'For many unions, EWCs represent an increasingly important source of information about company plans for European-scale restructuring and about the growing number of cross-border mergers and acquisitions' (Vitols, 1993:53). Unlike their European counterparts, employ-ers, managers and trade unions in the US and the UK will increasingly need to adapt to the re-emergence of participation, alongside the hitherto stronger trends in involvement. In America, a new federal-level political thrust is emerging in the field of participative industrial relations, whilst in the UK, the EU initiatives in this area refuse to be totally marginalized. We now turn our attention to exploring more comprehensively the rationales behind manage-rial and trade union thinking on involvement and participation approaches in the following chapter.

### Notes

1 Unification of Germany has had a dramatic impact on this situation, forcing German employers and unions to concentrate on problems on their doorstep. It is too early to make any realistic calculation as to the longer-term impact of the reunification of the 'two Germanies'. At the time of writing there is little objective evidence of a changing approach by the industrial rela-tions partners in Germany towards the social aspect of '1992'. However, the authors are aware of anecdotal evidence that suggests that there is increasing strain on the social consensus that underpins German industrial relations, including a growing antagonism in the West towards the cost of subsidizing East German industry. But, given the strong legislative backing to the German industrial relations system, attempts to directly weaken and marginalize the German trade unions, and the system of employee participation, seem an unlikely by-product of these ten-sions. This latter point implies that there will still remain a fairly strong dynamic within Germany pushing 'social dialogue' issues within the EU.

2 The remit of the Bullock Committee's enquiry was contested from the very beginning, as it 'accept[ed] the need for a radical extension of industrial democracy in the control of companies by means of representation on boards of directors' (CBI 1977:3). Whilst the majority report (representing the views of the Chairperson and the trade union and academic committee members) framed its recommendations within this context, a minority report (voicing the views of the employer members) objected that they had been forced to consider not *whether* but *how* employee directors should be appointed. More specifically, the minority report urged that board representatives should be drawn from the whole workforce (i.e. rather than solely representing trade union members in the organization), and that the system itself should be based on a two-tier model (as in Europe), with employee representatives located on a supervisory board (see the Bullock Report 1977; CBI 1977).

# 8

# Rationales for and Responses to Employee Involvement and Participation

So far, we have presented a primarily empirical account of trends and developments in employee involvement and participation during the latter part of the 1980s and the early 1990s. In this chapter, we go on to analyse more systematically the rationales and influences behind the growing utilization of involvement techniques, and the pressures surrounding the development of participatory policies.

The literature of this subject is potentially vast, especially if one includes the wave of studies based on concepts of production paradigms. 'Lean production' (see Womack et al. 1990), post-modern forms of organization reflecting global shifts in production organization, encapsulated principally in the idea of 'post-Fordism' (see e.g. Piore and Sabel 1984; Lash and Urry 1987), 'Japanization' (Wickens 1987; Oliver and Wilkinson 1992) and a host of new human resource management metaphors, notably the 'learning organization' (see e.g. Morgan 1993; Peters 1992; Dunn 1990; 1991; Keenoy 1991 on new metaphors in industrial relations), can all be said to have an important influence on the subject matter of this chapter. It is in fact almost impossible to avoid mentioning some of these concepts, or at least the language surrounding them, given their contemporary pervasiveness.

In many ways, these concepts share a core vision, which emphasizes the withering away of standard forms of organizational behaviour and structures, and the growing necessity to integrate employees and to devolve authority down through the organization. Large, bureaucratic structures, with top-heavy and directive management, should be, and (arguably) are being, replaced by post-modern forms of organization, with an emphasis on diversity and democratic decision-making. Post-Fordism develops this approach and directs it specifically at the point of production: 'Instead of Fordism's specialised machinery producing standardised products, we now have flexible, all-purpose machinery producing a variety of products', enabling economies of scale on small batch runs (Murray 1985:30). Ultimately, all of the above concepts contend that organizations need to create structures that are amenable to constant change, reflecting, and in part driving, the rapid and radical environmental shifts that we are witnessing as the twenty-first century approaches.

## Lean production, the learning organization and empowerment

Lean production has linked post-Fordism specifically to the concept of Japanization. Companies in the West, it is argued, must understand the lean production methods of the Japanese, in order to develop organizational structures that can compete successfully against the Nissans and Toyotas of this world (Womack et al. 1990). Stressing the hard element of this equation, lean production is based on: a zero-defect approach to production; integrated design, development and production systems; small-batch (i.e. non-standard or non-mass) production; a concomitant need for flexible technology to interface with a flexible workforce; and a rationalized hierarchy of suppliers, whereby first-tier suppliers work as an integral part of the development team, and second-tier suppliers are responsible for making the components required by the first tier. Underpinning this approach, it is argued that a 'creative tension' is produced within the workplace, which offers employees a challenging environment in which to thrive. (For a summary of the lean production concept see EIRR 1992b; and for a critique, see Williams et al. 1992.)

Critically, in order for companies to move from an inflexible, traditional (Fordist) base, to a flexible, lean production system, managers must change not only their ways of behaviour, but more fundamentally their ways of thinking. The learning organization, argue its advocates, is one in which managers perceive their position in the organization, and their relationship with subordinates, in a radically new way, utilizing new metaphors and ways of understanding. In the words of one of the learning organization's most lucid proponents: 'We are leaving the age of organized organizations and moving into an era where the ability to understand, facilitate, and encourage processes of self-organization will become a key competence' (Morgan 1993:xiii).

'Empowering' employees is the term contemporary management often use to encapsulate the micro-level dynamic enabling these macro- and meso-level post-Fordist or learning organization projects to reach fruition. In the following sections of this chapter, we examine the rationales and responses of the three key parties towards 'empowering' involvement and participation initiatives at the organizational level: management, employees and trade unions. To begin this exploration, we turn our focus to the nature of the issues typically discussed between the parties, to establish the relative importance of the various EI/EP forums which form the main features of contemporary employment relationships.

## Issues discussed in involvement and participation forums

The question of what issues get discussed and negotiated when employees have an influence on decision-making is important in that it offers an initial insight into the way that managerial rationales are expressed, modified and influenced through the filter of these forums.

Focusing specifically on evidence from the UK, once again we turn to WIRS as the single most reliable and substantial source of data to begin our analysis. Table 8.1 indicates the types of issues that are generally focused on in terms of information provision to employees and their representatives. As we move down the table, the nature of the issue tends to assume a more strategic connotation; hence whilst 'terms and conditions' are clearly of operational and non-strategic concern, 'investment' plans have inherent strategic implications. In the middle of the issues table, 'staffing and manpower plans' could be seen as operational and/or strategic. By 'strategic' we refer to those organizational activities which are long term in perspective, consciously, coherently and intentionally developed (Gospel and Palmer 1993:41), or policies which feed into these activities, such as financial information.

Table 8.1   *Information given to workers by management,[1] 1984 and 1990*

|  |  | Establishments (%) | |
|---|---|---|---|
|  |  | 1984 | 1990 |
| Operational |  |  |  |
|  | Terms and conditions | 66 | 62 |
|  | Health and safety | – | 66 |
|  | Work organization change | 70 | 68 |
|  | Staffing/manpower | 40 | 33 |
|  | Financial position (establishment) | 30 | 28 |
|  | Financial position (company) | 32 | 23 |
|  | Investment | 12 | 19 |
| Strategic |  |  |  |

[1]   The WIRS asked employee respondents to indicate how much information was given to them by establishment managements. The percentages in the table refer to the proportion of establishments in which managements provided 'a lot of information' on the listed issues. Whilst the WIRS failed to specify the type of forum through which information was provided, they did conclude that information provision was more common in larger and unionized establishments, suggesting that indirect forums would often be utilized, such as JCCs.

*Sources:* adapted from Millward and Stevens 1986; Millward et al. 1992

Those issues most likely to be focused upon are located in the top half of the table, falling into the non-strategic operational category. Hence whilst over 60 per cent of establishments gave information to employees on terms and conditions, health and safety and work organization changes in 1990, only one-third or fewer establishments considered it necessary or desirable to give information on strategic issues such as financial position and investment plans. Comparing the 1984 WIRS responses with 1990, information provision appears to have fallen slightly on nearly all issues except investment plans, where, perhaps surprisingly, provision has increased markedly from 12 to 19 per cent during the second half of the 1980s. This trend may be partly explained by the provisions in Section One of the Employment Act 1982 (explored in Chapter 5), which encourages companies to increase the awareness of employees on the financial position of the organization. If this is the case, then although the overall trend in information provision fell during the later 1980s, the 1982 Act may have had some positive influence, and indeed may well have offset a potentially sharper fall in information provision during this period.

In terms of consultation, WIRS results are less clear, indicating an increase in the extent of consultation over operational issues between 1984 and 1990, but surprisingly offering no data on the extent of strategic issue consultation (Millward et al. 1992:168–9). Work organization and health and safety issues were the two most common areas raised in consultation forums in 1990 (73 and 70 per cent of establishments respectively).

Size of establishment is an important factor in determining the extent of information provision and consultation, with larger companies of 500 or more employees being significantly more likely to provide information on both operational and strategic issues, and also more likely to have consultation practices on operational issues compared with smaller establishments. Establishments with 1,000 or more employees, in particular, were more likely to provide information on strategic issues to their workforce than smaller establishments, although WIRS points out that on staffing and manpower plans in 1990, managements were overall less likely, and much less likely in larger establishments, to give information or consultation rights compared with 1984 (Millward et al. 1992:170).

A further insight into the ways in which management approach operational and strategic issues in the various forums can be gained from the ACAS 1990 private sector survey, which examined the type of issue focused upon in four involvement and participatory forums: local-level joint consultation committees (LJCCs), local-level negotiating committees (LNCs), quality circles (QCs) and joint working parties (JWPs). In the following tables LJCCs and LNCs are differentiated from QCs and JWPs, the former being indirect or representational forms of involvement (LJCCs) and participation (LNCs), the latter being direct forms of involvement. Using this approach, we have grouped the issues into three broad clusters: basic employee, production and strategic. Issues discussed in QCs and JWPs are shown in Table 8.2; those discussed in consultation and negotiation forums are presented in Table 8.3.

As discussed in Chapter 5, production issues are the core focus in direct involvement forums. The ACAS survey found that production issues generally were discussed in 52 per cent of responding establishments, whilst production costs (72 per cent) and output (66 per cent) figured prominently on the agenda of quality circles (Table 8.2). Basic employee issues appear of no concern to quality circles (emphasizing the latter's diagnostic problem solving approach), except for health and safety, which interlinks directly with production issues. JWPs on the other hand tend to deal more with basic employee issues, and perhaps surprisingly, over a third of establishments claimed that pay was presented as an issue in this type of forum. Strategic issues, as expected, are not dealt with in direct involvement forums, with the possible exception of training, which may be a strategic issue when associated with organizational reforms. This latter point, however, indicates the some-

Table 8.2    *Issues discussed in local direct forums, 1990*

| Issue | Establishments (%) | |
| --- | --- | --- |
| | QCs | JWPs |
| *Basic employee* | | |
| Pay | | 35 |
| Safety | 47 | – |
| Grievance/discipline | | 25 |
| Absence | | 26 |
| Appraisal | | 21 |
| | | |
| *Production* | – | 52 |
| Quality | 95 | – |
| Output | 66 | – |
| Production costs | 72 | – |
| Job evaluation | – | 35 |
| Mgt/employee communication | 60 | – |
| Workgroup communication | 55 | – |
| | | |
| *Strategic* | | |
| Training | – | 28 |

*Source:* adapted from ACAS 1991

times complex nature of consultation, in that it can be difficult to draw a clear dividing line between operational and strategic issues. It is likely that the 28 per cent of establishment managements who responded that training was an issue in JWPs were thinking in terms of its operational aspects, rather than broader organizational change and manpower planning concerns. However, discussion of the narrower immediate production needs of training could easily lead into discussions on a broader level.

Not surprisingly, Table 8.3 indicates that basic employee issues such as pay (93 per cent) and redundancy (62 per cent) figure large as important issues for negotiation forums, although perhaps less obvious is the finding that welfare (65 per cent) and working conditions (50 per cent) still remain prominent in this context, given the trends noted elsewhere towards direct involvement managerial approaches. Moreover, the interface between issues dealt with in both representative and direct forums is unclear from this type of broad survey. Production issues were an important part of the agenda in both representational and direct forums. Most notably, quality (87 per cent) and output (82 per cent) were key issues in consultation committees (as well as in direct forums).

Compared to WIRS, the ACAS findings posit a much stronger picture of the proportion of establishments which focus on potentially strategic consultation issues in representative forums; for example, 83 per cent of management respondents claimed to consult over technology changes, and 78 per cent over training. Indeed at least two-thirds of respondents consulted over the four key strategic issues denoted in the survey. This is surprising

Table 8.3   *Issues discussed in local representative forums, 1990*

| | Establishments (%) | |
| Issue | LJCCs | LNCs |
| --- | --- | --- |
| *Basic employee* | | |
| Pay | 57 | 93 |
| Pensions | – | 22 |
| Safety | 72 | 35 |
| Work conditions | 89 | 50 |
| Redundancy | – | 62 |
| Welfare | 75 | 65 |
| | | |
| *Production* | | |
| Quality | 87 | – |
| Output | 82 | – |
| Work methods | 78 | – |
| | | |
| *Strategic* | | |
| Training | 78 | 19 |
| New technology | 83 | 28 |
| Staffing levels | 67 | 37 |
| Company finances | 66 | – |

*Source:* adapted from ACAS 1991

when we compare these findings with those of WIRS. The 1990 WIRS did not ask establishments to respond to the question of consultation rights on what we have termed strategic issues, but very few WIRS respondents even provide information on issues such as company finance, let alone offer consultation rights. Given that the ACAS survey concentrated solely on the private sector (manufacturing and services), this apparent disparity is even more surprising, as representative consultation rights and procedures are often seen as being more characteristic of the public than the private sector.

Though methodologically the WIRS and ACAS surveys are not comparable, particularly in terms of their respective scope, nevertheless rather different pictures emerge from the two sets of data. A partial explanation might be that the responses to WIRS refer to generally higher-level establishment forums, whilst respondents to ACAS are focusing on lower-level establishment committees. More importantly, both surveys are almost certainly failing to pick up important qualitative differences in managerial approaches to involvement and participation forums, especially in the handling of prospective strategic issues. In particular, there is no way of knowing from these types of surveys the degree of meaningful influence that the employees or trade union representatives can wield in the various forums. We return to this question after attempting to gain an insight into the relative importance attached to the various issues discussed in EI/EP forums.

**Importance of issues discussed in forums**

Whilst the above outline sheds some light on the relative likelihood of either operational or strategic issues being discussed in direct and representative forums, it offers little insight into the priorities given by management to the different issues dealt with. To the extent that time spent on issues is an indication of the relative importance attached to these issues, both the WIRS and ACAS surveys provide further evidence which helps inform our analysis of managerial rationales.

In terms of time spent, a mixture of basic employee and production issues appears to predominate. The ACAS survey found that the highest percentage of managers ranked working conditions as the most time consuming activity (32 per cent), followed by quality issues (31 per cent), pay (27 per cent) and welfare and output (26 per cent) (1991:11). The 1984 WIRS asked a comparable question (not apparently replicated in 1990) concerning the most important matter discussed by the principal consultative committee, and found that production issues were ranked first by establishment managers, followed by employee issues (Millward and Stevens 1986:148).

The 1990 WIRS also questioned management on the amount of information provided on various issues. Comparing these findings with data collected for the 1984 survey, a number of changes are noticeable. In 1984 most information was provided on terms and conditions and changes in working conditions, followed by staffing and manpower plans, the organization's financial position, and investment plans (see Millward and Stevens 1986:154–60). By 1990, whilst production and employment issues remained predominant in terms of the amount of information given by the highest proportion of establishments (18 and 12 per cent of establishments respectively), information on legislative and regulatory changes (such as employment legislation and local authority regulations) grew from almost zero in 1984 to 9 per cent in 1990. In manufacturing, direct involvement forums appear to be increasingly focused on working practices in terms of the amount of information and communication devoted to this issue, from 1 per cent of establishments in 1984 to 6 per cent in 1990 (see Millward et al. 1992:157–9).

The picture painted above tends to suggest that, in the UK at least, the issues focused upon in involvement and participation forums are diverse, and by no means restricted to operational matters. The ACAS survey, in particular, provides some insight into the extent that potentially strategic issues are dealt with, at least at local level. WIRS evidence indicates that at higher establishment level, strategic issues become less noticeable, and operational issues predominate.

It is interesting to note here the finding of an antipodean study, which argued that higher-level participation increases employee demand for more participation, whilst involvement in lower-level forums reduces the demand for higher-level involvement. The study concluded that shopfloor-level forums probably favoured managerial interests, whilst higher-level participatory programmes favoured employee interests (Drago and Wooden 1991). We speculate from these findings that management might direct certain issues into lower-level involvement forums, to discuss and negotiate these issues through a non-strategic mechanism, in order to limit the potential of these issues being discussed in a more meaningful strategic context.

However, this view implies a relatively clear-cut set of managerial rationales and responses to the utilization of involvement and participation forums, which, as we show below, is often far from the reality. Before returning to this issue, however, we focus our attention on the role of trade unions, which at least potentially may act as a further impediment to a unitary management-driven involvement agenda.

## Trade union approaches to involvement and participation

Critical to the ability of management to control the filtering mechanisms in dealing with involvement and participation issues is the position of trade unions. Theorizing on evidence collected during the 1970s, Poole argued that a combination of strong trade unions with legislative support was the key determinant in this context, rather than organizational or environmental factors (1986:147). Given the decline in union organization over the last decade, and research findings from Europe which indicate that the existence of legislation in itself does not appear to affect the degree of employee/union influence on organizational decision-making (see Chapter 7), we should now question whether this still holds true, in the context of the 'new industrial relations' of the 1990s.

In the USA and the UK (but less so in Europe), trade unions have historically expressed a wariness of becoming entangled in organizational decision-making, not only because of fear of contentious decisions emanating from involvement and participation forums, such as job reductions, but more generally because of the blurring of traditionally clearly demarcated management/union roles (see Chapter 7). During the 1980s, however, in the wake of rising unemployment and restrictive union legislation, union fears became increasingly concentrated on the marginalization issue, with EI being seen, either directly or indirectly, as a union avoidance mechanism (see Chapter 5).

By the late 1970s, and early 1980s, a number of academic researchers were positing this view of union marginalization in the context of involvement and participation trends, across the USA, the UK and Europe (e.g. Edwards 1978; Heller et al. 1979; Parker 1985; Wilson et al. 1982). In the US, Parker's (1985) study found that despite national leadership sponsorship of QWL programmes, many local union members perceived involvement and participation to be collaboratist, and located these new initiatives within the context of concessionary bargaining. Wilson et al.'s multi-sectoral survey of 30 firms across the UK found that union ability to influence the direction and outcome of participatory initiatives was negligible. A managerially driven agenda was pushing the unions to the fringe of decision-making, exacerbating the latter's traditional defensiveness towards non-collective bargaining methods of employee–management interaction. In the view of these researchers 'the relative impotence of union power, vis-à-vis managerial influence and control, is unavoidable under these circumstances' (1982:338).

In the face of continuous decline in membership and an increasingly unfavourable economic environment in the later 1980s and early 1990s, trade unions began to seriously reassess the issue of EI/EP, even though academic evidence was divided on the issue of marginalization. In the US, growing support was gained within the union movement for the idea that it needed to become more proactive in its approach to involvement and QWL change programmes, not least in an attempt to minimize job losses and protect working conditions (Heckscher 1988; Banks and Metzgar 1989). Deutsch and Schurman argue that in the 1990s, American unions now see the centrality of participatory forums for advancing employee and union influence, and conclude that: 'This recognition has led to a new approach that involves a focus on particular initiatives and specific efforts to restructure work and gain greater union and worker involvement' (1993:348). This shifting approach is augmented at national level in the USA with the Clinton administration's advocacy of employee rights and the strong emphasis, reflected in federal policies, on organizational-level participatory initiatives (see Chapters 5 and 7). At national level in the UK, a similar refocusing has been witnessed, away from nation-wide plans and towards micro-level initiatives.

In particular, although TUC and Labour Party documents continued to be produced throughout the 1980s on the issue of 'industrial democracy', by the latter 1980s their tone had undergone a significant shift. As the 1980s progressed, so too did the thinking of the TUC and Labour Party. A report written in the early 1980s (TUC–Labour Party Liaison Committee 1982) spoke of macro-level TUC involvement in national planning. But by the middle of the decade, a further joint report focused on European Union initiatives as a way to stem the increasing marginalization of unions in the UK, arguing for company-level rights supported legislatively (TUC–Labour Party Liaison Committee 1986). By the end of the decade, participation and financial involvement were encouraged not in the context of industrial democracy and worker rights, but to improve the economic well-being of organizations, industries and ultimately the country (Labour Party 1989). At the beginning of the 1990s, this shift in official labour movement attitude towards involvement was summed up by the then Deputy General Secretary of the TUC, who saw a fundamental symbiosis between the goals of trade unions and the stated objectives of the HRM project: 'The challenge to unions is to facilitate change while formulating positions which reflect their members' contributions to improved performance and lower unit costs' (Monks 1991:8).

Whilst there has been a significant shift during the 1980s at the level of national policy, it is important to contrast this with what was happening at the organizational level in the UK. The WIRS data make clear that union representation on principal (higher-level) and secondary JCCs remained constant during the second half of the 1980s (Millward et al. 1992:156–7). WIRS also showed that where unions were recognized and involved in EP/EI forums, information provision and bargaining rights were much more common, compared with establishments with weak or non-union arrangements. Unsurprisingly, bargaining in JCCs was especially associated with union presence; for example, public sector and private manufacturing establishments were twice as likely to engage in bargaining than the private services sector (1992:157–9). WIRS concluded that:

> trade unions were as involved in consultation arrangements in workplaces where union organization continued to be strong, but the fact that unionized workplaces were fewer in number in 1990 than before, meant that the involvement of the trade unions in consultation arrangements overall was smaller than previously. (Millward et al. 1992:157)

**Trade union responses to employee involvement at the workplace**

Where large-scale surveys, such as WIRS, are limited is in their ability to pick up on qualitative changes in the workplace, for which case study analyses are perhaps more appropriate.[1] The consensus which emerges from a number of case study examinations regarding attitudes and responses of trade unions at local level can be summarized in two ways. First, union representatives perceive individual and collective involvement initiatives not as bad things in themselves, but as offering the potential to some managements to bypass existing channels of communication, i.e. those underpinned by pluralistic union participation methods such as collective bargaining (e.g. Batstone 1988; Marchington 1990). Furthermore, work organization methods such as autonomous workgroups (AWGs) are perceived as creating a greater diversity of interests, as this form of work organization potentially erodes relatively homogeneous plant work patterns. For many trade unions, this may be seen as a threat to the pursuance of plant-wide collective agreements, for example on working hours and shift patterns (see e.g. Work Research Unit studies by Grayson 1990:12 and Russell and Dale 1989:12).

As yet, however, there is no clear-cut agreement on whether involvement initiatives are being used as a deliberate and direct managerial approach to marginalize trade unions. The Work Research Unit argues the case against, claiming that its studies indicate that quality circles, for instance, improve traditional industrial relations practice and strengthen the position of employee representatives (Russell and Dale 1989:12). Some case studies, on the other hand, point to a definite marginalization of shop stewards, especially when multi-involvement initiatives are introduced in the organization (Marchington and Parker 1990:222; Rowlinson et al. 1991).

To the extent that some organizations may use TQM and EI as weapons to (re)gain greater control over the workforce, the question is raised as to whether unions respond successfully to this threat. We would point to a number of American studies conducted on this issue, which stress the *potential* influence that a positive union response could have on HRM and EI initiatives within organizations (see e.g. Deutsch and Schurman 1993; Verma and McKersie 1987; Kochan et al. 1986). In the mid 1980s, Verma and McKersie urged a more constructive union approach to involvement and QWL initiatives, arguing that unions could increase their support and membership by co-sponsoring EI programmes, and indeed potentially gain a greater degree of employee identity with the union in the process (1987:566).

More recent empirical support for this view comes from a report on European works councils, which found that both management and unions were generally satisfied with arrangements for information provision and consultation, perceiving mutual benefits in organizational restructuring and in promoting a corporate identity. Union representatives stressed the importance of developing international contacts and collating group-wide information, which could then be used for local collective bargaining purposes (Gold and Hall 1990).

The UK has been the exception in this respect, as employers and senior management continue to be highly sceptical of European initiatives on the creation of Euro-level worker rights, especially regarding the European works council Directive (see Chapter 7). The UK's main employer body, the Confederation of British Industry, responded to the European Union's decision in 1994 to return to an 'enforceable' and universally applicable system of information and consultation rights for employees in European multinational companies, by planning to develop a Euro-wide business agenda to unite EU business leaders in opposition to what the CBI regarded as 'ill-conceived, disappointing and risible' policies emanating from Brussels (reported in *Financial Times* 20 April 1994). To counter UK employer resistance, the British TUC targeted the 1,000 or so transnational companies operating in the UK, which were likely to be affected by the EWC Directive, in order to push for the introduction of works councils in these organizations (*Financial Times* 11 April 1994).

More generally, however, there appears to be a major problem in respect of developing a considered and constructive union response to managerially driven EI initiatives because of a strong residue of indifference which manifests itself at local level. Aside from fears concerning potential union marginalization in decision-making, local union representatives tend not to be hostile to involvement initiatives *per se*, but rather see these schemes as legitimate areas of management prerogative, and do not therefore seek direct influence over the initiation of EI methods. A study of autonomous workgroups (AWGs), for example, found that shop stewards saw participative collective bargaining as the principal mechanism for improving the working conditions of their members, rather than involvement-oriented AWGs, and therefore left the introduction and running of new work organization forms to management (Grayson 1990:12). Another study quoted a shop steward on the issue of direct involvement schemes such as team briefings thus: 'the more informed we are the better it is. It saves us a hell of a lot of work because it's management's job to communicate' (Marchington and Parker 1990:150).

It seems, therefore, that despite the growing awareness of the potential positive outcomes of involvement initiatives, and the need to be active in their design, implementation and operation, unions have largely failed to make serious contributions to the involvement trend. The following conclusion is, perhaps, apposite: 'in the absence of both legislative and union pressure . . . management have been free to develop their own structures voluntarily' (Allen et al. 1991:11). But given this relative freedom of choice, what underpins managerial rationales towards EI? We turn our attention to two interrelated aspects here to explore this question: the concept of management strategy, and 'hard' and 'soft' human resource rationales.

**Management and strategy**

The concept of strategy is complex, but of critical importance to debates on participation and involvement, and more broadly in analyses of human resource management. Indeed, as we saw in Chapter 4, HRM is conceptually differentiated from personnel management on the basis of the former's strategic approach to employee relations, and the integration of HRM into broader organizational decision-making. The complexities in defining exactly what is meant by strategy have been usefully overviewed by Marchington and Parker, stressing in particular the degree to which decisions are made proactively and purposefully, the long-term and integrative nature of the decision, and the importance of assessing the extent to which strategic planning is reflected in successful implementation (1990:59). Added to this is the need to differentiate between varying levels of managerial decision-making, and the potential for contradictory and conflictual management goals to feed into and blur the strategic process. Purcell uses a three-tier 'political process' model of strategic decision-making to illustrate this point, arguing that: 'What actually happens in employee relations will be determined by decisions at all three levels and by the willingness and ability of local management to do what is intended in the context of specific environment conditions and forces' (1992:61). In other words, the different levels of organizational hierarchy can inherently limit the scope for effective integration of HRM. This need not necessarily lead us to conclude that strategy is largely missing from managerial approaches, although Marchington et al. (1992:54) point out a number of factors which often lead to an *ad hoc* managerial style, such as an over-reliance on consultants pushing a 'pop culture' onto the organization, and a concomitant attempt by some sections of management to gain in status by these superficial changes. But rather, analyses of managerial rationales in respect of involvement and participation must take on board, *a priori*, the existence not only of differentiated broad sectoral trends but also the possibility of a multi-patterned intra-sectoral and indeed intra-organizational set of rationales.[2] In a broad-ranging summary of some 70 different reports conducted across the EU, the European Foundation for the Improvement of Living and Working Conditions (EFILWC) concluded that 'Participation was often . . . a product of a changing coalition of inter-

ests defined by no single management level or distinct dominant aim'
(1988:37).

The debate over managerial rationales for introducing and utilizing
employee involvement and participation methods has taken a number of
interrelated forms in recent years. As we indicated in Chapter 1, Ramsay's
influential 'cycles' theory, which posited the view that management responded
to historical waves of worker opposition by enhancing consultation processes
and other forms of involvement to offset potential threats to managerial control (Ramsay 1977), still attracts critiques, most notably in the work of writers
who stress the opportunities opened to labour through this process (see e.g.
Ackers et al. 1992). Further, Ramsay's two key premises, a zero-sum employment relationship and an inherent (if often latent) challenging labour force, it
is argued, are sometimes valid assumptions but are by no means universally
applicable (Ackers et al. 1992).

It is interesting to note Ackers et al.'s observation that the zero-sum/con-
flictual relationship is more likely to be encountered in well-organized,
large-scale manufacturing settings, and least likely in private services, where
'quite different participations will occur' (1992:281). We have argued in earlier chapters that a dualism is developing in terms of the degree of formality
of involvement methods, with the former manufacturing type of organization
described by Ackers et al. as exhibiting a growing sophistication and formal-
ization in its utilization of JCCs, for example. On the other side of this
dualism, experiences in the private service sector are increasingly of an informal, more flexible and to some extent amorphous nature, with involvement
being more of a philosophical premise than a tangible set of methods.

The idea however that 'conflictual' employee relations tend to be primarily a large-company phenomenon is perhaps misleading. Methodologically it
is often difficult to survey smaller organizations, and even more difficult to
pick up on what is really happening in the small-company sector in terms of
employee relations. With the erosion of legislative support for employee rights
in the UK (reflected most recently in the abolition of wages councils) over the
last decade or so, and with the concomitant poor job security of many
employees in smaller organizations (and high levels of unemployment in the
early 1990s), it is quite likely that conflict in smaller companies is often
repressed and cannot find an institutional articulation, unlike in larger organizations, where an employee relations approach is more likely to exist in an
'adversarial-institutionalized' fashion (see Rainnie 1989).

Having noted these differentiated trends, we are still left with the problem
of understanding their underpinning rationale. The 'cycles' debate has on
the whole tended to become locked into a methodological impasse, especially over the balance between *a priori* theorizing and empirical observations,
in attempting to draw valid conclusions as to the meaning of trends in participation and involvement. This epistemological problem, however, has
remained with us, as the debate over managerial rationales has, to a large
extent, moved on from the 'cycles' debate, and into a more direct attempt to
assess the rationales of the key actors in the involvement and participation

context. In particular, a focus on 'hard' and 'soft' rationales for involvement (and HRM strategies more broadly) has been utilized to delve into the motives of management.

## Management rationales and hard and soft HRM

In Chapter 4, we noted that 'hard' and 'soft' styles of HRM have been identified. Whilst the hard and soft rationales of HRM are not mutually exclusive, and indeed share key characteristics which differentiate HRM from traditional approaches to people management (such as a drive towards flexibility and continuous change), a number of writers have focused in particular on the extent to which managerial rationales are shaped by pursuing the 'hard' aspects of HRM, such as increasing performance and output, compared with the 'softer' goals of enhancing employee motivation and commitment to the organization.

Attempts to evaluate a causal link between involvement and either hard or soft managerial rationales have tended to draw on evidence relating to the perceived outcomes of involvement initiatives, as indicated on the soft side through employee attitude surveys for example, and on the hard side by measurable performance indicators such as changes in productivity levels. This focus leaves unanswered the question of initial managerial rationales, but to the extent that final outcomes are linked to initial objectives, studies since the 1980s have, on the whole, demonstrated a much stronger relationship between the implementation of involvement techniques and the hard aspects of HRM.

In the UK, for instance, Fernie et al. make a strong case to challenge the view that the development of strategic HRM (incorporating EI) has a positive influence on the soft 'climatic' context of industrial and employee relations at the organizational level, arguing that 'HRM techniques and "new industrial relations" do not contribute to a better climate than that found in more traditional workplaces' (1994a:1). Similarly, Bradley and Hill (1987) in their study of American and British quality circles concluded that the most tangible benefits to those organizations they explored were economically based. Moreover, there was little evidence of an enhancement of quality of working life aspects such as developing a high-trust, high-commitment ethos within the workplace or of similar effects associated with soft HRM (1987:81).

A very different perspective is put forward by total quality commentators such as Tom Peters, who argue that the point of open-participative management is essentially philosophical, and that attempting to evaluate the impact this form of management has on the hard elements of HRM such as cost control and work rationalization not only is almost impossible, but also misses the point. If an organization is unable to understand the inherent developmental and empowering value exemplified in involvement approaches, then it has failed to grasp what management gurus like Peters have been arguing for over a decade now (see for example Peters and Waterman 1982; Peters 1987; 1992).

McKinlay and Starkey see HRM policies in terms of 'non-rational' aspects of organizational behaviour, such as 'harnessing employee commitment to company goals' (1992:121). This perspective, as that expressed by Peters above, tends to assume a 'virtuous circle' effect, whereby cause and effect become blurred, and in many ways unimportant, compared with the positive effect involvement techniques and improved performance can exercise on each other.

One factor which complicates the competing views expressed above derives from the difficulty in isolating the influences of what are often multi-faceted change programmes circulating within an organization at any given point in time. For example, the implementation of involvement techniques is typically accompanied by changes in technology (see below), and by 'flattening' hierarchical managerial structures. In this context, measuring the specific impact of one of these factors, such as the introduction of a systematic involvement programme, is extremely problematic.

A further uncertainty in this debate may well stem from the complex nature of contemporary managerial rationales, which can be shaped, at least in part, by position in the organizational hierarchy. Although based on a total of only 10 companies, a study conducted between 1981 and 1982 by Bradley and Hill (1987) mirrors points made in a number of later studies regarding the diverse motivations which can exist between different levels of management. For example, in all of their case study organizations, it was found that senior management initiated the introduction of quality circles, and that this level of management was in every case responsible for production and/or quality (1987:71). Middle management, on the other hand, appeared uniformly either hostile or at least wary of their introduction. In particular, this level of management feared employee involvement on the grounds of erosion of managerial prerogative, and had to be pressured from above into accepting what were at the time innovatory involvement techniques (1987:74–5).

Over the last decade, middle- and lower-level management have increasingly come to fear the potentially radical impact of participatory management, which threatens not only to modify their traditional role (i.e. primarily supervisory, with a clear structure of authority in a hierarchical relationship with other employees) but possibly to make it totally redundant. Line and supervisory management especially have often been faced with a change agenda emphasizing the coaching and mentoring nature of their roles in the new post-modern continuously learning organization (see e.g. Morgan 1993).

## New technology and involvement rationales

The various production paradigms mentioned at the start of this chapter share the basic assumption that global economic changes have created the conditions that necessitate the erosion of traditional pyramidal managerial hierarchies, and the development of flatter organizational structures and radically new forms of participatory management. According to many post-modern theories, technology too impacts upon management functions and in turn provides a critical input into the trends towards involvement.

This point is reflected in several otherwise diverse perspectives on information technology. Both Drucker (1992) and Buchanan (1992), for example, see the new wave of flexible information technology eroding the base of middle management, who it is argued were primarily information transmitters. The new information technology will be utilized much more effectively to take on this transmission role, thus making redundant several layers of managerial hierarchies and thereby creating flatter organizational structures. Whilst Drucker stresses the increased knowledge base required amongst the remaining (core) employees at the lower end of the organization, Buchanan focuses on what he perceives as the concomitant shift of control towards employees and away from a previously hierarchically oriented management.

Whilst these analyses illustrate macro-level trends, case study surveys have focused on the differential goals of management in the context of changing technology. The European Foundation for the Improvement of Living and Working Conditions (1988), for example, noted four main contextual forces which influence stated managerial rationales, again ultimately reflecting both hard and soft motives in utilizing involvement methods. The four pressures arise from cost, control, quality and developmental needs. In response to adverse market conditions, *cost* and *control* pressures focus management's attention on budgetary constraints, and, as a consequence, tend to push management into attempts to (re)gain a greater degree of control at the point of production. These attempts marginalize employee and union inputs in decision-making at this level, and imply a more limited and adversarial use of involvement methods. In contrast to cost and control pressures, innovations stemming from *quality* and *developmental* pressures 'laid greater stress upon raising commitment to management plans and gaining an enterprise or unit consciousness amongst the workforce that allowed common interests to flower' (1988:38). Management, in this context, would utilize involvement techniques as a consensus building device, and as a means to broaden the scope for employees to be involved in diagnostic problem solving issues at the point of production.

## Employee attitudes to involvement and participation

A little explored, but critical insight into the soft and hard motivations of management can be gained from an examination of employee perceptions towards new management initiatives on involvement. Pounsford, for example, has argued that a tentative causal link can be found between employee involvement and organizational performance, by comparing employee attitudes in high- and low-performing companies.

> the results suggest certain aspects of involvement that do seem related to improved performance, and this tends to reflect perceived characteristics of relationships

with immediate managers, including the extent to which managers delegate, or jobs are structured, to make the most of employees' abilities. (1991:5)

The above study goes on to highlight key factors enhancing the causal link between performance and involvement such as managerial consistency and a strong employee development ethos. Changes in technology and restructuring of work organization, in particular, are typically introduced in tandem with innovative methods of EI, putting great stress on the new line and middle manager roles.

Marchington et al. (1992) provide some small-scale evidence on employee opinion, with just over 600 employees in 25 organizations responding with their perceptions of management aims in introducing involvement practices. Their findings are shown in Tables 8.4 and 8.5. From the evidence in Table 8.4, we can see that employees feel that the goal of management is focused not on the employee *per se*, such as to increase satisfaction or recognize employee efforts, but rather on organizational improvements, with increases in efficiency being the principal perceived goal (44 per cent of employees). In other words, the perceptions of employees tend to be of management emphasis on the harder aspects of the human resource management project, rather than its softer side. *A priori*, employee attitudes concerning the impact of involvement initiatives will be closely related to their perceptions of managerial rationales in introducing these methods into the organization.

Table 8.4  *Employee perceptions of management rationales*

| Perception | Response (%) |
|---|---|
| Increase efficiency | 44 |
| Improve customer service | 20 |
| Work harder | 18 |
| Increase satisfaction | 15 |
| Employee recognition | 3 |

*Source:* Marchington et al. 1992

Using data derived from the same source as for the previous table, Table 8.5 outlines the responses of employees towards the introduction of team briefings. The criteria in Table 8.5 are focused on 'soft' managerial goals in the context of EI and HRM. Unlike the impact on 'hard' HRM aspects, such as raising efficiency levels, it could reasonably be argued that employees should generally be aware of any change in the 'soft' aspects mentioned above, such as increased commitment from the workforce or greater management openness. However, on all the criteria measured, only the amount of information received was perceived by employees to have risen significantly (59 per cent of respondents). It should also be noted that the same study found that briefing sessions were, in any case, viewed by employees as relatively insignificant communication channels for receiving information; one-to-one discussions with line managers and the 'grapevine' were seen as the more important information provision channels (1992:34, Table 5.3).

Table 8.5 *Employee perceptions of impact of team briefings (in per cent)*

| Impact on | Increase | Decrease | No change |
|-----------|----------|----------|-----------|
| Information received | 59 | 4 | 37 |
| Understanding mgt | 29 | 5 | 66 |
| Commitment | 19 | 4 | 77 |
| Upward communication | 31 | 6 | 61 |
| Mgt openness | 27 | 8 | 65 |

*Source:* Marchington et al. 1992

Fernie et al. support this finding, arguing that the industrial relations climate will not be improved by simply briefing or cascading information down the management chain: 'To achieve better management–employee relations communication must be a two-way process: management must listen to its workers, not simply bombard them with information' (1994a:13). The most important managerial goal in terms of the 'soft' aspect of EI is to raise commitment, which connects with a host of other 'soft' goals, such as increasing loyalty to the company. However, the evidence presented in Table 8.5 clearly indicates that raised commitment is not necessarily seen as an identifiable effect in the eyes of the majority of the workforce, with only 19 per cent of employee respondents seeing increased commitment as an outcome of team briefing initiatives, for example.

From this albeit limited survey, it seems doubtful whether management initiatives are having the kind of impact that many managers would envisage or hope for. If this is the case, we should not, however, assume that employees are necessarily attaching much weight to this managerial goal. What then might employees be looking for in the context of involvement?

Two studies on quality circles (Brossard 1990; Wilson 1989) found that employees (even those not directly involved in circles) are just as interested in the 'hard' goals of EI as management, and are sensitive to the interlinkages between quality improvements, market results and improved working conditions. Brossard concluded that 'workers are seeking far more psychological rewards in exchange for their involvement' (1990:16).

Similarly, the European Foundation for the Improvement of Living and Working Conditions (1988) review saw employees (either as individuals or as groups) responding to involvement and participation initiatives mainly on the basis of the potential of these initiatives to provide a base for achieving substantive gains, rather than as an end in itself. Immediate job concerns related to issues such as working environment, and with outcomes highly reminiscent of share scheme attractions to employees described in Chapter 6, bonuses tended to be the focus for employees. We need, therefore, to differentiate the motives not only of management in different contexts, but also employees, who are likely to respond to, and interact with, the introduction and practice of participatory management in a number of complex ways. One factor of particular importance in this respect is differential access to decision-making forums and organizational influence between female and male employees.

**Gender and employee access to workplace influence**

The various approaches to employee influence considered so far have tended to identify three main contributors to productive work, namely employers, managers and employees. A central argument has been that power and control reside with the employers and their senior managers: employees may contest (or contribute towards) aspects of managerial control as a uniform group or through involvement, individual employees may be granted enhanced work-based discretion arising from the exercise of specific involvement programmes. What has not been considered are potential divisions between employees in gaining access to either source of influence at work, and especially the gender-based power divide which separates women from men.

In this respect we should note that women are disadvantaged in several ways. First, within the ranks of employees, women have tended to face occupational segregation, and despite universal growth in activity rates, continue to occupy the lower levels of the jobs' hierarchy where opportunities to express their occupational, individual or gender interests are most restricted. Further, there is evidence that involvement exercises such as appraisal have the potential to positively disfavour women who are largely assessed by their male managers (see, for example, Freedland 1993; Grint 1993). An acute manifestation of the power divide between men and women at work is shown by the prevalence of sexual harassment and the limited actions which have been taken by employers to combat this hidden but pervasive form of women's suppression.

Moreover, as potential beneficiaries of collective participative activity, women have seldom achieved equality or been represented as a distinct group within the priorities of the labour movement. A recent report showed that in Britain, only four out of 75 union general secretaries were women. Under-representation was also demonstrated in membership of executive committees, as delegates to union conferences (where union policies will be determined) and as paid officials (Labour Research Department:1991). A Danish speaker at a conference, when expounding her experiences as a representative within the Danish union system, identified the point clearly: 'We had only been working with one contrast. The contrast between the worker and the employer. We never discussed the contrast between the female worker and the male worker. Perhaps we had forgotten something' (Jensen 1994:68).

Whilst the voices of employees in organizational affairs are muted, there is little doubt that, both individually and collectively, women have been subordinated to the demands and interests expressed by male employees. In this sense they have gained comparatively less than men in participative exercises and arguably have lost more than men through managerial involvement programmes, whether through exclusion from benefits (for example, part-time employees are often excluded from share bonus schemes) or through relegation of their work to less secure or more poorly rewarded areas.

## Conclusions

In this chapter, we have explored the question of rationales and responses to involvement and participation in four ways: first, by examining the types of issues discussed, and the importance attached to various involvement and participation forums; second, by examining the role played by trade unions in the process of involvement initiatives; third, by exploring the concept of managerial strategies, and looking in particular at hard and soft aspects of the human resource management project; and fourth, by noting employee attitudes and perceptions towards the introduction of managerially driven involvement methods, highlighting in particular gender differences within the workforce.

We found that the types of issues discussed in the various forums are diverse, and by no means confined to operational matters; potential strategic issues were of concern in a number of forums. However, we have argued that if they are to be discussed, management may attempt to channel these issues into lower-level and production-oriented involvement forums, to avoid their being discussed at higher, essentially strategic, levels of the organization.

We have argued that trade unions at national level are reassessing their attitudes towards new forms of work organization, and HRM generally, but at local level have tended to see involvement initiatives as an area of management prerogative, and hence have not attempted to become closely involved in their implementation and routine operation. However, whilst a number of involvement techniques associated with HRM ostensibly stress the importance of enhancing the softer aspects of the working environment, such as job satisfaction, motivation and commitment, the balance of evidence points more to a direct link between the harder managerial goals of HRM, such as increased performance and output.

We have also highlighted apparent differences in expectations and perceptions between management and employees. In particular, whilst a number of studies have attempted to identify links between hard and soft involvement methods and improved employee and organizational performance, we have argued that employees themselves tend to experience the harder aspects of these initiatives, and do not necessarily perceive a link with the softer goals of the human resource management project.

Taking this latter point further, the hard and soft aspects of HRM may become blurred and difficult to disentangle, and perhaps for many managements, irrelevant in any case. *A priori*, it could be argued that the cause and effect relationship between participatory management, increased employee performance and motivation is less important than the possible virtuous cycle these factors might create when organizations embark on a total quality change programme. However, the limited access to organizational decision-making available to some sectors of the workforce, especially female employees, raises serious questions as to the overall motivational and performance impact of such change processes.

In the final substantive chapter of this book, we turn our attention to another key influencing factor on involvement and participatory rationales, namely, the impact of employee relations practices of inward investor multinational organizations, based in, and operating from, the USA, Japan, the UK and Europe.

## Notes

1     WIRS also has a tendency to play down the overall significance of compositional change. As we demonstrated in Chapter 3, the enormous structural shifts that have taken place in the economy have left trade unions in a much weaker position in the 1990s compared with 15 or so years ago. The strengths and weaknesses of the survey method of data collection in the field of HRM and industrial relations have been usefully overviewed by Morris and Wood (1991).

2     There is also an organizational-psychological aspect to this problem, beyond the scope of the present study, but succinctly elucidated by Argyris (1992) who argues that senior managers often avoid explicitly raising issues that they perceive will be conflictual and problematic in terms of interpersonal manager–employee relationships.

# 9

# The Influence of Foreign Inward Investment

The influence of multinational and transnational companies (MNCs/TNCs) has received increasing attention throughout the decades since the Second World War as their importance in the world economy has grown. Indeed, by the early 1990s, MNC/TNC overseas investment had overtaken world trade in magnitude, with direct investment reaching $5.5 trillion, compared with $4 trillion in total world exports. Controlling about one-third of global private sector productive assets, the stock of foreign investment totalled $2 trillion in 1992. In value terms, the USA, the UK and Japan were the three most important countries of MNC/TNC origin, with $474 billion, $259 billion and $251 billion of assets respectively. Of the 20 largest MNCs/TNCs, seven were American, three Japanese, one from the UK, two joint UK/Dutch, and seven European (UNCTAD 1993).

Amongst these global companies model involvement managerial styles have been commonplace, practised, for example, by IBM, Unilever (see Chapter 5), Asea Brown Boveri (see Peters 1992), Volkswagen and Elf Aquitaine (see Chapter 7). There has nevertheless been a recurring debate, since the 1970s, about the activities of MNCs/TNCs in the world economy, and in particular their influence on the host countries in which they operate. Following on from Chapter 8's discussion of rationales and responses to the implementation and practice of EI and EP, we devote this chapter to an analysis of the contemporary influence of foreign inward investment in host countries: in particular we focus on the activities of North American and Japanese MNCs/TNCs and their overseas operations.

Specifically, we explore three main themes. First, we examine the common assumption that each inward investor country of origin has a homogeneous style of industrial relations. We question the degree to which a distinctive or consistent home-based approach to EI/EP can be distinguished, especially in the case of the USA and Japan. Second, we present empirical evidence of 'implanted' EI/EP practices, and explore the extent to which MNCs/TNCs either directly transplant their home-based model into the host country, or adapt to host country industrial relations patterns. And finally, we briefly outline the diverse and changing nature of global enterprises, and the implications this has for the implementation and practice of involvement and participation.

**Involvement and participation in Japan and the USA : homogeneity, diversity and change**

Analyses of the influence of inward investors into host countries will natu-rally, and to some extent justifiably, tend to stress homogeneity in home country approaches to EI and EP. For Guest, inward investment helps to shape managerial choice in the UK, in respect of employee relations styles, along four main paradigms: (i) a unitarist-individualistic (non-union) style, typified by American MNCs/TNCs; (ii) a unitarist-consultative (works coun-cil based) approach, largely a Japanese variant; (iii) a constrained pluralism (e.g. based on single-union deals), again typified by Japanese inward investors adapting to the UK context; and (iv) a traditional pluralistic style, European in orientation (1989:48).

*The Japanese approach: lean model or myth?*

Japan, in particular, has been characterized as having a highly homoge-neous industrial relations system, which Japanese MNCs/TNCs have implanted in their overseas operations. A number of early studies (see e.g. Ouchi 1981; Dore 1973) identified five pillars of Japanese management, namely: lifetime employment; compliant company unions (90 per cent of unions in Japan are enterprise based); consensus management (with a sys-tematic emphasis on employee involvement); total quality awareness; and a seniority-based reward and promotion system. All of these factors, it was argued, created the basis for high levels of employee motivation and loyalty to the company.

Whilst distinct, relatively homogeneous employee relations styles have been associated with Japan, this country has in fact experienced significant change during the 1980s and early 1990s, making it increasingly problematic to gen-eralize as to model approaches. During the 1980s, Japanese methods of management, encapsulated in the term *kaizen* (continuous change and improvement), developed a high profile across the globe, particularly in the USA and the UK, due both to Japan's own economic success and to the growing number of Japanese companies entering America and the UK during that decade. Indeed the American owned Ford Motor Company in the early 1980s entitled its campaign for greater competitiveness 'After Japan'. In the influential Massachusetts Institute of Technology (MIT) study of the world car industry, the Japanese approach, labelled 'lean production', was seen as the model for all other countries, not least the USA, to follow if they wished to remain globally competitive. The old Taylorist, scientific management mass production methods, exemplified by Ford in the USA since the early twentieth century, had been replaced in Japan by the new concept of lean pro-duction, the model, it is argued, for global production in the twenty-first century. Moreover, the main authors of the report emanating from the MIT study claim that: 'We've become convinced that the principle of lean produc-tion can be applied equally in every industry across the globe and that

conversion to lean production will have a profound effect on human society –
it will truly change the world' (Womack et al. 1990:8).

Quality is seen as the central goal underpinning Japanese production, inte-
grally linked to the employee involvement methods utilized by Japanese
enterprises. Total quality control systems, e.g. just-in-time stock control, quality circles, statistical process control and flexible working practices such as
team-based organized production methods, all reflect the interrelationship
between involvement and quality production. These methods are not
achieved purely by management dictate, but rely on the active involvement
and initiative of individuals and groups of employees. As Clegg notes, managerial rationales in Japan are based on 'deepening' the technological
knowledge base amongst the workforce, rather than constantly updating
technology with state-of-the-art equipment (1992:165). The importance given
to 'team' work is also critical, as it has long been accepted in Japan that efficient production methods, employee commitment and high morale, are only
possible within a small-team structure (i.e. of between 10 and 15 members):
'Within Japanese organizational practices, work in the internal labour market
seems to be designed with an eye to the collective worker rather than in opposition to the collective worker' (Clegg 1992:168). Conceptually, *kaizen* implies
continuous striving for improvement in every aspect of the organization's
business through the genuine involvement of all its employees. Hence for
Japanese management, the workforce is seen as a key strategic resource, and
it is from this starting point that one can best understand 'Japan's' approach
to employee involvement.

However, two points regarding this apparent homogeneity in Japanese
employment practices need stressing here. First, only about one-third of the
Japanese workforce have ever enjoyed lifetime employment, normally in the
very large MNC/TNC sector; and as we noted in Chapter 5, when discussing
the efficacy of quality circles in Japan, loyalty and motivation stem precisely
from such instrumental factors as lifetime employment and seniority-based
promotion (Watanabe 1991). Two-thirds of the Japanese workforce have,
throughout the post-1945 period, been engaged in smaller, satellite company
operations, often employed on short-term contracts, and have always been
subject to the market needs of the larger core companies, and hence more vulnerable to the vagaries of market competition and to unemployment.

Overlaying this dualistic system, by the late 1980s significant changes were
evident across the Japanese economy and society. Recent studies have stressed
the maturing of the Japanese economy, and organizations are coming under
increasing pressure on a number of fronts. For example, the annual wage
round (*shunto*) has tended to produce wage increases which have been little
related to productivity increases, and have either kept pace with or outstripped
inflation. At the societal level, a different kind of problem has also come to
light in the 1990s, namely *karoshi*, or death through overwork. Work-related
stress has become a contentious issue in Japan, and some commentators argue
that the younger generation of Japanese workers are generally no longer willing to work as hard as the immediate post-war generation (see *Industrial*

*Relations Review and Report* 1993b:4–16 for a brief overview of these factors).

Whittaker (1990) has highlighted five main pressures leading to 'a significant evolution' of Japanese organizational behaviour. First, youth attitudes are no longer adhering to a strict work ethic, and it is claimed by some Japanese commentators that 'passivity', rather than 'rebellion', has characterized the relationship of young Japanese employees to the world of work. This passivity may well herald a new challenge to Japanese organizations as they attempt to inculcate greater initiative and autonomy into their workforces. Second, a rise in female employment has necessitated multi-track employment paths, and more diversified approaches to personnel issues. Third, changes in technology have led to the need to introduce more flexible training packages for employees, which in turn has raised the prospect of greater labour mobility. Fourth, internationalization of the Japanese economy is creating a more cosmopolitan managerial stratum, bringing a greater diversity of ideas into large Japanese organizations. And finally, the growth of the service sector, with a concomitant increase in more flexible and less secure employment patterns, may be leading to a 'polarization in employment forms' in Japan. In response to these changes, Whittaker (1990) notes the trends towards rewarding ability rather than length of service; multi-track internal labour markets, whereby internal career paths are made more flexible; 'group employment', through which large companies and their supplier satellites loan out employees to each other; and most importantly, the increasing importance of external labour markets in Japan.

A number of Japanese specialists in the early 1990s have argued against the idea of a revolutionary transformation in Japanese employment and employee relations (note that Whittaker uses the term 'evolution'), and in particular, lifetime employment still remains a central pillar of the Japanese system (Schregle 1993), but this view is becoming less tenable as the 1990s progress. Increasingly harsh global market pressures on Japanese companies, at home and abroad, are creating a severe strain on organizational abilities to retain employment security as a dominant feature of Japanese personnel and industrial relations policies.

Cyclical market trends have led to cutbacks in Japanese organizations at home and abroad. For instance, at the end of 1993, Nissan UK announced it was seeking large-scale voluntary redundancies at its operations in the northeast of England, reflecting a sharp fall in European car sales. And in Japan itself, Nissan, Mitsubishi and Mazda all announced losses in 1994, leading the last company to freeze the usual spring intake of new employees (reported in *Financial Times*, 1 June 1994:32). Whilst not too much should be read into these relatively short-term measures, they may have significant long-term implications for styles of Japanese employee and industrial relations, when added to the structural changes noted above.

Furthermore, pressures on Japanese organizational employment levels are not confined to short-term cyclical trends. A 1992 survey conducted by the Japan Productivity Centre found that manufacturing companies would have to eliminate 39 per cent of their staff to reach US productivity levels per employee. The main problem, it was argued, lay in white-collar areas in Japanese organizations, where staffing levels spiralled during the 1980s, in contrast to the stable, or falling, levels of blue-collar employment (reported in *Financial Times* 23 May 1994).

Unlike the legislated European approach, there is no statutory support for involvement or participation in Japanese organizations. In practice, Japanese methods are focused almost solely on the shopfloor, and involve employees primarily in production and technical issues. There is no participative board-level representation of employees, and in fact representation tends to be downplayed in favour of direct individual and small-group involvement. This makes Japanese organizations and employees particularly vulnerable to the changes indicated above, as there are few higher-level structures in place, comparable to the European works council system, to balance or counteract pressures felt at organizational level.

### The different strands of American involvement and participation

Change is also evident in US industrial relations. In the decades following the Second World War, America could be characterized as having a dual indus-trial relations approach, adversarial in the more traditional, engineering and manufacturing sectors, such as steel-making and automobiles; and integrative in other sectors, such as high technology, bearing comparisons with the Japanese integrative style, and putting great emphasis on the quality ethos.

During the 1980s, however, attitudinal changes amongst the main parties operating within the more traditional sectors became apparent, expressed in a desire for a more participatory and consensual form of employee relations. In particular, union leaders came to see the limitations of collective bargain-ing, which allowed for no real involvement in strategic decision-making in American organizations (Kochan et al. 1986:182).

We have argued in earlier chapters that changes in approach towards EI and EP in the United States can be seen at both workplace and higher (com-pany and industry) decision-making levels. In the former case, the introduction of involvement schemes in the early 1980s very often centred on the 'team' method of production. As in the Japanese case, this is a critical point, as it created an interface between changes in work organization and an increase in employee decision-making and responsibility. Kochan et al. (1986) distinguished five involvement and participation trends, namely: corporate campaigns; grass-roots involvement initiatives (see Chapter 5); strategic involvement through stock ownership (see Chapter 6); industry-level interac-tions; and formal board representation (see Chapter 7).

To reiterate briefly from previous chapters, these initiatives have diverse implications for EI and EP in America. First, *industry-level interactions* have tended to take place in highly competitive sectors composed of large numbers of employing organizations, with a small number of recognized unions, and are essentially aimed at raising issues for discussion which normally fall outside the remit of collective bargaining. *Board representation* of union members typically occurred in a number of companies during the 1980s in the context of severe economic crises (such as in the airline industry). Given the recessionary context, it is not surprising that this type of development was negotiated as part of a collective bargaining agreement which involved wages and conditions concessions on the part of the unions (concession bargaining). *Stock ownership* has steadily become more significant in America, starting in a small way in the 1950s, and gaining legislative support in the Employee Retirement and Income Security Act 1974. A new type of stock ownership came into vogue in the early 1980s, in the form of employee share ownership plans (ESOPs), for example in the trucking industry, where between 1983 and 1985 there were 16 conversions to employee stock ownership. These conversions also introduced board-level representation for employees. The attractiveness to companies of share schemes stemmed from tax-based incentives, but ESOPs are also seen as a mechanism to stave off hostile takeover bids from other companies, and are a low-cost benefit to employees. Despite this trend, in the trucking industry at least, the Teamsters union, whilst supporting ESOPs, has retained a strong adversarial collective bargaining approach (Kochan et al. 1986:183–95).

*Corporate campaigns* are essentially attempts by unions to influence strategic organizational decision-making indirectly, by embarking on specific public relations exercises designed to put pressure on a company – often over the issue of union recognition. However, this approach has rarely achieved longer-term participation in the enterprise (Kochan et al. 1986:195–7). The final approach, *grass-roots initiatives*, sprung up in the mid 1980s, often as an outgrowth of non-strategic employee participation schemes introduced in the early 1980s. The General Motors (GM) Saturn Project is the best known example of this development. Seeking to emulate the 'lean production' approach of the Japanese, the unions agreed with GM to implement a plan which sought to create a high level of shopfloor participation. This approach included worker representatives taking part in forums to discuss changes in work organization, accompanied by a 'strategic advisory committee' to be engaged in long-term planning (Rehder 1994:2).

Summarizing the meaning of this plurality of trends, in the mid 1980s, Kochan et al. concluded that:

> American labor and management are clearly moving through an important period of experimentation with new strategies in organizational governance – strategies that if diffused and institutionalized, will represent a fundamental departure from the New Deal model of collective bargaining and industrial relations. (1986:204)

When these trends are added to the demise of well-established integrative models of employee relations, symbolically represented most notably by worldwide job cuts in companies like IBM and Xerox in the early 1990s, US-based MNCs/TNCs operating abroad are likely to export a multiplicity of approaches from their home base, making it increasingly difficult to generalize a typical American organizational model of involvement and participation.

*Summary: Japan and the USA in transition*

In Japan, a unitarist-integration approach remains the dominant although increasingly pressurized model in most industries and sectors. In America, however, this approach tends to co-exist alongside the continuation of a more adversarial collective bargaining system, similar to the UK, where both human resource management and collectively organized industrial relations exist alongside each other in the same organization. In both Japan and the States in the 1990s, involvement and participative methods tend to focus on immediate work-related issues, such as the need for quality improvements in production, and generally on technical matters arising on the shopfloor, in which case it could be argued that 'participation' approaches are directly geared towards the achievement of managerial goals. However, unlike in Japan, the US is experiencing a renewed federal-level interest in EI and EP, which overlays the organizational-level initiatives described above.

In the 1990s, therefore, involvement and participation in both the USA and Japan can be said to be largely characterized by an integration approach that implies relatively little employee influence on strategic areas of organizational decision-making, with its stress on drawing the employees into a systematically planned organizational culture. In other words, the involvement approach described in earlier chapters predominates in these countries. Given this context, how do MNCs/TNCs from America and Japan behave in their operations overseas? In particular, to what extent do they simply implant home-based models of EI and EP, or adapt their approach to the traditions and norms of the host country in which they operate? It is to these questions that we now turn.

### The influence of inward investors on involvement and participation: implantation or adaptation?

Research in this area has tended to focus on two interrelated, but distinct, issues. The first is the influence of foreign inward investment on the host country, through the direct transplantation of managerial practices in overseas operations of MNCs/TNCs. Owing to the perceived importance of the Japanese 'model' for global production, elaborated above, most research in this area has centred on Japanese organizations, especially in their operations in the USA and the UK. Much of this work has suggested a tendency towards implantation of patterns of work organization, but more of an inclination towards adaptation of employee relations practices to the norms existing in host countries. The second area of research has concentrated on the indirect influence of inward investors on managerial practices in the host economy more generally. These studies have tended to examine the extent of convergence or divergence in patterns of human resource practices between domestic and foreign owned organizations.

*Implantation and work organization*

First we examine the issue of direct influence of MNC/TNC overseas operations. In the USA, Florida and Kenney (1991), arguing against the idea of cultural specificity, claim that the car industry has experienced successful transplantation of Japanese production and work organization methods, through inward investment. Since the early 1980s, seven Japanese car manufacturers, and an approximate 270 Japanese or US–Japanese joint venture automotive supplier companies, have established what amounts to a 'second automobile industry in the US', according to these authors (1991:181).

However, on closer inspection, it can be seen that the extent to which Japanese human resource management methods have been introduced into American establishments varies quite considerably. Florida and Kenney themselves note three patterns in the transplantation of Japanese company ideas into US operations. First, the system of work and production organization has been introduced into America with few modifications. Semi-autonomous teams, job rotation, quality circles, relatively few job classifications, have in particular been adopted wholesale by both assembler and supplier establishments. Second, employee remuneration and other personnel issues have been introduced in a modified fashion in transplant companies. For example, unlike in Japan, individual bonuses were used only marginally in the pay systems for shopfloor workers in both assembly and supplier plants in the US, with a standard rate of pay being the preferred norm. Again in contrast to the post-war Japanese car industry, employment security was low in US supplier transplants. In assembly plants, informal employer/union agreements were often in place, with the aim of minimizing the risk of layoffs through mechanisms such as wages reductions during downturns in trade, and the use of temporary workers during peak production periods. The personnel issues in which transplant companies followed the Japanese approach most closely were the use of 'rigorous recruitment and training systems', in stark contrast to American car industry traditions of 'hiring off the street', low levels of induction and lack of continuous training. Third, employee/industrial relations have been adapted to the American unionized car industry context, especially in the large assembly plants (1991:193). We return to the issue of inward investors and trade unionism below.

The patterns described in the US car industry echo a number of studies conducted in the UK regarding the differential extent to which various aspects of the Japanese approach are implanted into host country operations. In particular, work organization methods associated with Japanese production systems tend to be introduced but less attention is paid to implementing a particular style of employee relations. Oliver and Wilkinson's (1989) well-known study of 'Japanization' in the UK, conducted in the late 1980s, showed that most of the above-mentioned Japanese involvement and production methods are in common use in their multi/transnational operations in Britain. For example, a total quality control system was in use, or implementation was being planned in all companies surveyed. Group/team working was in use or planned in 93 per cent of Japanese UK enterprises, and statistical process control was in place in 79 per cent of companies. Communicating to the workforce is another key approach in ensuring that the various involvement techniques work effectively, and indeed is a form of involvement itself. The same study found that 83 per cent of Japanese companies in the UK used or planned to use sophisticated employee communication methods, such as team briefings (1989:76, Table 2).

American MNCs/TNCs have had greater opportunities to exert direct influence on host country practices than the Japanese, given the scale of US owned overseas operations, and the much longer history of US company global activities. In the high-technology sector, the homogeneous world-wide character of organizations such as IBM is well known (see e.g. Evans and Lorange 1989). Further evidence of the implantation approach can be seen in the car industry. The US owned General Motors Holden and Ford Australia's use of systematic EI initiatives as the bedrock for a radical restructuring of their work organization (Lansbury and Davis 1992) mirrors similar trends in the home-based US car industry outlined earlier in this chapter.

*Inward investors and employee relations adaptation*

In terms of employee relations, the behaviour of inward investors tends to be more circumspect: they often make adaptations to host country traditions and norms rather than impose external systems. Broad, for instance, denotes the evolution of four methods of employee/management consultation in Japanese transplants in the UK (1994:27–8). First, in smaller plants (possibly in the early stage of the organization's life cycle), 'informal' consultation is the norm, whereby management rely on face-to-face discussions with individuals or small groups of employees. Second, the 'substitution' approach is used, where Japanese transplants replace trade unions and collective bargaining with company councils, with the latter rarely being granted extensive influence on basic issues such as pay and conditions. Third, a brown-field site 'separation' model is utilized, whereby traditional collective bargaining co-exists with newer forms of consultation through such methods as company councils. Stressing the adaptive nature of many Japanese organizations, Broad notes that 'these Japanese owned firms operate along similar lines of conventional British custom where unions are strongly organised' (1994:28). Single-union agreements, mostly on green-field sites, are the fourth approach commonly practised by Japanese companies in the UK.[1]

Drawing on mid-1980s evidence, Purcell et al. (1987) found that foreign owned companies were just as likely to recognize trade unions for bargaining purposes as their UK counterparts. At the end of the 1980s, Guest (1989) reached a similar conclusion about foreign owned companies operating in the UK, arguing that human resource management approaches are primarily a green-field site phenomenon, and that traditional industrial relations practices remain relatively unaffected in established economic sectors. However, in certain industries, noticeably in the high-technology sector, green-field site operations follow a distinctly non-union model in the UK. Focusing on the prevalence of non-unionism in American MNCs/TNCs, and citing a Scottish Development Agency (now Scottish Enterprise) survey, which found that none of the US electronic high-technology companies set up in the so-called Silicon Glen during the 1980s had been unionized, Guest argues that: 'It seems plausible to expect that American companies, reflecting their home culture of anti-unionism, individualism, and familiarity with HRM, will generally pursue the non-union path' (1989:48).

Some small-scale evidence emerged in the early 1990s from the north-east of England, to support Guest's contention that American MNCs/TNCs largely adhere to a non-union model in the UK. This evidence is presented in Table 9.1. The table shows that American companies operating in the north-east of England clearly adopt a non-union approach (88 per cent). Far Eastern multinationals, including Japanese, were more likely to have single-union deals (33 per cent) than the other foreign-based establishments, but were on the whole non-union in orientation (67 per cent).[2]

Table 9.1    *Union status in companies in the north-east of England by country of origin*

| Origin | Number of companies operating with: | | |
| | Multi union | Single union | No union |
| --- | --- | --- | --- |
| America | 1 | 1 | 14 |
| Far East | 0 | 6 | 12 |
| UK | 4 | 4 | 13 |

*Source:* adapted from Peck and Stone 1992

### Inward investor influence on the host economy: divergence

The above noted growth of non-unionism (experienced not only in the UK, but across the industrialized world in the 1990s) raises the issue as to what extent inward investor practices indirectly influence host country trends in EI/EP (and human resource management more generally). UK evidence points to a significant degree of divergence between the practices of foreign and UK owned companies in this respect.

Results from the 1990 ACAS survey, shown in Table 9.2, disaggregate types of involvement methods, and compare these with establishment country of ownership. The survey focuses on four commonly used methods (see Chapters 5 and 7), namely: written forms of communication, team briefings (TBs), quality circles (QCs) and joint working parties (JWPs). The table shows that foreign-owned establishments are much more likely to utilize all four methods of involvement than UK companies. Written communication (75 per cent) and team briefings (75 per cent) in particular were commonly used by foreign owned firms, compared with UK companies (48 per cent and 51 per cent respectively). It is also interesting to note the findings on joint working parties which, as we noted in Chapter 7, are more oriented to bargaining compared with other methods of involvement. Perhaps for this reason, both UK and foreign owned non-union establishments were less likely to utilize this type of method, compared with unionized organizations. But again in terms of ownership, joint working parties were more common in foreign than UK establishments. Again, this provides further evidence that foreign owned companies make significant adaptations to the still relatively unionized environment of the UK.

Table 9.2    *Establishments using various involvement methods by type of ownership, 1990 (per cent)*

| Method | UK | Foreign | All |
|---|---|---|---|
| Written | 48 | 75 | 53 |
| TBs | 51 | 75 | 55 |
| QCs | 23 | 40 | 27 |
| JWPs[1] | 23/49 | 37/65 | 30/52 |

[1]    Figures for JWPs refer to non-union/union establishments respectively.
*Source:* adapted from ACAS 1991

The ACAS survey offers us further evidence of the union/non-union divide, according to country of ownership of the organization. Table 9.3 shows the relatively high utilization by foreign subsidiaries of consultation forums, compared with UK organizations, in terms of the number of issues discussed. Again, we can see that irrespective of union status, foreign owned establishments were more likely to engage employees over a relatively larger number of consultation issues, compared with UK owned organizations. In unionized establishments, 85 per cent of foreign owned establishments fell into this category, compared with 73 per cent of UK owned companies. In the non-union sector, the respective figures for foreign and UK owned establishments were 40 and 26 per cent. The ACAS results therefore support earlier findings of Purcell et al., who concluded that: 'Rather more foreign owned than British owned firms used a wide variety of methods to communicate with employees and adopt methods to gain employee loyalty and commitment such as quality circles' (1987:136).

Table 9.3    *Establishments reporting an above average number of issues for consultation,[1] by type of ownership and union status, 1990 (per cent)*

| | UK | Foreign | All |
|---|---|---|---|
| Non-union | 26 | 40 | 29 |
| Union | 73 | 85 | 76 |
| All | 52 | 68 | |

[1]    The median number of issues, in the ACAS survey, on which managers reported that they consulted employees prior to making decisions was six.
*Source:* ACAS 1991

It appears therefore that, in the UK context at least, there is evidence of divergence between the practices of inward investor companies and those of domestically owned organizations. This divergence might be partly explained by evidence which suggests that the example presented by inward investors in developing a strategic human resource management style rarely has a direct causal effect on the behaviour and policies of indigenous managements (outside foreign owned transplant establishments). In particular, a large question mark remains over the extent that UK-based management act strategically in taking on board foreign-inspired EI initiatives. Alternatively, do UK companies simply introduce new methods on an *ad hoc* basis, believing that techniques, such as team briefings, by themselves improve employee relations and organizational performance, at little overall cost to the company in financial or organizational terms?

The weight of evidence points to a lack of direct inward investor influence on UK companies, and suggests that the latter tend to promote EI initiatives in a non-strategic fashion. For example, the study of the north-east of England cited above found that established companies which had experimented with 'new' techniques had not been directly influenced by inward investor companies. Rather, new ideas had primarily entered the organization through management consultants and corporate sources nationally (Peck and Stone 1992). Whilst it may be reasonable to speculate that an indirect correlation might exist here (for example management consultants and corporate executives may themselves be influenced by the practices of inward investors), there is little specific evidence to demonstrate a causal relationship.

A number of studies questioning the extent of the so-called Japanization of UK employee relations have argued in a similar vein. Oliver and Wilkinson (1992; 1989), as noted above, found a significant degree of comparability between UK and Japanese management approaches. For example, 88 per cent of 'emulator' UK companies had in place Japanese-style EI methods (1989:83). But the same authors also noted that many new-style employee relations practices in UK organizations, such as in-house communications forums, significantly pre-dated the emulation of Japanese production methods, and in fact were often introduced prior to the surge of inward investment by Japanese companies in the 1980s (1989:5). Marchington and Parker produced similar findings in their case study observations, concluding 'that the development of employment practices has more to do with commercial objectives and pressures than to the transplantation of ideas from elsewhere' (1988:279). Purcell et al. found that foreign owned companies were more likely to have deliberately encouraged EI methods as a matter of corporate policy, compared with UK organizations, and that more resources were devoted to personnel management to achieve these goals (1987:136–7). Oliver and Wilkinson also found that there was a noticeable lack of synchronization between UK management's increasing Japanese-style personnel policies, and broader production techniques, compared with Japanese companies operating in the UK (1989:87), indicating a lack of strategic thinking on the part of typical UK management. Indeed, the same authors argued that Japanese companies themselves tended to gain more through setting up green-field operations than being strategically adept in turning round established employee relations practices (1989:87).

### Global organizations, involvement and participation

The debates explored above tend to be focused primarily on the influence associated with large inward investor organizations, and for this reason, up to now, we have conflated the terms MNC and TNC. In the final section of this chapter, we turn our attention to the increasingly complex internal character of contemporary global organizations, and the implications that this complexity may have for their approaches to EI and EP. Three models have emerged in the literature over the past 25 years on the subject of global companies: the implanted model (most closely associated with the concept of the multinational corporation or MNC), the adaptive model (increasingly linked with the transnational corporation or TNC) and, most recently, the partnership or joint venture enterprise.

### *MNCs: the implanted model*

Multinational corporations are characterized as organizations with integrated, centrally planned global business strategies, tightly controlled by the home country headquarters (Ferner 1994). In employee relations, this approach is represented by a strategy of home country implantation in which a common culture and organizational structures are imposed upon the organization's satellite operations.

During the 1970s, the politico-economic aspects of MNC activities came under growing scrutiny as two main views emerged. Some feared that MNCs were becoming more powerful than the nation states in which they operated (Murray 1971), and others believed that the state (or combination of states acting in unison) ultimately still exercised a veto on the activities of global companies (Warren 1971).

As an integral part of this debate industrial relations researchers turned their attention to the specific effects that MNCs may have on labour relations in the host country (see e.g. Gennard and Steuer 1971; Forsyth 1973; Roberts 1973; Flanagan and Weber 1974). In summarizing these studies, union, academic and political fears were expressed along the following lines:

1   MNCs did not follow well-established local or national patterns of industrial relations and collective bargaining.
2   A number of leading global companies tended not to recognize trade unions, implanting their home-based model of unitarist employee relations directly on the host country (e.g. the North American owned IBM and Kodak).
3   MNCs could exercise power within the guest country, especially in terms

of production switching (i.e. pulling out of one country when better opportunities were present elsewhere).

4   Trade unions found it difficult to tap into the appropriate level of management in order to effectively bargain and discuss issues of mutual concern.

5   Global companies were able to 'price-fix', (i.e. shift paper profits around the world to avoid tax liabilities and obscure union understanding of the real level of organizational performance for bargaining purposes).

6   Many MNCs set up assembly line plants in their foreign operations, and retained research and development facilities in their home base – a practice, it was argued, that had important implications for the structure and stability of employment in the guest country.

During the 1980s, host country fears were increasingly matched by union concerns in the country of MNC origin, that a net outflow of capital from their home base would result in large-scale job losses, as production switched from high-labour-cost countries to low-cost Third World states. The fears of host and home-based countries have continued into the 1990s, although new issues have come to the fore, not only as the structure of globalization has become more complex (in Europe, for example, within the context of the Single European Market and the Social Chapter), but also as our understanding of the patterns of MNC activities has become increasingly multi-dimensional.

The changing character of MNCs presents a further problematic aspect in analysing the way in which global organizations behave in host countries. Pundits in the 1970s tended to assume a fairly static multinational organization model, whereby companies retained a strong national identity, and would seek to implant a clearly definable home-based industrial relations or human resource management approach in their overseas operations. But by the 1990s, the internationalization of capital and the increasingly competitive nature of world product markets have led to two main developments away from this static model. First has been the evolution of a different model of global enterprise, away from the highly centralized and homogeneous MNC towards a more decentralized, heterogeneous TNC model (see Bartett and Ghoshal 1989; Ferner 1994). And second, as a number of UK and North American authorities have noted (see e.g. Beaumont 1993:211–14; J. W. Walker 1992:93–5), has been the growth of what might be termed 'partnership' operations, in which organizations enter into joint ventures and other forms of alliances, as a key strategy in order to meet the imperatives of contemporary global competition.

*TNCs: the adaptive model*

The development of the transnational company has been systematically overviewed by Ferner, who argues that TNCs are characterized by considerable subsidiary autonomy, with control and knowledge base (research and development) globally diffused (1994:80–1). *Ceteris paribus*, approaches to employee involvement and participation in the polycentric TNC will be more diverse and adaptive to host country norms, compared with the ethnocentric MNC approach which is more likely to be characterized by home country model implantation. Moreover, 'divisionalization' of TNC operations implies relatively decentralized human resource management styles, especially if it is accompanied by a high level of integrated production functions (Ferner 1994:82; Marginson et al. 1993). Indeed, in a functional context, human resource management practices will tend to be more diverse in transnational companies than in most other areas of operation, as the management of people will be inherently sensitive to host country norms (see Laurent 1986:97).

This MNC/TNC dichotomy is counterbalanced by a number of complex influencing factors, not least of these being pressures exerted on polycentric organizations to converge their operations globally. Ferner notes the case of the Swiss-Swedish TNC Asea Brown Boveri (ABB), seen by a number of commentators as one of the most dynamic polycentric organizations of the 1990s (see e.g. Peters 1992). The otherwise diverse human resource management style of ABB world-wide has been partly offset by a homogeneous moulding of its approach through its 'T50' programme. This aims to halve all lead times in its global activities within 12 months, by decentralizing work responsibilities and broadening individual and team-based skills (Ferner 1994:83–4).

*Partnership global enterprises: the fluid model*

Whilst the MNC and TNC represent relatively clear-cut models for an analysis of the likely approaches to be adopted towards EI/EP, a more fluid trend in global enterprises has emerged in the last decade of the twentieth century in the form of joint venture partnerships. Cross-national partnerships are not in themselves a new development: for example, state-backed companies in the defence/aerospace industries in Europe have collaborated in the past in the design and production of aircraft. But in the 1990s, private sector organizations, especially in capital intensive industries, have increasingly formed alliances in research and development and production of leading-edge products. In the telecommunications industry, for example, plans for an ambitious global partnership were unveiled in summer 1994, involving France Télécom and Deutsche Telekom, together buying a 20 per cent stake in the third largest US long-distance telecommunications carrier, Sprint. This alliance was aimed at creating an enterprise capable of servicing the technical communications requirements of the extremely large MNC/TNC sector and followed quickly on the heels of an earlier joint venture in the same industry between British Telecommunications and MCI, North America's second largest carrier (reported in *Financial Times*, 15 June 1994).

The partnership type of operation creates a more complex and multi-dimensional basis for involvement and participation, as two or more TNCs seek to develop their managerial approaches within a cross-cultural setting, amidst widespread spatial locations. Within this context, adaptation and innovation, rather than implantation, tend to result. Indeed, partnership operations may be consciously entered into with the goal of breaking away from home-based models to learn new ways of managing, including new forms of organizational decision-making. Beaumont (1993), for example, describes a Japanese/UK parent company joint venture conforming to this model, within which employee relations, or human resource management, has been developed independently of parent company approaches. Within the (non-union) joint venture establishment, a policy mix has resulted which includes a strong emphasis on two-way communications (primarily through team briefing), and performance appraisal for all employees (1993:212–13).

The growing trend towards joint venture operations does contain inherent problems, as partnerships are broken relatively easily, sometimes contentiously, as in the case of the UK's former Rover Group car company. Rover entered into a partnership with Japan's Honda organization in 1979, initially in a fairly limited licensing deal, but subsequently in a more full-blooded venture in 1991 with the agreement between the two companies to collaborate on the development and production of new car ranges throughout the 1990s. Inspired by the integrative involvement style of its Japanese partners, management at Rover introduced a total quality improvement programme in 1987, aimed in part at encouraging a much greater level of employee input in the process of change and quality enhancement. In 1991, a 'new deal' was initiated between the company and its 35,000 employees, based on the introduction of single-status terms and conditions, greater emphasis on team working, full flexibility, job security and a streamlined trade union agreement (*Industrial Relations Review and Report* 1992b:12–15).

UK/Japanese collaboration helped lead to a revival in Rover's fortunes in the latter 1980s, due not least to the adoption of substantially new forms of production and work organization, relying heavily on the involvement approaches outlined in Chapter 5. However, in 1994 the German car makers BMW bought Rover from its UK parent, British Aerospace, in a move that was principally characterized by a complete lack of consultation with Honda management. At the time of writing it is too early to assess the effect this ownership change will have on Rover's Japanese-inspired human resource management style, but nevertheless this case study illustrates the dynamism, and potential fragility, of the partnership type of global enterprise, and is a long way from the relatively static image of the MNC implanting its home-based practices overseas.

**Conclusions**

In this chapter, we have argued that inward investor organizations will either implant their home-based models of involvement or participation, or adapt to local host country traditions and norms, depending on the management culture of the global enterprise and perhaps also on the specific context in which it is operating. In particular, whilst patterns of work organization and involvement tend to be implanted in a company specific fashion into the host country operation of foreign owned enterprises, styles of employee relations are more likely to be adapted, sometimes significantly, to host country norms. We have further argued that there is little evidence of a direct causal link between foreign owned company practices and indigenous managerial approaches to employee relations.

We would speculate, however, that the different approaches towards EI and EP utilized by inward investors together have some indirect influence on changes within the operation of domestic industrial relations and human resource management, particularly as these approaches often appear to be compatible with employee relations changes that domestic employers are wishing to make in any case.

## Notes

1   Japanese utilization of single-union deals has been a contentious issue in the UK, and it is not clear to what extent some of these agreements allow for a robust trade unionism to flourish in the establishment. Wilkinson et al., for example, argue that single-union deals in Japanese companies in Wales are characterized by a distinctly unitarist managerial philosophy, 'where fundamental differences of interest between employer and employee are not admitted' (1993:282).

2   We are cautious in drawing too generalized conclusions from this regional study as, for example, broader-based studies have found that over half of Japanese manufacturing companies in the UK recognize trade unions, predominantly within a single-union context (see Oliver and Wilkinson 1992:266–71; Hove et al. 1990). However, company representative bodies that exist in many Japanese plants, for example at Toshiba and Nissan, are based on consensus building, although in theory almost any subject can be discussed in these forums. In Nissan, for example, a Company Council was established in its plant in north-east England, and meets four times per year. This is an all-purpose body, which deals with consultative, negotiating and grievance issues (Nissan 1988). But overall, the north-east of England findings may well indicate that Japanese organizations would favour a non-union framework of employee relations, where feasible in the context of local conditions. Evidence from America would support this view. As noted earlier in this chapter, Florida and Kenney (1991), for example, found that a non-union model predominated in the car supplier sector in Japanese owned companies, in contrast to heavily unionized Japanese owned assembly plant operations.

# 10

# Forwards or Backwards for Employee Influence at Work?

In our opening chapters we described three main routes that channels for employee influence can follow and categorized these as industrial democracy, employee participation and employee involvement respectively. We went on to state that the more radical ID route has been largely cut off in contemporary industrial societies, and socialist ideas of worker power have subsequently stagnated or been displaced by more pragmatic programmes for worker interventions. This shift has accelerated in recent years with the distortion and ultimate collapse of socialist practice in Eastern Europe, compounded by the current domination of free market and competitive relations ideologies circulating in both mature and emergent industrial societies.

The disintegration of social democratic visions for popular workplace control has left involvement and participation as the two dominant channels for the provision of employee inputs into decision-making at work, and the directions and effects of these processes have formed the main focus of the present study.

This final chapter is composed of two main sections. First, from our findings we conclude that employee participation is in danger of marginalization as employee involvement practices are becoming more prevalent. We then draw upon these findings to argue that, as a consequence of these changes, the means available for the bulk of employees to articulate their interests at work are becoming restricted to management designed and instigated involvement forums, at a time when the policies and practice of employment relations become increasingly individualized and deregulated.

## Pressures facing representative participation at work

Our conclusions from this study of contemporary patterns of employee involvement and participation derive from three main themes which emerge. The first is that, in concept, involvement and participation have significantly different characteristics. Nevertheless, though they should be seen as distinct processes, involvement and participation can be subject to manipulation by either employers or employees, the extent and directions depending upon the environment in which they are located. As Poole has argued, the potential (or latent) power resources accessible to either party are drawn from the wider (political and economic) and internal (managerial, organizational and technological) environments (1986:Chapter 7); it is these resources which serve to structure the extent to which specific programmes for involvement and participation progress in terms of implementation, adaptation and withdrawal. In general, those programmes which are closest to a middle ground between EI and EP, such as joint consultation, are most sensitive.

The second concluding theme is that, under current economic and political circumstances, an accumulating body of evidence indicates that employee participation has been subject to considerable pressure from employers (and hostile governments). In some cases, participation has been displaced by competing involvement techniques or simply withdrawn. The third conclusion is that there is ample evidence of an expansion in the deployment of employee involvement techniques by a growing number of employers.

## The character of involvement and participation

In the early chapters of this book we outlined key characteristics which in our view differentiate employee involvement from participation, concluding that principal distinctions can be found in their origins, implementation and prime intended beneficiaries. With regard to involvement, we state that techniques originate with management, are organized by management and are primarily intended to raise individual worker effectiveness, either through direct application (e.g. performance-related pay), or indirectly through modifying employee attitudes. Conversely, participation tends to originate either with government policies which aim to provide collective protection for employees, or through the efforts of employees themselves to erect defensive structures. Whilst EI tends to be individually oriented, reflecting management's concern to highlight and reinforce individual employee relationships, some well-established involvement initiatives such as joint consultation are founded upon a representative basis, and we have termed these initiatives as 'collective' or 'representative' involvement in order to distinguish them from genuine participative exercises. At times of labour market buoyancy, these 'boundary' approaches can become 'contested terrain' between EI and EP, and its is perhaps not surprising that employer use of collective involvement exercises has declined over the past few years with falls in union membership, contraction in the number of recognition agreements and growing restrictions imposed by employers over collective bargaining arrangements (see e.g. Gall and McKay 1994; Terry 1994). More commonly seen under contemporary economic conditions have been employer attempts to redirect participative initiatives into new or existing systems of involvement.

The early chapters of this book offer an analysis of the changing environmental conditions under which employing organizations operate and which have tended to give support to managerial EI efforts. The main influence has unquestionably been the rise in the competitive climate which in turn has stimulated employers to review, perhaps on an ongoing basis, their organizational structures and employment arrangements. Whereas in Europe there has been a call for a uniform framework of participative collective rights, motivated in part by the need to represent employee interests in the change process, this call has been dismissed by Britain's Conservative government in its endeavours to dismantle 'barriers to employment'. The erection of collective employee defences against expressions of managerial control initiatives are interpreted by the government as a major restraint upon productivity, operational efficiency and macroeconomic performance.

From within this new competitive framework have arisen major changes to industrial and occupational structures, as uncompetitive industries have been scaled down and given way to new configurations of market-responsive, smaller-scale and service-oriented enterprises, accompanied by occupational shifts compatible with these changes. Reforms in education, partly stimulated by changing industrial needs, have helped to raise both aggregate skill levels and the educational profile of the workforce as older, less qualified workers drop out (or are driven out) from active labour market participation. In combination, these changing labour supply characteristics can encourage employers to restructure their operations through adopting cultures of 'lean production' and 'learning organization', and lead them also to consider approaches to employee management consistent with and facilitative of these broad developments.

We indicated that one expression of increased managerial attention to employee relationships has been the emergence of human resource management in both its 'hard' or calculative and 'soft' or integrative manifestations. We pointed out that although many employee involvement techniques predate the ascendancy of HRM, they do nevertheless comprise a solid conceptual core to this latter development. We also noted the apparent absence of any tangible participative thrust to HRM, which has led some trade unions to observe both EI and HRM with a somewhat sceptical eye (see Monks 1994).

### The decline of employee participation

Current trends point either to employer hostility to collective arrangements (as evidenced for example with the demise of collective share schemes in Scandinavia and the precipitous decline in the number of bargaining units in some sections of British industry) or to attempts to restrict the scope of participative forums. These attempted inhibitions might also apply to collective involvement-oriented joint consultation, whose usage has declined in recent years. Participative collective bargaining in the UK and America is experiencing similar tensions and is becoming increasingly circumscribed by involvement techniques. Chapter 7 examines these pressures facing EP, and we can conclude that in the absence of supportive legislation and institutional arrangements acceptable to the major interest groups, participation is always prone to be ineffective as a countervailing influence over managerial decision-making or vulnerable to unmitigating and destabilizing pressures.

One problem for employees is that any participative initiative which is acceptable to management, either in policy terms or in practical operation, is also likely to make little impact in shaping the main directions or outcomes of managerial decision-making.

In the UK we find, for example, evidence of employer modification of the participative intent of works councils towards an involvement mode. In Germany, birthplace and stronghold of works councils, influence has been found to be weakest when these bodies attempt to confront issues of business policy. Similar problems have been experienced by employee trustees of occupational pension fund trusts in Britain, thereby fatally undermining the notion that employee ownership of productive capital is necessarily associated with its deployment and control.

The concept of worker directors, another main branch of European participation practice identified (along with works councils, collective bargaining and collective share schemes), was universally rejected by British industry. In the handful of experiments to be conducted, their original countervailing intent was confounded through a combination of management hostility and union confusion. It should be borne in mind that the successful resistance by employers to the imposition of Bullock-style participation, and the problems experienced by those union directors who were appointed, occurred at a time of acknowledged union confidence based upon strength in numbers, a sympathetic government in office, and strong workplace bargaining structures in place. Even in this favourable climate, non-collective bargaining participation was unable to gain any substantial foothold. Notwithstanding the wealth of European experience of boardroom participation, practice demonstrates that even when tolerated by employers, worker directors can also become isolated from strategic decisions through restrictions on their numbers or formal curtailment of their range of activities. In summary, it seems that participative intent can often emerge as involvement reality.

### The rise of employee involvement

Our review of developments in employee involvement demonstrates both steady growth in the proportion of employers adopting EI techniques and an increase in the range of practices which employers operate. In particular increased use of combinations of EI approaches was noted. Use of involvement also appears to be extending to smaller enterprises and establishments, particularly through informal communicative procedures. We also saw little visible evidence to connect individual EI techniques with any measurable effects upon employee behaviour, though very little attempt appears to be made by managers either to monitor or to evaluate the outcomes of EI usage. This pragmatism was especially apparent in the use of employee share schemes.

Three critical questions are raised by these involvement developments. First, what are the reasons behind this expansion? Second, does the expansion provide evidence for a more strategic role for employment relations in corporate affairs? And third, what are the behavioural effects of employee involvement? We summarize our conclusions to each of these issues below.

*Reasons for expansion in employee involvement*

It would appear that a number of influences may be identified which separately, or in combination, can induce managers to adopt forms of employee involvement.

First, legislation can act as an incentive to employers to adopt involvement techniques. In the UK, the original provisions of the Employment Act 1982 which require employers to report regularly on steps taken with regard to employee involvement have lent to it a perspective of 'positive employment practice' over which 'good' employers would be expected to take action. Whilst only a minority of employers surveyed concede that statutorily supported tax concessions have been a major inducement in encouraging them to adopt individual share schemes, closer analysis through case studies does point to this factor as being at least partly responsible for this adoption. The rise of ESOPs in America is strongly associated with the legislation which encouraged their introduction.

Second, in a number of countries there has been continuous government exhortation in support of EI. In the UK this support derives from governmental concern to construct a solid wall of involvement 'facts' with which to confront European enthusiasm for the imposition of a common framework of employee participation rights. Equally relevant is the UK government's stated belief that voluntarily implemented involvement provides a direct and accessible route toward employee commitment, flexibility and efficiency. The decline of collective ideology and activity, in pursuit of which the UK's Conservative government has played an enthusiastic part, also stimulated state promotion of alternative and more restrictive measures for employee influence to be exercised within an increasingly unitarist framework.

In some involvement areas, the government has been able to go further and use its position as both employer *and* financial controller to ensure that desired specific techniques, such as performance appraisal and performance-related pay, are implemented as a condition for additional funding, as happened, for example, in universities and for some health service occupations.

Third, some commentators attribute the rise in EI, and in particular specific practices, to the influence (either direct or indirect) of inward investing industry. There is little doubt that the high profile enjoyed by systems of communication, quality programmes, flexibility, innovative reward systems, alternative forms of workforce representation and the like, owe something to the favourable publicity given to Japanese companies like Nissan, or American enterprises such as Hewlett Packard. Indeed, the success which these have enjoyed in operating productively (at least, until very recently) has helped to reinforce the positive image of 'value added' by EI to these companies' working practices.

Fourth, there is little doubt that managers associate certain desirable production attainments with the deployment of specific techniques. Hence a company wishing to raise its output quality may well consider ways by which this may be addressed through the application of appropriate techniques of involvement, and indeed it is not unreasonable to suppose that the factors discussed above may help to narrow down the range of options considered by managers. Technological innovation contemplated by the organization may also stimulate managers to think about desirable involvement techniques to accompany the changes.

### A strategic role for employee involvement?

The use of 'strategic' human resource management terminology is now commonplace and it generally assumes that management direction of employees is purposeful, allied to organizational objectives, and long term in perspective rather than opportunistic and reactive. Within this framework is contained the notion of treating individual employees as a key and flexible organizational resource. It is further assumed that development and investment in this human resource will lead to long-term organizational benefit.

The conclusions which emerge from our review raise a number of doubts with regard to the applicability of this strategic model to involvement experience. Our scepticism is based upon the following factors. Whilst the vision of senior management with regard to organizational objectives may be mobilizing EI in coherent directions, the commitment, enthusiasm and competence of middle managers and supervisors to implement and efficiently operate systems of EI can be questioned. Further, employees can recognize that the operational objectives of EI focus upon management rather than employee concerns. Compatibility between softer-edged EI practice and existing employee relations traditions may also be problematic for line managers and supervisors.

Senior managers are the key to organizational change, and there are indications that in recent years they have shifted from a position of detachment from labour matters to formulating and imposing 'a view' about desired directions for their systems of employee relations (Storey 1992:266). The same author, however, harbours doubts about the extent to which these desires translate into action. Contradictory messages emanating from senior management with regard to appropriate styles of management are certainly not uncommon, particularly as significant organizational change is invariably associated with significant cost, and cheaper and more superficial models may, therefore, be more attractive.

Nevertheless, these managerial intentions tend to be unfocused and are seldom reported to integrate with policies for internal organizational developments. Research from Marchington et al. (1993a) confirms the informal and *ad hoc* nature of much EI implementation; many involvement techniques are introduced as a result of individual managers championing particular techniques or as a result of new managerial enthusiasms, a common reason for the introduction of individual share schemes, for example. In consequence, a range of techniques might operate contemporaneously, though at different stages of endorsement or promotion. Second, an element of faddishness often accompanies the launch of EI techniques, assisted perhaps by the ministrations of employee relations consultants.

In this sense, we doubt whether EI could be regarded as a strategic element of employer action. These doubts are strengthened by our examination of inward investor influence: in both American and Japanese companies EI techniques can be commonly found, and the range of approach shows little apparent variation from their UK counterparts. The main differences are to be found in the coherence, intent and corporate culture of the overseas companies, who also demonstrate these attributes by devoting more resources to their personnel activities than UK companies and are more likely to integrate these personnel activities within a broader corporate strategy.

## *The behavioural effects of employee involvement*

A major problem for senior management is that their plans and objectives are delivered and operated through a network of line managers and supervisors whose views on labour relations may lead them to distort or neglect new, and possibly challenging, approaches to employee management. Equally, some managers may simply not be competent to adopt new styles of management (which, of course, may well result in the same neglect of, or resentment towards, involvement initiatives). Certainly, training for management in the application of new involvement initiatives does not appear to be extensive (Marchington et al. 1993b:573; Thompson 1993).

A recent study ascribes the reasons for decline of individual involvement programmes chiefly to 'supervisory apathy or opposition' (Marchington et al. 1993b:564), especially when the initiative emerges from distant senior management or personnel sources. Some involvement projects were seen by line managers as either inappropriate to their circumstances or even competitive with other (involvement) steps taken by local plant managers or functional services personnel, such as sales, who had launched separate programmes (1993b:565). Possibly, for these reasons, it was within 'centralised private sector companies that supervisory and middle-management resistance or dislike of centrally derived EI schemes' was most apparent (1993b:567).

All-employee share schemes offer similar examples of the schism which can develop between senior manager originators of schemes and middle- and lower-order managers, who may see share provision to subordinates (which might imply an altered status relationship with employees who also become nominal owners) as a perk unrelated to, and possibly destructive of, the employer–employee effort bargain, upon which much of their traditional motivational ideas and authority relations are located. A slightly resentful middle manager in a company researched by one of the authors was quoted (not untypically) as saying: 'Seventy per cent of employees see shares as something they get, whether they work hard or not. We need to put more play into it; it's not used as a motivational part of the management of the company' (quoted in Baddon et al. 1989:193).

Similarly, a recent company case study where quality circles had been introduced demonstrates how competing management cultures can serve to restrict the operation of this form of involvement. The HRM department was keen to offer discretion to the circles in the issues that circle members chose to research and in their ways of operation. Both the general manager and production managers were unimpressed and successfully undermined the initiative, which they saw as too erosive of their traditional, disciplinary, sources of authority and control (Geary 1993). Hunter and Beaumont describe the difficulties in introducing total quality management into a manufacturing company: 'The overwhelming impression conveyed to us was of supervisors and charge hands who were very production, as opposed to employee, centred in their orientation. Is such an orientation compatible with successful introduction to TQM?' (1993:326).

With regard to the preparation of managers in order to undertake involvement responsibilities, contemporary research has identified inadequately trained managers as a significant factor in the failure of performance-related pay schemes to motivate employees (Thompson 1993). Again, this failure must put a question mark over the commitment and control by senior managers over the directions taken by the involvement process and in turn the progress of HRM, which is highly dependent upon all levels of management for its direction and application (see Legge 1989).

### Employee involvement and human resource management

We have shown in Chapter 4 that observers of the human resource management scene are united that, in concept at least, involvement occupies a pivotal status within the formulation of strategic HRM, to an extent that it would appear doubtful whether HRM could legitimately be defined as a practical feature of management strategy without evidence of a substantial and integrated EI contribution. In this section, it would be helpful to 'unwrap' HRM a little in order to locate more precisely the putative role of EI within its framework.

A popular framework is the HRM 'cycle' offered by Storey (1989). In this cycle, the principal elements of HRM activities link coherently to the achievement and enhancement of employee performance. Performance is thus assessed through appraisal, which offers both rewards and individual development opportunities to employees. Reward further motivates performance and development heightens employee capabilities to perform well (1989:7). In this cycle involvement is not offered a specific label, but its components are clearly identifiable among the 'appraisal' and 'developmental' elements which feed into the 'performance' and 'rewards' aspects of the model. These involvement elements are further developed in Storey's later formulation contrasting HRM with personnel management characteristics. In this model EI features strongly as an identifiable distinguishing feature between the two managerial modes (Storey 1992:35). Further, it will be recalled from Chapter 4 that Beaumont (1992) also included 'relatively high levels of individual employee and work group participation in task related decisions' as a main dimension of HRM.

One conclusion that we arrive at from the contrast between an EI profile and the practical operation of EI is that the situation with regard to the status and practice of HRM is by no means clear. If, as seems the case in many companies, involvement techniques are being injected with minimal systematic relationship to one another or to the broader organizational context in which they are supposed to operate; if the management line is unprepared or hostile towards the altered status relationships inherent in many EI programmes; if little attempt is made to monitor and assess progress of techniques; if indeed, their impact is neither as comprehensive nor as profound as some of their advocates would like to see; then there are severe doubts as to whether EI, acting either alone or as part of a wider HRM programme, may be capable of 'bridging the gap' in interests which pluralist writers typify for relations between employers and employees. As Guest and his colleagues have indicated: 'If EI fails to increase identification with, and commitment to the organization, then arguably it is failing in its objectives of reducing the sense of "them and us"' (1993:192).

Under circumstances of EI failure to alter the beliefs and values of individual employees or collectivities of employees, then other explanations for the observed fluctuations in contemporary employee relations may need to be explored. For employers, there will be the question of confronting the awkward fact that observed changes to employee behaviour may be more amenable and attributable to solid contemporary economic realities than the involvement programmes which have occupied a large part of their policy-making to 'change hearts and minds' over the past 10 years. In other words, there is a danger of attributing positive effects to one factor cluster (involvement) when employee behaviour is under severe restraint from a range of sources, including high levels of unemployment, persistent uncertainty about future prospects (perhaps promulgated in part through employee communications media), relaxation of protective legislation, curbs on union activity, and ideology drift from a rights-based employment agenda to one founded more on principles of economic efficiency. Certainly it seems that few employees harbour illusions about the efficiency-driven purpose of involvement. As we saw in Chapter 5, a majority of employees believe that management objectives for EI are to increase efficiency or to encourage people to work harder. Even share schemes are largely seen by employees in bonus terms. By contrast, only a small minority of employees believe that the bottom-line purpose of involvement is to improve employee satisfaction. For politicians, there may be the realization that rather than having removed the vestiges of oppositional industrial relations, these remain, but may wait to express themselves in different patterns of individual and collective manifestations of discontent than was the case when trade union influence was more openly embraced by both government and employers.

## The rise of empowerment as a form of involvement

Associated with deregulation and flexibility, EI may be seen as a means of intensifying work, with no commensurate increase given to pay, status or security. The recent hype afforded to EI-oriented 'empowerment' illustrates this possibility strongly. Whilst the boundaries surrounding empowerment seem rather fluid at present, its main feature appears to involve individual job ownership by employees: 'so that they can take personal interest in improving the performance of the organization' (Byham 1988:viii). Other practical management guides point in the same direction (see Scott and Jaffe 1991; Mitchell Stewart 1994).

A look at case studies reveals a rather different picture. These indicate that empowerment tends to be introduced in companies which have removed layers of supervisory management and is used to cover existing tasks with fewer staff (Pickard 1993), with any 'reward' being intrinsic to the added responsibilities associated with the 'empowered' jobs. This makes individual employees vulnerable in at least two ways: first, added responsibility invariably increases stress levels; and second, 'empowered' employees are held responsible for the efficiency of their work, but job boundary protection in the form of job descriptions and employee specifications becomes less evident. Any performance failures can then be attributed to the 'empowered' employees rather than the poverty of managerial or organizational support. Basically and critically, empowerment becomes a euphemism for work intensification.

## Future developments in employee influence: the route blocked?

Despite the unproven capacity for involvement exercises to thrust employee influence beyond the reach of immediate task-based decision-making, there seems to be little doubt that involvement practice will continue to evolve and proliferate. First, the lack of penetration of earlier approaches encourages involvement innovations in a continuing spiral of activity; and second, because the very lack of influence offered to 'involved' employees by these same processes is attractive to company managers. There is equally little doubt that pressures on participative action will intensify, even in those countries whose governments formally espouse participative access to employees. In all countries, scope for participative action among employers will be circumscribed by market and competitive pressures.

Under these circumstances, employees will have diminishing collective resources available to confront or influence employer policies, and singular reliance upon individualized involvement techniques within increasingly unitarist organizations may be the sole, highly restricted opening available to employees to exercise influence. The weaknesses of involvement to act as an instrument of employee influence have been thoroughly rehearsed in the course of this book and can be summarized as follows.

First, there is little evidence that employee influence over corporate decisions which affect them has been, or can ever be, enhanced through contemporary configurations of involvement. In other words, whilst involvement might increase individual task discretion or open up channels for communication, the involvement programme is not designed to offer opportunities for employees to gain or consolidate control over the broader environment in which their work is located.

Second, with continuing attention afforded to involvement exercises at work, there is a danger that collective means to influence employer and managerial decisions will become further eroded, especially when combined with broader government or employer campaigns against participation. Employee ability to resist or offset potentially damaging decisions to their well-being will ultimately be damaged.

Third, EI is linked functionally and operationally with employee flexibility within increasingly deregulated labour markets. This raises further doubts about the capability of involvement to serve as a vehicle for the expression of employee interests:

1   EI is tied in with programmes whose objectives are directed to the attainment of management goals. Employee intervention in choosing or supervising these programmes would be rejected on grounds of expertise, violation of meritocratic principles, hierarchy or interference with the rationality of market forces.

2   Essentially the objective of deregulation and workforce flexibility is to remove controls which affect the deployment and remuneration of labour and which serve to prevent management from taking unilateral action over issues which materially affect employees or their welfare, such as work intensification. Involvement will be introduced in the hope of reinforcing the control process, rather than reverse it.

3   Deregulatory activities do not necessarily exert a uniform effect across the workforce: indeed, they can compound existing inequalities and deprivations, including impeding access to decision-making and to rewarding jobs and careers. In particular, deregulation exercises are tending to adversely affect women to a greater extent than men in that women are more likely than men to become part-time or temporary workers, are more likely to be offered atypical contracts of employment and are concentrated in insecure occupations and industries. For example, wages councils, which set statutory minimum employment terms for 2.5 million vulnerable workers in the UK, have now been abolished: 80 per cent of employees in wages council industries were women. Though patterns of female activity vary across countries, inequality is a phenomenon which is occurring throughout Europe (Rubery and Fagan 1994) including Sweden, despite its highly regarded policies for equality of treatment (Gonäs and Westin 1993), and in the USA (Bamber and Whitehouse 1993:300–1). At the same time gender segregation at work ensures that women continue to occupy inferior status and authority positions.

## Conclusions

Throughout the industrial era, encompassing some 200 years, control and authority over the destiny and lives of a large majority have been vested in a minority of owners and their managers. This domination has inspired attempts by workers themselves, often in association with their political supporters, to provide mechanisms through which managerial control could be mediated.

Mature democracies have invariably progressed in terms of political democracy to embrace universal representative suffrage, often moving hand in hand with educational progress and social reforms. The lack of popular self-expression at work has contrasted sharply with the evolution of political self-determination at local and national levels in the affairs of state as well as in voluntary associations, including the governance of trade unions. In these same democracies, there has been an assumption by many that representative participation would not only extend to industry, but in time would progress, despite employer opposition, to provide a stable source of countervailing power to confront that enjoyed by employers. Whilst ultimate employer authority would be retained, it would be applied through the dynamic of pluralistic participation. It was in this sense that Poole wrote optimistically about 'the long march towards industrial democracy' (1986:179) and Bean was able to suggest that consensus exists towards the rights of working people 'to participate in the making of decisions which critically affect their working lives' (1994:160), the quote with which we opened this book.

In contrast, we have argued that processes of employee participation face continuing harassment from employers and that employee involvement has become, in many industrial settings, the principal focus and outlet for the expression of employee influence at work. In previous years, when pluralist pressures appeared to be a permanent and growing feature of the industrial-political landscape, it could be assumed that demands for employee influence would exert a progressive ratchet effect, ultimately allowing 'the long march' to reach its destination: but a significant question now concerns the direction in which this march is leading, especially as at the head of the marchers can be seen the banner of commercial and managerial objectives rather than that of employee interests. Industrial democracy, both as a set of ideas and in practice, has largely disintegrated. Even employee participation, in its diverse forms, is under threat as an increasingly impotent counter to management initiatives and strategies. Employees are increasingly being left with management-inspired and -controlled involvement as their main, or even sole, source of information, communication and action. In an increasingly individualized and deregulated labour market, with global competitiveness acting as the prime motor for management practice, it seems likely that the bulk of employees will be left with few resources either to query or to contest the directions taken by management control despite the rhetoric of empowerment, involvement and the host of other metaphors being raised to disguise workers' growing occupational impoverishment.

These pessimistic prognostications should, however, be tempered by a number of background developments whose cumulative effects indicate that future systems of employee relationships will not necessarily conform to the patterns of management ascendancy described above. First, the economic doctrine predicated upon flexible market relations is now under serious scrutiny as skill levels in liberal economic conditions remain obstinately low. As a consequence of accumulating doubts, a change in the employee relations' political climate is now perceptible in the USA. Kochan and Weinstein observe that the Dunlop Commission on the Future of Worker–Management Relations, established in 1993, has been 'presented with considerable evidence pertaining to the negative side of contemporary labour relations'. This 'negative' picture includes an increase in union repression, legal or otherwise, by employers and a growth in litigation over disputes, leading the Commission to emphasize 'the interdependence of employee participation, employee representation and dispute resolution' (1994:498). Kochan and Weinstein are convinced that the Commission will 'propose mechanisms to legitimize broader forms of employee participation and to remedy the demonstrated weaknesses in the enforcement of employee rights to join a union and achieve collective bargaining coverage', perhaps even through 'experimentation with American versions of European-style works councils' (1994:498).

A similarly potent factor within the European Union is of course that the Union is standing firm in its allegiance to employee participation. It is the UK which increasingly appears out of line in its opposition to worker rights and employer obligations. Whilst acknowledging that Western European countries 'have seen an abrupt loss of trade union membership and influence, and a new assertiveness on the part of management' (1995:26), R. Hyman identifies three important influences which constrain endorsement of unregulated labour market behaviour within the EU. First, mainstream politics has rejected 'unqualified ideological commitment to market liberalism', enthusiasm for which is restricted to 'minority parties' (1995:29). Second, collective relationships in which a 'social partnership' is prominent continue to be recognized both conceptually and ideologically. Third, long-standing political-legal values give vital sustenance to this collective framework (1995: 29–30). Of particular importance also is the expansion of the European Union, following the inclusion of Sweden, Austria and Finland, countries which are familiar with politically and legally sanctioned social partnership arrangements.

Finally, EU sanctioned works councils are starting to receive endorsement by UK multinationals with operations in Europe despite the opposition of government ministers. Even the giant United Biscuits company, with a European workforce in excess of 25,000 employees, and a long-standing corporate supporter of Conservative administrations, has acknowledged the pragmatic justification for incorporation of worker rights within a collective framework which is additional to collective bargaining machinery. Many of the UK's largest companies have strong European connections and will have to comply with the directive on worker rights in their continental plants, and many accept that it will not be feasible to exclude their domestic plants from establishing parallel arrangements, notwithstanding the opt-out clause negotiated by the UK government at Maastricht.

Employers will undoubtedly press on with their plans for individually inspired involvement programmes, but whether these are implemented in isolation from collective influences or adjacent to them will depend heavily upon the impact of broader national and international political and economic dynamics. Of growing significance is that the direction of these forces is rather more sympathetic to the collective voice of employee interests than that of employers alone.

# References

ACAS (1988) *Employee Appraisal*, London, ACAS.

ACAS (1991) *Consultation and Communication: the 1990 ACAS Survey*, Occasional Paper No. 49, Work Research Unit, London, ACAS.

Ackers, P., Marchington, M., Wilkinson, A. and Goodman, P. (1992) 'The use of cycles? Explaining employee involvement in the 1990s', *Industrial Relations Journal*, Vol. 23, No. 4, Winter, pp.268–83.

Ainley, J. (1992) 'Asking staff to survey management style', *Involvement and Participation*, No. 612, Winter/February, pp.10–11 and 19.

Allen, C., Cunningham, I. and McArdle, L. (1991) *Employee Participation and Involvement in the 1990s*, Stockton, Jim Conway Foundation.

Anderson, G. (1992) 'Performance appraisal' in B. Towers (ed.) *The Handbook of Human Resource Management*, Oxford, Blackwell, pp. 186–207.

Argyris, C. (1992) 'A leadership dilemma: skilled incompetence' in G. Salaman (ed.) *Human Resource Strategies*, London, Sage, pp.82–94.

Armstrong, P. (1989) 'Limits and possibilities for HRM in an age of management accountancy' in J. Storey (ed.) *New Perspectives in Human Resource Management*, London, Routledge, pp.154–66.

Atkinson, J. (1985) *Flexibility, Uncertainty and Manpower Management*, IMS Report 89, Sussex, Institute of Manpower Studies.

Baddon, L., Hunter, L., Hyman, J., Leopold, J. and Ramsay, H. (1987) 'Developments in profit-sharing and employee share ownership', Survey Report, University of Glasgow, Centre for Research into Industrial Democracy and Participation.

Baddon, L., Hunter, L., Hyman, J., Leopold, J. and Ramsay, H. (1989) *People's Capitalism? A Critical Analysis of Profit Sharing and Employee Share Ownership*, London, Routledge.

Baglioni, G. and Crouch, C. (eds) (1991) *European Industrial Relations*, London, Sage.

Balcombe, J. (1988) *Successful Suggestion Schemes Update 1988*, London, The Industrial Society.

Bamber, G.J. and Whitehouse, G. (1993) 'Appendix' in G. Bamber and R.D. Lansbury (eds) *International and Comparative Industrial Relations*, 2nd edn, London, Routledge.

Banks, A. and Metzgar, J. (1989) 'Participating in management: union organizing on a new terrain', *Labor Research Review*, Vol. 14, No. 1.

*Bargaining Report* (1993) 'Works councils in the UK', No. 127, April, Labour Research Department, pp.11–14.

Bartett, C. and Ghoshal, S. (1989) *Managing across Borders*, London, Hutchinson.

Batstone, E. (1984) *Working Order*, Oxford, Blackwell.

Batstone, E. (1988) *The Reform of Workplace Industrial Relations*, Oxford, Clarendon Press.

Batstone, E., Ferner, A. and Terry, M. (1985) 'Unions on the Post Office Board' in W.E.J. McCarthy (ed.) *Trade Unions*, 2nd edn, Harmondsworth, Pelican, pp.109–23.

Bean, R. (1994) *Comparative Industrial Relations*, 2nd edn, London, Routledge.

Beaumont, P. (1988) *The Decline of Trade Union Organisation*, London, Croom Helm.

Beaumont, P.B. (1992) 'Annual review article 1991', *British Journal of Industrial Relations*, Vol. 30, No. 1, pp. 107–26.

Beaumont, P.B. (1993) *Human Resource Management: Key Concepts and Skills*, London, Sage.

Beer, M. and Spector, B. (1985) 'Corporate wide transformation in human resource management' in R.E. Walton and P.R. Lawrence (eds) *Human Resource Management Trends and Challenges*, Boston, MA, Harvard Business School Press, pp.123–46.

Bell, D.W. and Hanson, C.G. (1987) *Profit Sharing and Profitability*, London, Kogan Page.

Besse, D. (1992) 'Personnel management in France', *Personnel Management*, August, pp.40–6.

Bevan, S. and Thompson, D. (1991) 'Performance management at the crossroads', *Personnel Management*, November, pp.36–9.

Blanchflower, D.G. and Oswald, A.J. (1986) *Profit-Sharing – Can it Work?*, New Bridge Consultants.

Blasi, J. and Kruse, D. (1991) *The New Owners*, New York, Harper Business.

Blumberg, P. (1968) *Industrial Democracy: the Sociology of Participation*, London, Constable.

Blyton, P. (1992) 'Flexible times? Recent developments in temporal flexibility', *Industrial Relations Journal*, Vol. 23, No. 1, Spring, pp. 26–36.

Blyton, P. and Turnbull, P. (1992) 'HRM: debates, dilemmas and contradictions' in P. Blyton and P. Turnbull (eds) *Reassessing Human Resource Management*, London, Sage, pp.1–15.

Bougen, P.D., Ogden, S.G. and Qutram, Q. (1988) 'Profit sharing and the cycle of control', *Sociology*, Vol. 22, No. 3.

Bowey, A. and Thorpe, R. (1986) *Payment Systems and Productivity*, London, Macmillan.

Bradley, K. and Hill, S. (1987) 'Quality circles and managerial interests', *Industrial Relations*, Vol. 26, No. 1, Winter, pp. 68–82.

Brannen, P. (1983) *Authority and Participation in Industry*, London, Batsford.

Bregn, K. and Jeppesen, H.J. (1991) 'Profit-sharing schemes: partner or opponent to the Danish labour market', paper presented to conference on *Changes in Labour Markets and Industrial Relations in Europe*, Aalborg, Denmark.

Brenan, G. (1950) *The Spanish Labyrinth: an Account of the Social and Political Background of the Spanish Civil War*, 2nd edn, Cambridge, Cambridge University Press.

Brewster, C. and Hegewisch, A. (1993) 'Employee communication and participation' *P+ European Participation Monitor*, No. 7, pp.14–18.

Brewster, C. and Smith, C. (1990) 'Corporate strategy: a no-go area for personnel?', *Personnel Management*, July, pp.36–40.

Brewster, C., Gill, C. and Richbell, S. (1981) 'Developing an analytical approach to industrial relations policy', *Personnel Review*, Vol 10, No. 2, pp. 3–10.

Bristow, E. (1974) 'Profit-sharing, socialism and labour unrest' in K.D. Brown (ed.) *Essays in Anti-Labour History*, London, Macmillan.

Broad, G. (1994) 'Japan in Britain: the dynamics of joint consultation', *Industrial Relations Journal*, Vol.25, No.1, March, pp.26–38.

Brossard, M. (1990) 'Workers' objectives in quality improvement', *Employee Relations*, Vol. 12, No. 6, pp.11–16.

Brown, W. and Walsh, J. (1991) 'Pay determination in the 1980s: the anatomy of decentralization', *Oxford Review of Economic Policy*, Vol. 7, No. 1.

Buchanan, D. (1992) 'High performance: new boundaries of acceptability in worker control' in G. Salaman (ed.) *Human Resource Strategies*, London, Sage, pp.138–55.

Bullock Report (1977) *Report of the Committee of Inquiry on Industrial Democracy*, Chairman Lord Bullock, Cmnd 6706, London, HMSO.

Burke, T. and Moss, J. (1990) 'Right place, right time, right staff', *Times Higher Education Supplement*, 6 April, p. 15.

Byham, W.C. (1988) *Zapp, the Lightning of Empowerment*, New York, Fawcett Columbine.

CAITS (1994) *Rethinking Worker Democracy*, Sheffield (UK), Centre for Alternative Industrial and Technological Systems.

Casey, B., Lakey, J. and White, M. (1992) *Payment Systems: a Look at Current Practice*, Research Series No. 5, October, Department of Employment.

Cassels, J. (1990) *Britain's Real Skill Shortage*, London, Policy Studies Institute.

CBI (1977) *In Place of Bullock*, London, Confederation of British Industry.

*CBI News* (1990) 'A nation of shareholders', November, pp.8–10.

Clarke, O. (1993) 'Conclusions: towards a synthesis of international and comparative experience of nine countries' in G.J. Bamber and R.D. Lansbury (eds) *International and Comparative Industrial Relations*, 2nd edn, London, Routledge.

Claydon, T. (1989) 'Union derecognition in Britain in the 1980s', *British Journal of Industrial Relations*, Vol. 27, No. 2, July, pp.214–24.

Clegg, H. (1960) *A New Approach to Industrial Democracy*, London, Blackwell.

Clegg, H. (1985) 'Trade unions as an opposition which can never become a government' in W.E.J. McCarthy (ed.) *Trade Unions*, 2nd edn, Harmondsworth, Pelican, pp.83–91.

Clegg, S. (1992) 'Modernist and post modernist organization' in G. Salaman (ed.) *Human Resource Strategies*, London, Sage, pp.156–88.

Cole, G.D.H. (1972) *Self Government in Industry*, London, Hutchinson.

Cooke, W. (1990) *Labour–Management Co-operation*, Kalamazoo, MI, W.E. Upjohn Institute for Employment Research.

Copeman, G., Moore, P. and Arrowsmith, C. (1984) *Share Ownership*, Aldershot, Gower.

Cornell, C. (1992) 'Employee suggestion programmes', *Human Resource Professional*, March.

Cox, J. and Kriegbaum, H. (1989) *Innovation and Industrial Strength*, London, Policy Studies Institute.

Creigh, S., Donaldson, N. and Hawthorn, E. (1981) 'A stake in the firm', *Employment Gazette*, May, pp.229–36.

Cressey, P. (1992) 'Technology and banking' in M. Beirne and H. Ramsay (eds) *Information Technology and Workplace Democracy*, London, Routledge, pp. 173–92.

Cressey, P., Eldridge, J. and MacInnes, J. (1985) *Just Managing*, Milton Keynes, Open University Press.

Cressey, P., Eldridge, J., MacInnes, J. and Norris, G. (1981) 'Industrial democracy and participation: a Scottish study', Research Paper no. 28, Department of Employment.

*Current Sweden* (1983) 'The employee fund issue moves toward a decision', No. 309, October.

*Current Sweden* (1991) 'The economic policies of Sweden's political parties', No. 383, June.

Dann, C. (1992) 'Involving people in achieving change', *Involvement and Participation*, No.612, Winter/February, pp.2–3 and 20.

Delbridge, R. and Turnbull, P. (1992) 'Human resource maximization: the management of labour under just-in-time manufacturing systems' in P. Blyton and P. Turnbull (eds) *Reassessing Human Resource Management*, London, Sage, pp.56–73.

Deming, W.E. (1982) *Quality, Productivity and Competitive Position*, Cambridge, MA, MIT Press.

Department of Trade and Industry (1985) *Quality Circles*, National Quality Campaign, London, DTI.

Deutsch, S. (1993) 'Introduction to the United States labour scene', *Economic and Industrial Democracy*, Vol.14, No.3, pp.327–32.

Deutsch, S. and Schurman, S. (1993) 'Labour initiatives for worker participation and quality of working life', *Economic and Industrial Democracy*, Vol.14, No.3, pp.345–54.

Devine, A. (1992) 'Suggestion schemes: a critical analysis of the schemes in use at Royal Insurance (UK) Ltd, Scotland' MSc Dissertation, University of Strathclyde.

Dølvik, J.E. and Stockland, D. (1992) 'Norway: the "Norwegian Model" in transition' in A. Ferner and R. Hyman (eds) *Industrial Relations in the New Europe*, Oxford University Press, pp. 143–68.

Donovan Report (1968) *Royal Commission on Trade Unions and Employers' Associations 1965–1968*, Cmnd 3623, London, HMSO.

Dore, R. (1973) *British Factory, Japanese Factory: the Origins of National Diversity in Industrial Relations*, London, Allen and Unwin.

Dore, R. and Sako, M. (1989) *How the Japanese Learn to Work*, London, Routledge.

Drago, R. (1988) 'Quality circle survival: an exploratory analysis', *Industrial Relations*, Vol. 27, No. 3, Fall, pp.336–51.

Drago, R. and Wooden, M. (1991) 'The determinants of participatory management', *British Journal of Industrial Relations*, Vol. 29, No. 2, June, pp.177–204.

Drucker, P. (1968) *The Practice of Management*, London, Pan Books.

Drucker, P. (1976) *The Unseen Revolution: How Pension Fund Socialism Came to America*, London, Heinemann.

Drucker, P. (1992) 'The coming of the new organization' in G. Salaman (ed.) *Human Resource Strategies*, London, Sage, pp.128–37.

Dunn, S. (1990) 'Root metaphor in the old and new industrial relations', *British Industrial Relations Journal*, Vol. 28, No. 1, March, pp.1–31.

Dunn, S. (1991) 'Root metaphor in industrial relations: a reply to Tom Keenoy', *British Industrial Relations Journal*, Vol. 29, No. 2, June, pp.329–36.

Dunn, W.N. and Obradovic, J. (eds) (1978) *Workers' Self-Management and Organizational Power in Yugoslavia*, University of Pittsburgh.

Eaton, A. and Voos, P. (1992) 'Unions and contemporary innovations in work organization, compensation and employee participation' in L. Mishel and P. Voos (eds) *Unions and Economic Competitiveness*, Armonk, NY, M.E. Sharpe.

Eccleston, B. (1989) *State and Society in Post-War Japan*, Cambridge, UK, Polity Press.

Edwards, C. (1978) 'Measuring union power: a comparison of two methods applied to the study of local union power in the coal industry', *British Journal of Industrial Relations*, Vol. 16, No. 1, March, pp.1–15.

EGOR Group (1990) *Training and Employment of Engineers in Europe*, Paris.

EIRR (1990a) *Employee Participation in Europe*, European Industrial Relations Review, Report No. 4.

EIRR (1990b) 'Sweden: the full employment "miracle"', *European Industrial Relations Review*, No. 193, February, pp.20–3.

EIRR (1991a) 'Survey of board-level employee representation', *European Industrial Relations Review*, No. 205, February, pp.20–5.

EIRR (1991b) 'The E.W.C. Directive and previous participation initiatives', *European Industrial Relations Review*, No. 207, April, pp. 23–7.

EIRR (1991c) 'European information and consultation at Elf Aquitaine', *European Industrial Relations Review*, No. 211, August, pp.10–12.

EIRR (1991d) 'Europipe – the European Company Statute in action?', *European Industrial Relations Review*, No. 213, October, pp.12–14.

EIRR (1991e) 'Sweden: new government – new industrial relations?', *European Industrial Relations Review*, No. 214, November, pp.11–13.

EIRR (1992a) 'Airbus Industrie Staff Council – a disputed agreement', *European Industrial Relations Review*, No. 218, March, pp.13–14.

EIRR (1992b) 'Employee participation in European statutes', *European Industrial Relations Review*, No. 223, August, pp.25–9.

EIRR (1993a) 'European-level consultation at Bull', *European Industrial Relations Review*, No. 228, January, pp.20–1.

EIRR (1993b) 'Information and consultation in European multinationals – part one', *European Industrial Relations Review*, No. 228, January, pp.13–19.

EIRR (1993c) 'Information and consultation in European multinationals – part two', *European Industrial Relations Review*, No. 229, February, pp.14–20.

Eldridge, J., Cressey, P. and MacInnes, J. (1991) *Industrial Sociology and Economic Crisis*, Hemel Hempstead, Harvester.

Employment Department (1989) *People and Companies: Employee Involvement in Britain*, HMSO.

Employment Department (1990) *Labour Market and Skill Trends 1991/92*, Sheffield.

Employment Department (1991) *Labour Market and Skill Trends 1992/93*, Sheffield.

*Employment Gazette* (1987) 'Involving the staff', March, pp.147–9.

*Employment Gazette* (1988) 'Employee involvement', October, pp.573–5.

*Employment Gazette* (1991) 'Employee involvement: a recent survey', December, pp.659–64.

*Employment for the 1990s* (1988) White Paper, CM. 540, December.

Engels, F. (1892) *The Condition of the Working Class in England*, London, Granada.

European Foundation for the Improvement of Living and Working Conditions (1988) *Participation Review: a Review of Foundation Studies on Participation*, Dublin, EFILWC, November.

European Trade Union Institute (1990) *The Social Dimension of the Internal Market, Part III, The Representation of Workers in the Workplace in Western Europe*, Info 32, Brussels, ETUI.

European Trade Union Institute (1991) *The Social Dimension of the Internal Market, Part IV, European Works Councils*, Info 33, Brussels, ETUI.

Evans, P. and Lorange, P. (1989) 'The two logics behind human resource management' in P. Evans, Y. Doz and A. Laurent (eds) (1989) *Human Resource Management in International Firms: Change, Globalization, Innovation*, Basingstoke, Macmillan.

Ferner, A. (1994) 'Management: An overview of research issues', *Human Resource Management Journal*, Vol.4, No.3, Spring, pp.79–102.

Ferner, A. and Colling, T. (1991) 'Privatization, regulation and industrial relations', *British Journal of Industrial Relations*, Vol. 29, No. 3, pp.391–410.

Fernie, S., Metcalf, D. and Woodland, S. (1994a) *Does Human Resource Management Boost Employee–Management Relations?*, London, London School of Economics, Working Paper 584, February.

Fernie, S., Metcalf, D. and Woodland, S. (1994b) 'What has human resource management achieved in the workplace?' *Employment Policy Institute: Economic Report*, May, Vol. 8, No. 3.

Findlay, P. (1993) 'Union recognition and non-recognition: shifting fortunes in the electronics industry in Scotland', *Industrial Relations Journal*, Vol. 24, No. 1, pp.28–43.

Finegold, D. and Soskice, D. (1988) 'The failure of training in Britain: analysis and prescription', *Oxford Review of Economic Policy*, Vol. 4, No. 3, Autumn.

Flanagan, R. and Weber, A. (eds) (1974) *Bargaining without Boundaries*, Chicago, University of Chicago Press.

Fletcher, C. and Williams, R. (1992) 'The route to performance management', *Personnel Management*, October, pp.42–7.

Florida, R. and Kenney, M. (1991) 'Organization vs. culture: Japanese automotive plants in the US', *Industrial Relations Journal*, Vol.22, No.3, Autumn, pp.181–98.

Flude, M. and Hammer, M. (eds) (1990) *The Education Reform Act 1988*, London, Falmer.

Fogarty, M. and Brooks, D. (1986) *Trade Unions and British Industrial Development*, London, Policy Studies Institute.

Fogarty, M. and White, M. (1988) *Share Schemes – As Workers See Them*, London, Policy Studies Institute.

Forsyth, D. (1973) 'Foreign-owned firms and labour relations: a regional perspective', *British Journal of Industrial Relations*, Vol.11, No.1, March, pp.20–8.

Foster, J. and Woolfson, C. (1986) *The Politics of the UCS Work-In*, London, Lawrence and Wishart.

Fowler, A. (1987) 'When chief executives discover HRM', *Personnel Management*, Vol. 19, No. 1, p.3.

Fowler, A. (1988) 'New directions in performance pay', *Personnel Management*, November, pp.30–7.

Fox, A. (1971) *A Sociology of Work in Industry*, London, Collier Macmillan.

Fox, A. (1974) *Beyond Contract: Work, Power and Trust Relations*, London, Faber.

Fox, A. (1985) *History and Heritage*, London, Allen and Unwin.

Freedland, M. (1993) 'Performance appraisal and disciplinary action: the case for control of abuses' *International Labour Review*, Vol.132, No.4, pp.491–506.

Fuerstenberg, F. (1987) 'The Federal Republic of Germany' in G. Bamber, and R. Lansbury, (eds) *International and Comparative Industrial Relations*, London, Unwin Hyman, pp.165–86.

Gall, G. and McKay, S. (1994) 'Trade union derecognition in Britain 1988–1994', *British Journal of Industrial Relations*, Vol.32, No.3, September, pp.433–49.

Geary, G.F. (1993) 'New forms of work organisation and employee involvement in two case study sites: plural, mixed and protean', *Economic and Industrial Democracy*, Vol. 14, No. 4, pp.511–34.

Gellerman, S.W. and Hodgson, W.G. (1988) 'Cyanamid's new take on performance appraisal' in *Manage People, Not Personnel* (1990), Harvard Business Review Books.

Gennard, J. and Steuer, M. (1971) 'The industrial relations of foreign owned subsidiaries in the UK', *British Journal of Industrial Relations*, Vol.9, No.2, July, pp.143–59.

George, G. (1986) 'Appraisal in the public sector: dispensing with the big stick', *Personnel Management*, May, pp.32–5.

Giddens, A. (1971) *Capitalism and Modern Social Theory*, Cambridge, Cambridge University Press.

Giles, E. and Williams, R. (1991) 'Can the personnel department survive quality management?', *Personnel Management*, April, pp. 28–33.

Gold, M. and Hall, M. (1990) *Legal Regulation and the Practice of Employee Participation in the European Community*, Working Paper No. EF/WP/90/41/EN, Dublin, EFILWC.

Gonäs, L. and Westin, H. (1993) 'Industrial restructuring and gendered labour market processes', *Economic and Industrial Democracy*, Vol.14, No.3, pp.423–57.

Gospel, H. and Palmer, G. (1993) *British Industrial Relations*, 2nd edn, London, Routledge.

Grayson, D. (1990) *Self Regulating Work Groups – an Aspect of Organisational Change*, Occasional Paper No. 46, Work Research Unit, London ACAS, July.

Grint, K. (1993) 'What's wrong with performance appraisals? A critique and a suggestion', *Human Resource Management Journal*, Vol.3, No.3, pp.61–77.

Grummitt, J. (1983) *Team Briefing*, London, Industrial Society.

Guest, D. E. (1989) 'Human resource management: its implications for industrial relations and trade unions' in J. Storey (ed.) *New Perspectives in Human Resource Management*, London, Routledge, pp.41–55.

Guest, D.E. (1991) 'Personnel management: the end of orthodoxy', *British Journal of Industrial Relations*, Vol. 29, No. 2, pp.149–75.

Guest, D.E. (1993) 'The impact of employee involvement on organisational commitment and "them and us" attitudes', *Industrial Relations Journal*, Vol. 24, No. 3, pp.191–200.

Hakim, C. (1989) 'Identifying fast grow small firms', *Employment Gazette*, January.

Hall, M. (1992) 'Behind the European Works Councils Directives: the European Commission's legislative strategy', *British Journal of Industrial Relations*, Vol. 30, No. 4, December, pp.547–66.

Hallock, M. (1993) 'Unions and US labour policy', *Economic and Industrial Democracy*, Vol.14, No.3, pp.333–44.

Hammer, T.H. and Stern, R.N. (1986) 'A yo-yo model of co-operation: union participation at the Rath Packing Company', *Industrial and Labor Relations Review*, Vol. 39, April, pp.337–49.

Handy, C., Gordon, C., Gow, I. and Randlesome, C. (1988) *Making Managers*, London, Pitman.

Hanford, T.J. and Grasso, P.G. (1991) 'Participation and corporate performance in E.S.O.P. firms' in R. Russell and V. Rus (eds) *International Handbook of Participation in Organisations*, Vol. II *Ownership v. Participation*, Oxford University Press, pp. 221–31.

Hare, P.G. (1991) 'Eastern Europe: the transition to a market economy', *The Royal Bank of Scotland Review*, No. 169, March, pp. 3–16.

Harvard Business School (1981) *General Motors and the United States Auto Workers*, Boston, MA, Harvard Business School.

Hayek, F.A. (1985) 'The trade unions and Britain's economic decline' in W.E.J. McCarthy (ed.) *Trade Unions*, 2nd edn, Harmondsworth, Pelican, pp.357–64.

Heckscher, C. (1988) *The New Unionism: Employee Involvement in the Changing Corporation*, New York, Basic Books.

Heller, F., Wilders, M., Abell, P. and Warner, M. (1979) *What Do the British Want from Participation and Industrial Democracy?*, London, Anglo-German Foundation.

Hepple, B. (1991) 'Comparative trade union rights in the EC: threats and challenges presented by the Single Market' in R. Trask (ed.) *Trade Union Rights in the Single Market*, London, International Centre for Trade Union Rights, pp. 9–21.

Herzberg, F. (1968) *Work and the Nature of Man*, London, Staples Press.

Hill, B. (1988) 'Agriculture' in P. Johnson (ed.) *The Structure of British Industry*, 2nd edn, London, Unwin Hyman.

Hill, S. (1991) 'Why quality circles failed but total quality management might succeed', *British Journal of Industrial Relations*, Vol. 29, No. 4, December, pp.541–68.

HMSO (1989) *People and Companies: Employee Involvement in Britain*, London.

HMSO (1991a) *Higher Education: a New Framework*, CM. 1541, London.

HMSO (1991b) *Education and Training for the 21st Century*, CM. 1536, Vol. 1, May, London.

Hobbs, P. and Jeffries, K. (1990) 'So how many co-operatives are there?' in G. Jenkins and M. Poole (eds) *New Forms of Ownership, Management and Employment*, London, Routledge.

Horvat, B. (1969) *An Essay on Yugoslav Society*, White Plains: International Arts and Science Press.

Hove, T., Cunningham, G., Tucker, T. and Liddle, D. (1990) *The Japanese Business and Investment Survey*, London, Economic Development Briefing.

Hughes, S. (1992) 'Living with the past: trade unionism in Hungary since political pluralism', *Industrial Relations Journal*, Vol.23, No.4, Winter, pp.293–303.

*Human Resources Europe* (1991) 'Recruitment issues in France', No. 10, August/September.

Hunter, L.C. and Beaumont, P.B. (1993) 'Implementing TQM: top down or bottom up' *Industrial Relations Journal*, Vol. 24, No. 4, pp.318–27.

Hunter, L.C. and MacInnes, J. (1991) *Employers' Labour Use Strategies – Case Studies*, Research Paper No. 87, Department of Employment.

Hurly, S. (1992) 'How works councils could work for multinationals', *Involvement and Participation*, No. 613, Spring/May, pp.6–9.

Hyman, J. (1992) *Training at Work*, London, Routledge.

Hyman, J, and Beaumont, P. (1985) 'Personnel and welfare: the case of the problem drinker at work', *Employee Relations*, Vol.7, No.1.

Hyman, J., Ramsay, H., Leopold, J., Baddon, L. and Hunter, L.C. (1989) 'The impact of employee share ownership', *Employee Relations*, Vol. 11, No. 4, pp.9–16.

Hyman, R. (1971) *Marxism and the Sociology of Trade Unionism*, London, Pluto.

Hyman, R. (1995) 'Industrial relations in Europe: theory and practice', *European Journal of Industrial Relations*, Vol. 1, No. 1, pp.17–46.

Incomes Data Services (1987) 'Performance appraisal of manual workers', IDS Study No. 390, July.

Incomes Data Services (1989) 'Employee share ownership plans', IDS Study No. 438, July.

Incomes Data Services (1990a) 'Profit sharing and share options', IDS Study No. 468, October.

Incomes Data Services (1990b) 'Total quality management', IDS Study No. 457, May.

*Industrial Relations Review and Report* (1984) 'Flexibility agreements: the end of who does what?', No. 316, March.

*Industrial Relations Review and Report* (1987a) 'Employee involvement statements – current practice', No. 396, July, pp.2–7.

*Industrial Relations Review and Report* (1987b) 'Manual workers' appraisal – a growing trend surveyed', No. 398, August, pp.2–12.

*Industrial Relations Review and Report* (1992a) 'European works councils', No. 511, May, pp.12–15.

*Industrial Relations Review and Report* (1992b) 'Lean production – and Rover's "new deal"', No. 514, June, pp.12–15.

*Industrial Relations Review and Report* (1993a) 'Single union deals survey: 1', No. 528, January, pp.3–15.

*Industrial Relations Review and Report* (1993b) 'The impact of Japanese firms on working and employment practices in British manufacturing industry', No. 540, July, pp.4–16.

Industrial Society (1986) *Quality Circles: a Survey of QCs in the UK*, Industrial Society New Series No. 5.

IPM/IPA (1990) *Employee Involvement and Participation in the United Kingdom*, the IPM/IPA Code, Institute of Personnel Management/Involvement and Participation Association.

IPA (1990) 'BR takes the PRP line', *Involvement and Participation*, No. 607, Autumn, pp.12–13 and 17, Involvement and Participation Association.

Jacobi, O., Keller, B. and Muller-Jentsch, W. (1992) 'Germany: codetermining the future' in A. Ferner and R. Hyman (eds) *Industrial Relations in the New Europe*, Oxford, Blackwell, pp.218–69.

James, G. (1988) *Performance Appraisal*, Occasional Paper No. 40, Work Research Unit, London, ACAS.

James, G. (1991) *Quality of Working Life and Total Quality Management*, Occasional Paper No. 50, Work Research Unit, London, ACAS, November.

Jensen, A. (1994) 'Rethinking worker democracy: reclaiming the rights of working people', report of a conference organized by the Centre for Alternative Industrial and Technological Systems, 18–19 February.

Jones, D.C. and Kato, T. (1993) 'The scope, nature and effects of employee stock ownership plans in Japan', *Industrial and Labour Relations Review*, Vol.46, No.2, pp.352–67.

Kanter, R.M. (1983) *The Change Masters*, London, Routledge.

Kanter, R.M. (1989) *When Giants Learn to Dance*, London, Routledge.

Keenoy, T. (1991) 'The roots of metaphor in the old and the new industrial relations', *British Journal of Industrial Relations*, Vol. 29, No. 2, June, pp.313–28.

Keep, E. (1989) 'Corporate training strategies: the vital component?' in J. Storey (ed.) *New Perspectives on Human Resource Management*, London, Routledge, pp.109–25.

Kelley, M. and Harrison, B. (1992) 'Unions, technology and labour–management co-operation', in L. Mishel and P. Voos (eds) *Unions and Economic Competitiveness*, Armonk, NY, M.E. Sharpe.

Kelly, J. (1988) *Trade Unions and Socialist Politics*, London, Verso.

Kelly, J. and Kelly, C. (1991) '"Them and us": social psychology of "the new industrial relations"', *British Journal of Industrial Relations*, Vol. 29, No. 1, pp. 25–48.

Kelso, L. and Adler, M. (1958) *the Capitalist Manifesto*, London, Random House.

Kirkpatrick, I., Davies, A. and Oliver, N. (1992) 'Decentralisation: friend or foe of HRM?' in P. Blyton and P. Turnbull (eds) *Reassessing Human Resource Management*, London, Sage, pp.131–48.

Kjellberg, A. (1992) 'Sweden: can the model survive?' in A. Ferner and R. Hyman (eds) *Industrial Relations in the New Europe*, Oxford, Blackwell, pp. 88–142.

Klein, K.J. and Rosen, C. (1986) 'Employee stock ownership in the United States' in R.N. Stern and S. McCarthy (eds) *International Yearbook of Organisational Democracy*, Vol. III, New York, Wiley, pp. 387–406.

Kochan, L. (1966) *Russia in Revolution 1890–1918*, London, Weidenfield and Nicolson.

Kochan, T., Katz, H. and McKersie, R. (1986) *The Transformation of American Industrial Relations*, New York, Basic Books.

Kochan, T. and Weinstein, M. (1994) 'Recent developments in US industrial relations', *British Journal of Industrial Relations*, Vol. 32, No. 4, pp.483–504.

Kollantai, A. (1921) *The Workers' Opposition in Russia*, Chicago, Industrial Workers of the World.

*Labour Market Quarterly Report* (1992), Department of Employment, May.

Labour Party (1989) *Meet the Challenge, Make the Change – A New Agenda for Britain*, London, Labour Party.

*Labour Research* (1987) 'Big fish grab sell-off shares', September, pp.7–8.

*Labour Research* (1990) 'Uncertain future for employee share ownership', May, pp. 21–3.

*Labour Research* (1991a) 'A shareholding democracy', March, pp.21–3.

*Labour Research* (1991b) 'The UK's employment involvement test', April, pp.12–14.

*Labour Research* (1992) 'The union derecognition band-wagon', November, pp.6–8.

*Labour Research* (1994) 'Strategy mapped out to tackle HRM', June, p.5.

Labour Research Department (1991) *Women in Trade Unions*, March.

Lane, C. (1989) *Management and Labour in Europe*, Aldershot, Edward Elgar.

Langeland, O. (1991) 'Profit sharing and employee ownership in Norway', paper presented to conference on *Changes in Labour Markets and Industrial Relations in Europe*, Aalborg, Denmark.

Langeland, O. (1993) 'Employees on the capital market', *Economic and Industrial Democracy*, Vol. 14, No. 2, May, pp. 217–32.

Lansbury, R. and Davis, E. (1992) 'Employee participation: some Australian cases', *International Labour Review*, Vol.131, No.2, pp.231–48.

Lash, S. and Urry, J. (1987) *The End of Organized Capitalism*, Cambridge, Polity Press.

Laurent, A. (1986) 'The cross-cultural puzzle of international human resource management', *Human Resource Management*, Vol.25, No.1, pp.91–102.

Lawler, E.E. (1986) *High Involvement Management*, San Francisco, Jossey-Bass.

Legge, K. (1989) 'Human resource management: a critical analysis' in J. Storey (ed.) *New Perspectives on Human Resource Management*, London, Routledge, pp.19–40.

Legge, K. (1994) 'Managing culture: fact or fiction?' in K. Sisson (ed.) *Personnel Management*, 2nd edn, Oxford, Blackwell.

Lind, O. (1979) 'Employee participation in Sweden', *Employee Relations*, Vol. 1, No. 1, pp. 11–16.

Long, R. (1986) 'Recent patterns in Swedish industrial democracy' in R. Stern and S. McCarthy (eds) *International Yearbook of Organizational Democracy*, Vol. III, New York, Wiley.

Lucio, M. and Weston, S. (1992) 'Human resource management and trade union responses: bringing the politics of the workplace into the debate' in G. Salaman (ed.) *Human Resource Strategies*, London, Sage, pp.215–32.

Maaløe, E. (1993) 'How to become a successful worker-owner: a study of long-term change of UK employee buy-outs', *Economic and Industrial Democracy*, Vol. 14, pp. 133–48.

MacInnes, J. (1985) 'Conjuring up consultation: the role and extent of joint consultation in post-war private manufacturing industry', *British Journal of Industrial Relations*, Vol. 23, No. 1, March, pp.93–113.

MacInnes, J. (1987) *Thatcherism at Work*, Milton Keynes, Open University Press.

MacKay, L. and Torrington, D. (1986) *The Changing Nature of Personnel Management*, London, Institute of Personnel Management.

McKinlay, A. and Starkey, K. (1992) 'Competitive strategies and organizational change' in G. Salaman (ed.) *Human Resource Strategies*, London, Sage, pp.107–24.

Marchington, M. (1987) 'A review and critique of research on developments in joint consultation' *British Journal of Industrial Relations*, Vol. 25, No. 3, November, pp.339–52.

Marchington, M. (1990) 'Unions on the margin?', *Employee Relations*, Vol.12, No.5, pp.1–24.

Marchington, M. (1992) *Managing the Team*, Oxford, Blackwell.

Marchington, M., Goodman, J., Wilkinson, A. and Ackers, P. (1992) *New Developments in Employee Involvement*, Research Series No. 2, May, Employment Department.

Marchington, M. and Parker, P. (1988) 'Japanisation: a lack of chemical reaction?', *Industrial Relations Journal*, Vol. 19, No. 4, Winter, pp.272–85.

Marchington, M. and Parker, P. (1990) *Changing Patterns of Employee Relations*, Hemel Hempstead, Harvester Wheatsheaf.

Marchington, M., Wilkinson, A. and Ackers, P. (1993a) 'Waving or drowning in participation', *Personnel Management*, March, pp.46–50.

Marchington, M., Wilkinson, A., Ackers, P. and Goodman, J. (1993b) 'The influence of managerial relations on waves of employee involvement', *British Journal of Industrial Relations*, Vol. 31, No. 4, pp.553–76.

Marginson, P., Armstrong, P., Edwards, P., Purcell, J. and Hubbard, N. (1993) The Control of Industrial Relations in Large Companies: an Initial Analysis of the Second Company Level Industrial Relations Survey', Warwick Papers in Industrial Relations, No.45, December, Coventry, IRRU.

Marginson, P., Edwards, P.K., Martin, R., Purcell, J. and Sisson, K. (1988) *Beyond the Workplace: Managing Industrial Relations in the Multi-Establishment Enterprise*, Oxford, Blackwell.

Martin, A. (1984) 'Trade unions in Sweden: strategic response to change and crisis' in P. Gourevitch, A. Martin, G. Ross, S. Bernstein, A. Markvots, and C. Allen (eds) *Unions and Economic Crisis*, London, George Allen and Unwin.

Marx, K. and Engels, F. (1848) 'Manifesto of the Communist Party' in *The Revolutions of 1848*, Harmondsworth, Penguin, 1973.

Mason, B. (1994) 'The changing structures and strategies of employers' and employees' organisations: the case of central and eastern Europe' in T. Kauppinen and V. Koykka (eds) *The Changing Structures and Strategies of Employers' and Employees' Organisations,* proceedings from the IIRA 4th European Regional Congress, 24–26 August, Helsinki, Finnish Labour Relations Association, pp.97–123.

Mayhew, K. (1991) 'The UK labour market in the 1980s', *Oxford Review of Economic Policy*, Vol. 7, No.1, Spring, pp. 1–17.

Metcalf, D. (1989) 'Water notes dry up', *British Journal of Industrial Relations*, Vol. 27, No. 1, pp. 1–31.

Metcalf, D. (1990) 'Union presence and labour productivity in British manufacturing industry', *British Journal of Industrial Relations*, Vol. 28, No. 2, pp. 249–66.

Meyer, D. and Cooke, W. (1993) 'US labour relations in transition', *British Journal of Industrial Relations*, Vol.31, No.4, pp.531–52.

Millward, N. (1994) *The New Industrial Relations?*, London, Policy Studies Institute.

Millward, N. and Stevens, M. (1986) *British Workplace Industrial Relations 1980–1984*, Aldershot, Gower.

Millward, N., Stevens, M., Smart, D. and Hawes, W.R. (1992) *Workplace Industrial Relations in Transition*, Aldershot, Dartmouth.

Minford, P. (1982) 'Trade unions destroy a million jobs', *Journal of Economic Affairs*, No. 2, January, pp.73–9.

Minns, R. (1980) *Pension Fund and British Capitalism*, London, Heinemann.

Mitchell Stewart A. (1994) *Empowering People*, London, Pitman.

Monks, J. (1991) 'Unions come to terms with HRM', *Involvement and Participation*, No. 610, Summer/Autumn, pp.8–9.

Monks, J. (1994) 'The union response to HRM: fraud or opportunity', *Personnel Management*, September, pp.42–7.

Morgan, G. (1993) *Imaginization*, London, Sage.

Morris, R. and Wood, S. (1991) 'Testing the survey method: continuity and change in British industrial relations', *Work, Employment and Society*, Vol.5, No.2, pp.259–82.

Murray, R. (1971) 'The internationalization of capital and the nation state', *New Left Review*, No.67, May–June, pp.84–109.

Murray, R. (1985) 'Benetton Britain', *Marxism Today*, November, pp.28-32.

NALGO (1993) 'Trade union recognition, recruitment and retention in the water industry', April, London, NALGO.

National Institute for Economic and Social Research (1989) *Productivity, Education and Training*, London.

Nichols, T. and O'Connell Davidson, J. (1992) 'Employee shareholders in two privatised utilities', *Industrial Relations Journal*, Vol. 23, No. 2, pp. 107–19.

Nissan (1988) *Information*, Nissan Motor Company (UK) Ltd.

Niven, M. (1967) *Personnel Management 1913–63*, London, Institute of Personnel Management.

Nolan, P. and Marginson, P. (1990) 'Skating on thin ice? Metcalf, D. on trade unions and productivity', *British Journal of Industrial Relations*, Vol. 28, No. 2, July, pp. 227–48.

Oliver, N. and Wilkinson, B. (1989) 'Japanese manufacturing techniques and personnel and industrial relations practices in Britain: evidence and implications', *British Journal of Industrial Relations*, Vol. 27, No. 1, March, pp.73–92.

Oliver, N. and Wilkinson, B. (1992) *The Japanization of British Industry*, 2nd edn, Oxford, Blackwell.

Osterman, P. (1994) 'How common is workplace transformation and who adopts it?' *Industrial and Labor Relations Review*, Vol. 47, No. 2, January, pp.173–88.

Othen, R. (1990) 'Assessing attitudes', *Involvement and Participation*, No. 606, Summer, pp. 11 and 23.

Ouchi, W. (1981) *Theory Z: How American Business Can Meet the Japanese Challenge*, Boston, Addison-Wesley.

Parker, M. (1985) *Inside the Circle: A Union Guide to QWL*, Boston, MA, South End Press.

Pateman, C. (1983) 'Some reflections on participation and democratic theory' in C. Crouch and F. Heller (eds) *International Yearbook of Organizational Democracy*, Vol.I, Chichester, Wiley.

Peck, F. and Stone, I. (1992) *New Inward Investment and the Northern Region Labour Market*, Research Series No.6, October, Employment Department.

*Personnel Management* (1990) *Total Quality*, Factsheet 29, May.

*Personnel Management Plus* (1990), Vol. 1, No. 3, September.

*Personnel Management Plus* (1994) 'Robust research – or just headline-seeking analysis?' June, Vol. 5, No. 6, p.9.

Peters, T.J. (1987) *Thriving on Chaos: Handbook for a Managerial Revolution*, New York, Knopf.

Peters, T.J. (1992) *Liberation Management*, New York, Knopf.

Peters, T.J. and Waterman, R.H. (1982) *In Search of Excellence*, New York, Harper and Row.

Pickard, J. (1993) 'The real meaning of empowerment', *Personnel Management*, November, pp.28–33.

Pieper, R. (ed.) (1990) *Human Resource Management: An International Comparison*, Berlin, Walter de Gruyter.

Piore, M. and Sabel, C. (1984) *The Second Industrial Divide: Possibilities for Prosperity*, New York, Basic Books.

Pollert, A. (1988) 'The flexible firm: fixation or fact', *Work, Employment and Society*, Vol. 2, No. 3, pp. 281–316.

Pollert, A. and Hradecka, I. (1994) 'Privatisation in transition: the Czech experience', *Industrial Relations Journal*, Vol. 25, No. 4, pp.52–63.

Poole, M. (1986) *Towards a New Industrial Democracy*, London, Routledge.

Poole, M. and Mansfield, R. (1992) 'Managers attitudes to human resource management: rhetoric and reality' in P. Blyton and P. Turnbull (eds) *Reassessing Human Resource Management*, London, Sage, pp.200–15.

Pounsford, M. (1991) 'The meaning and value of employee involvement', *Involvement and Participation*, No. 611, Autumn, pp.405 and 415.

Pravda, A. and Ruble, B. (eds) (1986) *Trade Unions in Communist States*, London, Allen and Unwin.

Purcell, J. (1992) 'The impact of corporate strategy on human resource management' in G. Salaman (ed.) *Human Resource Strategies*, London, Sage, pp.59–81.

Purcell, J., Marginson, P., Edwards, P. and Sisson, K. (1987) 'The industrial relations practices of multi-plant foreign-owned firms', *Industrial Relations Journal*, Vol. 18, No. 2, Summer, pp.130–37.

Purcell, J. and Sisson, K. (1983) 'Strategies and practice in the management of industrial relations' in G.S. Bain (ed.) *Industrial Relations in Britain*, Oxford, Blackwell.

Rainnie, A. (1989) *Industrial Relations in Small Firms*, London, Routledge.

Rajan, A. (1990) *1992: a Zero Sum Game*, London, Industrial Society.

Ramsay, H. (1976) 'Participation: the shopfloor view', *British Journal of Industrial Relations*, Vol.XII, No.2, pp.128–41.

Ramsay, H. (1977) 'Cycles of control: worker participation in sociological and historical perspectives', *Sociology*, Vol. 11, No. 3, September, pp.481–506.

Ramsay, H. (1990) *The Joint Consultation Debate: Soft Soap and Hard Cases*, Discussion Paper No. 17, Centre for Research in Industrial Democracy and Participation, University of Glasgow.

Ramsay, H. (1991) 'The community, the multi-national, its workers and their charter: a modern tale of industrial democracy', *Work, Employment and Society*, Vol. 5, No. 4, pp.541–66.

Ramsay, H. (1992) 'Swedish and Japanese work methods – comparisons and contrasts', *European Participation Monitor*, No. 3, pp. 37–40.

Ramsay, H. (1994) *Euro-Unionism and the Great Auction: an Assessment of the Prospects for Organised Labour Post-Maastricht*, Occasional Paper No. 5, University of Strathclyde, Department of Human Resource Management, February.

Ramsay, H., Hyman, J.. Baddon, L., Hunter, L. and Leopold, J. (1990) 'Options for workers: owner or employee?' in G. Jenkins and M. Poole (eds) *New Forms of Ownership, Management and Employment*, London, Routledge.

Randell, G. (1989) 'Employee appraisal' in K. Sisson (ed.) *Personnel Management in Britain*, Oxford, Blackwell, pp. 149–76.

Rehder, R. (1994) 'Saturn, Uddevalla and the Japanese lean systems: paradoxical prototypes of the 21st century', *International Journal of Human Resource Management*, Vol.5, No.1, pp.1–31.

Rehn, G. and Viklund, B. (1990) 'Changes in the Swedish model' in G. Baglioni and C. Crouch (eds) *European Industrial Relations*, London, Sage, pp. 300–25.

Roberts, B.C. (1973) 'Multi-national collective bargaining: a European prospect?', *British Journal of Industrial Relations*, Vol.11, No.1, March, pp.1–19.

Roberts, I. (1993) 'Where are the European works councils? – an update', *Industrial Relations Journal*, Vol. 24, No. 3, September, pp.178–81.

Rose, J.B. and Chaison, G.N. (1993) 'Convergence in international unionism', *British Journal of Industrial Relations*, Vol.31, No.2, pp.293–98.

Rose, M. (1988) *Industrial Behaviour*, 2nd edn, London, Penguin.

Rowlinson, M., McArdle, L., Hassard, J., Procter, S. and Forrester, P. (1991) 'The changing face of industrial democracy: evidence from the UK electronics industry', paper presented to meeting on *Future of Employment Relations: International Comparisons in the Age of Uncertainty*, Cardiff Business School, September.

Rubery, J. and Fagan, C. (1994) 'Does feminization mean a flexible labour force?' in R. Hyman, and A. Ferner (eds) *New Frontiers in European Industrial Relations*, Oxford, Blackwell.

Russell, R. (1989) 'Taking stock of the E.S.O.P.s' in C.J. Lammers and G. Széll (eds) *International Yearbook of Participation in Organizations*, Vol. 1, Oxford, Oxford University Press.

Russell, S. and Dale, B. (1989) *Quality Circles – a Broader Perspective*, Occasional Paper No. 43, Work Research Unit, London, ACAS, May.

Sapsed, G. (1991) 'Appraisal the IBM way', *Involvement and Participation*, No. 608, Winter/February, pp.8–9 and 14.

Schneider, T.J. and Comfort, A.F. (1993) 'Employee participation gets high profile in USA' *Involvement and Participation*, No. 619, Autumn/November, pp.14–17.

Schregle, J. (1993) 'Dismissal protection in Japan', *International Labour Review*, Vol.132, No.4, pp.507–20.

Schuller, T. and Hyman, J. (1986) 'Economic democracy and pension funds' in R. Stern and S. McCarthy (eds) *International Yearbook of Organizational Democracy*, New York, Wiley.

Scott, C.D. and Jaffe, D.T. (1991) *Empowerment*, Menlo Park, CA, Crisp.

Singh, R. (1992) 'Human resource management: a sceptical look' in B. Towers (ed.) *The Handbook of Human Resource Management*, Oxford, Blackwell, pp.127–43.

Sisson, K. (1989) 'Personnel management in perspective' in K. Sisson (ed.) *Personnel Management in Britain*, Oxford, Blackwell.

Sisson, K. (1990) 'Introducing the *Human Resource Management Journal*', *Human Resource Management Journal*, Vol. 1, No. 1, pp.1–11.

Sisson, K. (1994) 'Introduction', in K. Sisson (ed.) *Personnel Management*, 2nd edn, Oxford, Blackwell.

Sisson, K. and Timperley, S. (1994) 'From manpower planning to strategic human resource management?' in K. Sisson (ed.) *Personnel Management*, 2nd edn, Oxford, Blackwell, pp.153–84.

Sisson, K., Waddington, J. and Whitson, C. (1992) 'Company size in the European Community', *Human Resource Management Journal*, Vol. 2, No. 1, Autumn, pp.94–109.

Skinner, W. (1981) 'Big hat – no cattle: managing human resources', *Harvard Business Review*, Vol.59, pp.106–14.

Smith, G. (1993) 'Employee share schemes in Britain', *Employment Gazette*, April, pp. 149–54.

Sproull, A. and MacInnes, J. (1989) 'Union recognition and employment change in Scottish electronics', *Industrial Relations Journal*, Vol. 20, No. 1, pp.33–46.

Spry, C. (1991) 'Big bang hits the Health Service', *Personnel Management*, January, pp. 23–5.

Spurr, I. (1990) 'Are house journals just hot air?', *Involvement and Participation*, No. 607, Autumn, pp.14–17.

Steedman, H. and Wagner, K. (1987) 'Productivity, machinery and skills in a sample of British and German manufacturing plants. Results of a pilot inquiry', *National Institute Economic Review*, No. 122.

Stevens, B. (1991/2) 'Employee ownership and participation in the USA', *Industrial Participation*, Winter, pp. 16–19.

Storey, J. (ed.) (1989) *New Perspectives on Human Resource Management*, London, Routledge.

Storey, J. (1992) *Developments in the Management of Human Resources*, Oxford, Blackwell.

Storey, J. (1994) 'Management development', in K. Sisson (ed.) *Personnel Management*, Oxford, Blackwell.

Strauss, G. (1992) 'Human resource management in the USA' in B. Towers (ed.) *Handbook of Human Resource Management*, Oxford, Blackwell.

Szell, G. (1988) 'Participation, workers' control and self-management', *Current Sociology*, Vol.36, No.3, Winter.

Taylor, D. and Snell, M.W. (1986) 'The Post Office experiment: an analysis of industrial democracy meetings' in R. Stern and S. McCarthy (eds) *International Yearbook of Organizational Democracy*, New York, Wiley, pp.75–104.

Terkel, S. (1977) *Working*, Harmondsworth, Penguin.

Terry, M. (1983) 'Shop stewards through expansion and recession', *Industrial Relations Journal*, Vol. 14, No. 3, pp.49–58.

Terry, M. (1994) 'Workplace unionism: redefining structures and objectives' in R. Hyman and A. Ferner (eds) *New Frontiers in European Industrial Relations*, Oxford, Blackwell.

Tillsley, C. (1994) 'Employee involvement: employees' views', *Employment Gazette*, June, pp.211–16.

Thomas, H. (1977) *The Spanish Civil War*, 3rd edn, Harmondsworth, Penguin.

Thomas, R.J. (1988) 'Review article: what is human resource management?', *Work, Employment and Society*, Vol.2, No.3, pp.392–402.

Thompson, M. (1993) *Pay and Performance: the Employee Experience*, Report No. 258, Institute of Manpower Studies.

Thompson, P. and Smith, C. (1992) 'Socialism and the labour process' in C. Smith and P. Thompson (eds) *Labour in Transition*, London, Routledge, pp. 3–33.

Torrington, D. (1989) 'Human resource management in the personnel function' in J. Storey (ed.) *New Perspectives on Human Resource Management*, London, Routledge.

Towers, B. (1992) *Choosing Bargaining Levels: UK Experience and Implications*, Issues in People Management No. 2, Institute of Personnel Management.

Townley, B. (1989) 'Selection and appraisal: reconstituting "social relations?"' in J. Storey (ed.) *New Perspectives on Human Resource Management*, London, Routledge, pp. 92–108.

Training Agency (1989) 'From quality circles to total quality management at Prestwick Circuits Ltd', *Investing in People II*, HMSO, February.

Troy, L. (1992) 'Convergence on international unionism', *British Journal of Industrial Relations*, Vol.30, No.1, pp.1–44.

TUC–Labour Party Liaison Committee (1982) *Economic Planning and Industrial Democracy – The Framework for Full Employment*, London, Labour Party.

TUC–Labour Party Liaison Committee (1986) *People at Work: New Rights, New Responsibilities*, London, Labour Party.

Tyson, S. (1987) 'The management of the personnel function' *Journal of Management Studies*, Vol.21, No.5, pp.523–32.

Tyson, S. and Fell, A. (1986) *Evaluating the Personnel Function*, London, Hutchinson.

UNCTAD (1993) *World Investment Report 1993: Transnational Corporations and Integrated International Production*, New York, United Nations.

Unity Trust Bank (1990) *Employee Share Ownership Plans*.

Verma, A. and McKersie, R. (1987) 'Employee involvement: the implications of non-involvement by unions', *Industrial and Labor Relations Review*, Vol. 40, No. 4, July, pp.556–68.

Visser, J. (1992) 'The strength of union movements in advanced capitalist democracies: social and organisational variations' in M. Regini (ed.) *The Future of Labour Movements*, London, Sage, pp.17–52.

Vitols, S. (1993) 'European works councils – an overview', *P+ European Participation Monitor*, No. 6, pp.52–4.

Walker, J.W. (1992) *Human Resource Strategy*, New York, McGraw-Hill.

Walker, S. (1992) 'Empowerment: where human resources has to draw the line', *Human Resources*, Summer, pp. 98–100.

Walton, R.E. (1985) 'From control to commitment in the workplace' in *Manage People, Not Personnel* (1990), Harvard Business Review Books.

Warren, B. (1971) 'The internationalization of capital and the nation state: a comment', *New Left Review*, No.68, July–August, pp.83–8.

Watanabe, S. (1991) 'The Japanese quality control circle: why it works', *International Labour Review*, Vol. 130, No. 1, pp.57–80.

Wedderburn, W. (Lord) (1990) *The Social Charter, European Company and Employment Rights: An Outline Agenda*, The Institute of Employment Rights, February.

West, N. (1992) *The Impact of Demographic Change in Training*, Stockton-on-Tees, Jim Conway Foundation.

Wheeler, H.N. (1993) 'Industrial relations in the United States of America' in G.J. Bamber and R.D. Lansbury (eds) *International and Comparative Industrial Relations*, London, Routledge.

Whittaker, H. (1990) 'The end of Japanese-style management?', *Work Employment and Society*, Vol.4, No.3, pp.321–48.

Whyte, W.F. (1991) 'Learning from Móndragón' in R. Russell and V. Rus (eds) *International Handbook of Participation in Organisations*, Vol.II, Oxford, Oxford University Press.

Wickens, P. (1987) *The Road to Nissan*, Basingstoke, Macmillan.

Wilkinson, B., Morris, J. and Munday, M. (1993) 'Japan in Wales: a new industrial relations', *Industrial Relations Journal*, Vol.24, No.4, December, pp.273–83.

Williams, K., Haslam, C., Williams, J. and Cutler, T. with Adcroft, A. and Johal, S. (1992) 'Against lean production', *Economy and Society*, Vol. 21, No. 3, August, pp.321–54.

Wilson, D., Butler, R., Croy, D., Hickson, D. and Mallory, G. (1982) 'The limits of trade union power in organisational decision-making', *British Journal of Industrial Relations*, Vol.20, No.3, November, pp.322–42.

Wilson, F. (1989) 'Productive efficiency and the employment relationship: the case of quality circles', *Employee Relations*, Vol. 11, No. 1, pp.27–32.

Womack, J., Jones, D. and Roos, D. (1990) *The Machine that Changed the World*, New York, Rawson Associates.

Woodhall, M. (1987) 'Human capital concepts' in G. Esland (ed.) *Education, Training and Employment*, Vol. 2, Wokingham, Addison-Wesley, pp.27–34.

Wood, S. (1991) 'Japanisation and/or Toyotaism?' *Work, Employment and Society*, Vol. 5, No. 4, pp.567–600.

Wyatt Company (1990) *Performance Management*, London.

Young, T. (1991) 'Response to M. Weiss "The German Model of Workers' Participation: some lessons"' in R. Trask (ed.) *Trade Union Rights in the Single Market*, International Centre for Trade Union Rights, August, pp.67–84.

# Index